April 26, 2013

To Beverly,

Since you do know the new Shanghai, I am sure you will recognize some of the sites of Old Shanghai where I was born and raised.

Warm regards,

Lihone

Stateless
IN SHANGHAI

LILIANE WILLENS

Stateless in Shanghai

By Liliane Willens

ISBN-13: 978-988-18154-8-4

Published by
China Economic Review Publishing (HK) Limited for Earnshaw Books
1804, 18/F New Victory House,
93-103 Wing Lok Street, Sheung Wan, Hong Kong

First printing January 2010.
Second printing February 2010.
Third printing April 2010.

This book has been reset in 10pt Book Antiqua. Spellings and punctuations are left as in the original edition.

In Memory of my parents
Benjamin and Thaïs Willens
and
Old Amah, Shao Wang and Lao Papa

TABLE OF CONTENTS

CONTENTS

Acknowledgements

WHENEVER I mention to people that I was born in Shanghai, China, they look quite surprised, then inevitably say "How interesting", or "How come?" and often add "You don't look Chinese!" Hearing these comments repeatedly, I began to accept the idea that a European brought up in Asia was somewhat out of the ordinary, especially during the turbulent times of the 20th century. After my friends persistently urged me to write a book of my life in Shanghai, I asked myself, "Well, why not?"

And the long road to this finished product began. Fortunately, my mother related to me on tape her youth in Russia; I have the letters my father wrote to my mother while he was still in the People's Republic of China, and the diary of my younger sister Jacqueline where she described the last years of the Japanese occupation of Shanghai. I questioned many people who had lived in "our" Shanghai – relatives, friends and acquaintances – and interviewed a number of my former classmates now scattered around the world. They all filled many memory gaps – personal or otherwise – and in the process, reminded me of many other happenings and incidents. I am most grateful to all of them.

In addition to these personal reminiscences, I researched primary sources dealing with the history of China and "Old Shanghai" during the 19th and 20th centuries to put my experience in historical context. Throughout the book I have used the Wade-Giles English spelling of Chinese words, names and places prevalent in China during the era I describe, but I have also included their current names in *pinyin*, the official romanization system adopted by the People's Republic of China in 1958.

I wish to thank most heartily the following who read so diligently the various drafts of my manuscript and offered valuable suggestions – Jacqueline Arons, Carla Danziger, Tess Johnston, Renée Quimby and Marcia Ristaino (however, any error is of my own making); my Shanghai classmates Claude Daroso, Ginette Grillon, Jeanine Reynaud, Alla Rabinovich Herman and Bernard Saint-Oyant who reminded me of events I had forgotten; other Shanghailanders who clarified many points – Helene (Loula) Ballerand, Daofen Chen, Nikita Moravsky, Laura Topas, Yunshi Wang and Wanqiong Zhong; Robert Rowe who prepared the maps; my family who gave me much moral support, especially my first American-born niece, Roxanne Quimby; my friends who encouraged me along the way – Silvia Bertran, Blaine Carvalho, Norma Chaplain, Susan Coates, Dominique Dillenseger, Sylvia Firschein, Olga Koval, Marit Helliksen Kulak, Ruth Kurzbauer, Elvira May, Ania Piasecka and Matthew Sellers; and others who wished me "good luck" or helped me solve problems with my recalcitrant computer.

I am very grateful to the editors of Earnshaw Books – Derek Sandhaus who shepherded the transformation of my manuscript into book form, Andrew Chubb for his most insightful editing of this book, Alice Polk for her diligent proofing and Frank Zheng for his design. I would also like to thank Graham Earnshaw for his support throughout.

Xie, xie – Thank you

Liliane Willens
November 2009

Shanghai - 1941

Chinese Municipality of Greater Shanghai

Japanese Naval Depot and Landing Party Barracks

Hongkew District

Whangpoo River

Pootung

Whangpoo River

Chapei

Shanghai North Railway Station

Broadway Mansions

Garden Bridge

The Bund

Quai de France

Public Gardens

Cathay Hotel

Palace Hotel

Nanking Road

Avenue Edward VII

Boulevard des deux Républiques

Old Chinese City (Nantao)

Shanghai-Hangchow-Ningpo Railway

Soochow Creek

International Settlement

Shanghai Race Course

Bubbling Well Road

Kaiser Wilhelm Schule

Avenue Foch

Rue Ratard

Route Paul Henry

Avenue Joffre

Route Vallon

Collège Municipal Français

Université l'Aurore

Avenue Dubail

French Park-Koukaza

Route Rémi

Ecole Rémi

French Concession

St. John's University

Jessfield Park

Great Western Road

Route de Say Zoong

Route Pichon

Route Delastre

Shanghai American School

Avenue Pétain

Avenue Joffre

Avenue Haig

Towards Lunghwa Airport and Hungjao

🏠 = Houses where author lived with her parents and sisters

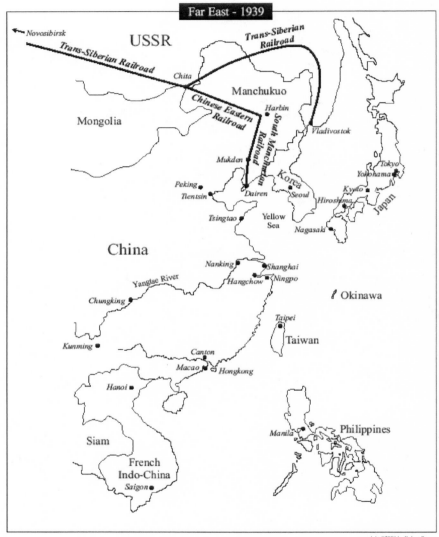

copyright ©2009 by Robert Rowe

Benjamin's Saga

1

MY FATHER Benjamin never told my sisters and me that he was born in Ukraine, then a part of the Russian Empire, and grew up in the small town of Radomyshel, about 60 miles west of Kiev. My mother warned us never to question him about his early years. His sister Sonia, who left Russia with him, never talked about their past – and we were not interested in questioning her. We knew that my father abhorred Stalin and the Soviet Union, and avoided wherever possible any association, social or political with Russia.

Venyamin (Benjamin) Vilensky was born in 1894 and grew up during the reign of Czar Nicholas II at a time when Russia was in economic and political turmoil, and pogroms – anti-Semitic violence sanctioned by the czars – erupted regularly. The *Yids* (a very derogatory term for Jews) were considered "game" to be hunted, caught and killed whenever the Cossack warriors, the elite corps of horsemen and other ultra-nationalists, entered the villages and towns in the Pale of Settlement, a vast region that today comprises Belarus, Lithuania, Moldova, Poland and the Ukraine. With rare exceptions, Jews like my father were obliged to live there until the 1917 Bolshevik revolution. The Pale was a creation of Catherine the Great in the last decade of the 18th century when she acquired her share of Poland and discovered to her surprise and disgust that she was also inheriting one million Jews.

I was able to gather information about the life led by my father, his parents and his five siblings in Radomyshel when in 1992 I went to Ukraine on a business assignment. I had discovered among my father's papers a brief letter written to him twenty years earlier by his nephew Leonid Vilensky, residing in Kiev. I decided to go to the address listed on the envelope for I was sure citizens of the former Soviet Union hardly ever moved out of the apartments assigned to them by the state. I walked up five flights of stairs, knocked on a door and knew that I had come to the right place when a man opened the door who closely resembled my father. There was no doubt he was my cousin Leonid. He seemed very startled to see someone on his doorstep who, by her clothing and accented Russian, was undoubtedly a foreigner. When I informed him that I was his cousin from America he yelled out to his wife Lyuda that the gods had sent him a very special gift on this day – which coincidentally was his birthday. After this initial visit I returned several times after work to reminisce about our relatives scattered around the world. At our get-togethers Leonid told me about the life of our respective grandparents, fathers, uncles and aunts in Radomyshel, where they had resided until the outbreak of the Bolshevik Revolution. Our grandfather was a small businessman while our grandmother stayed at home with the children, four boys and two girls all born in Radomyshel. Her greatest fear while her children were growing up was the possibility that military recruiters would seize and kidnap her sons for service in the czar's armed forces.

Leonid proudly showed me a raincoat my father had sent him in the early 1970s and which he was still able to wear. He related how he was ever grateful that during the great famine in Ukraine in the early 1930s under Stalin, his siblings and parents did not die of hunger thanks to the financial help they received from my father and his sister, Sonia, living in China. He explained to me that this enabled his parents to purchase food in special stores, the *torgovy sindikat* (commercial stores) known by the acronym *torgosin*, where purchases had to be paid for in US dollars. Leonid, then a child, went several times to these stores with his mother who, fearful of being attacked by starving people in the street, had to hire hefty men to help her carry home the bags of flour, rice and meat. Her bodyguards gladly received food for their service. As Leonid and Lyuda were telling me about the very difficult life they led during the Stalin era, World War II and later under various communist leaders, I could only think that there but for the grace of God, go I.

Since I expressed a strong interest in seeing my father's birthplace, one of Leonid's relatives drove us to Radomyshel, where the main square was dominated by a huge statue of Lenin. Leonid pointed out the place where once stood my grandparents' home, now replaced by a restaurant. He explained that their house was similar to the ones behind the square with their pre-Russian Revolution architecture of low roofs, windows reaching to the ground, and small vegetable gardens at the back. Another throwback to that era was the sight of horses pulling carts with peasants taking their vegetables and fruit to the market. We then entered a Russian Orthodox Church built towards the end of the 19th century with its onion-shaped blue dome, where in the darkened interior many parishioners, standing as is the Orthodox custom, were responding to the low tone of the priest's prayers. I was discretely taking pictures when a church official suddenly pounced on me, angrily informing me that this was forbidden. I did manage to calm him down when I explained that as a foreign visitor I was unaware of such a regulation and apologized. Many mixed emotions were churning in me, prying as I was into my father's birthplace, a secret he had guarded so well all his life.

When I left the church I felt I was leaving a prison. I imagined possible scenes of yore as I looked at the spot where my grandparents' home once stood facing the church and suddenly shuddered, although it was a warm and sunny day. During the Czarist era the bells of this church would ring daily, not only to call the faithful to religious services, but also to announce the latest *ukaz* (regulation) from the czars and the authorities in St. Petersburg. All news of a negative nature, whether economic or political, would eventually be blamed on the Jews, and the local populace surely listened with anger when their priests berated the Jews for all the maladies of the time, and worse, for killing their Savior, Jesus Christ. My father's family living in such close proximity to that church, I felt, must have been somewhat akin to Jews in Nazi Germany living near Gestapo headquarters.

As Leonid and I strolled around Radomyshel we talked about the violent anti-Semitic acts that occurred when my grandparents and their siblings lived in the Ukraine. Later we visited a memorial honoring the residents killed by the White and Bolshevik armies during the civil war. The lettering on the plain horizontal slab, in contrast with a nearby ornately-sculptured World War II memorial, briefly stated that White "bandits" had come through the town and massacred its people. No indication was made that the only victims in Radomyshel were Jews killed by the violently anti-Semitic Ukrainian National Republican Army and their allies, the Cossacks, led by their *Ataman* (chief) Sokolovek.

It is not surprising that Benjamin decided to leave Radomyshel for Vladivostok in 1916 after Czar Nicholas II sided with the Great Powers and declared war on Germany. Benjamin, then 22 years old, knew he would be conscripted immediately if he stayed, but in far-off Vladivostok he would be safe from military recruiters. The Russian authorities' only interest in Siberia and Russia's Far East was as an area for workers' colonies or as a place to send prisoners and revolutionaries, who paid for their dissent with hard labor in mines deep in the tundra and icy steppes. Benjamin managed to convince his younger sister Sonia to leave Radomyshel with him on the Trans-Siberian train to Vladivostok, thousands of miles away from European Russia.

Benjamin chose to go to Vladivostok because he was told that a number of British and German banks and trading firms were established in that city and that it was a busy trans-shipment port for goods from Manchuria to Japan and Korea. He found work in a German export company where he quickly learned the German language and, being linguistically inclined, also taught himself French. By now Benjamin spoke Russian, Yiddish, German and French and read ancient Hebrew, never imagining that one day he would have to learn another language, English, and of all places, in China.

However, when the civil war spread to Russia's Far East and the White and Red armies were battling for control of the area, Benjamin pulled up stakes once again and in 1919 left Vladivostok for Harbin, in Manchuria (Dongbei). He took a ship to Dairen (Dalian) then a train to Harbin, where his sister Sonia had gone two years earlier, married a pharmacist and led a very comfortable life thanks to her husband's thriving business.

Harbin had been transformed into a Russian provincial town at the end of the 19th century when Russia obtained territorial concessions from China to build the Chinese Eastern Railway that linked Harbin to their naval facilities at Port Arthur. Thousands of Russian engineers, architects and clerks were hired for the railroad administrative offices, repair shops and depots, lured by free housing and education for their children.

When Benjamin arrived in Harbin, the city was flourishing culturally, with concert halls, theaters and an opera house, and with a Russian population that had grown to 200,000, including the largest Jewish community in the Far East, numbering 15,000 people. Many of the latter had managed to leave the Pale of Settlement, the pogroms and the civil wars, and had trekked to Harbin where they could own land and where their children could attend Russian schools without any restrictions.

Benjamin felt at home intellectually and culturally in Harbin, where he stayed with his sister Sonia and her husband. However, he could not find any full-time work as a translator or clerk, although he was qualified to work for Harbin's main employer, the Chinese Eastern Railway. Jews were barred from this quasi-government operation run by anti-Semitic Whites who had left Russia before and after the Revolution. Benjamin decided to leave Harbin when he received a letter from a friend living in Shanghai who wrote that he could find work in that Europeanized city controlled by the Americans, the British and the French. This was an opportunity to distance himself from the simmering disputes in Harbin between the Japanese and the White Russians, the political opponents of the Bolsheviks in the Russian civil war.

In 1920, Benjamin took the train from Harbin to the port of Dairen and sailed south to Shanghai. He wanted to leave behind all matters relating to Russia and the Russians, hoping to find work in Shanghai as a clerk or a translator for a European firm or for the municipalities run by the English and the French. Soon after his arrival in Shanghai, Benjamin pulled down the curtain on his past in Czarist Russia, its civil war and the Bolsheviks, anglicized his family name and listed his place of birth as Chisinau in Romania's Bessarabia. He would later pay a high price for hiding the fact that he was born in Russia.

With his new identity as Benjamin Willens and calling himself a Romanian national, he was poised to tackle an alien culture in the city of Shanghai.

The Tale 2 of Thaïs

IN CONTRAST to my father, my mother Thaïs enjoyed telling us about her early years in Siberia in Novonicolaevsk, renamed Novosibirsk after the Revolution, where she was born in 1902. This town did not exist until Czar Alexander III ordered in 1893 that a bridge be built over the River Ob for the crossing of the Mid-Siberian Railway and the eventual continuation of the Trans-Siberian Railway to the port of Vladivostok. People from adjoining hamlets came to find work with the railroad or establish businesses, and the town very soon grew to 20,000 inhabitants thanks to the Trans-Siberian Railway, which transported goods to and from Moscow and Vladivostok. Novonicolaevsk became known in the Russian business world as the "Chicago of the North".

When in 2003 I visited Novosibirsk, the third-largest city in present-day Russia, it was no longer recognizable as the town my mother described with its wooden houses and the horse-drawn *troika* (carriage) which her family used for their outings. However, the massive red-brick Alexander Nevsky Cathedral, built at the end of the 19th century, which loomed close to Thaïs' family home on the River Ob, and the small Nicholas Chapel then dedicated in honor of Czar Nicholas II, were still there, having escaped communist destruction.

My mother Thaïs often spoke about her childhood and especially about her grandfather, Pavel Udalevitch, the family's very religious patriarch who was held in awe and reverence by his grandchildren. My great-grandfather Pavel was born in 1820 in present-day Belarus, where, at the age of eighteen, he was conscripted into the Russian army to serve the obligatory 25 years in the military. As with all Jewish veterans who served this length of time, he was given discharge documents that allowed him to live outside the Pale of Settlement. Pavel took advantage of the opportunity to distance himself from the Czarist authorities and settled in Siberia, away from the anti-Semitic violence and pogroms prevailing in European Russia. My mother always related with pride that her grandfather never abandoned his faith despite intense pressure during his military service to convert to Christianity.

Pavel claimed a homestead in the small town of Tatarsk in Siberia. There he married and had two children, one of whom would become my maternal grandmother Anna. Eventually Pavel and his family moved to the newly established town of Novonicolaevsk, where he opened a bakery which proved to be very successful since in the early years it was one of the few in town.

Pavel's daughter, Anna, married Samuel Vinokuroff, originally from Lithuania, who had wandered into Novonicolaevsk probably to avoid being drafted into the dreaded Czarist army. Samuel and Anna had six daughters, Fanya, Rebecca, Thaïs, Vera, Brania and Bessie, a son, Boris, and a set of twins who died in infancy. Samuel soon took over the bakery, and as his children grew up they helped him during the busy summer months. Once their chores ended, the children often rushed to the nearby Ob railway station to see the Trans-Siberian roaring into town from its long ride from Moscow and St. Petersburg. The attraction for these girls and their classmates was to see the disembarking passengers who had come from European Russia dressed in the latest finery, and, more important and exciting, to wave to the university students sitting quietly by the windows of their compartments. These young men in their distinctive school caps and shirts with high collars and young women dressed in nondescript clothing never left the train to walk about the station, which somewhat puzzled the children of Novonicolaevsk. They did not realize these young people had been accused of being revolutionaries and were being sent as political prisoners to work at backbreaking tasks in the frigid camps and mines in the outposts of Siberia, never to return to their homes in European Russia.

Although Thaïs' grandparents, parents and siblings lived during the reign of the obsessively anti-Semitic Czar Alexander III and his son Nicholas II, they did not suffer the consequences of the czars' repressive laws and the pogroms against Jews. Thaïs and her siblings attended the local Russian school, which would not have been possible in European Russia. Although Thaïs' grandfather and parents spoke Yiddish at home, the children spoke to them in Russian, the language they were studying in school and which they used with their servants and the help in the bakery. Since the Jewish population rarely exceeded 1,000 people in Novonicolaevsk and was as low as 700 during World War I due to military conscription, anti-Semitism was more prevalent in words than in action. Thaïs' brother Boris, however, was beaten by his classmates quite often because he was a small and frail *Yid*. His sisters were rarely harassed but Thaïs did recall one incident where some boys in her class tried to smear lard on her lips, knowing that Jews did not eat pork. She reported this incident to her teacher and subsequently was never bothered again.

My mother also remembered vividly how she and her friends were shocked when, in 1918, a teacher informed the class that Czar Nicolas II, his wife Alexandra and their five children had been executed in Yekaterinburg by the Bolsheviks. When I pressed my mother about her feelings towards the czar and his fanatically religious wife, both of whom condoned anti-Semitic acts, she answered without elaborating that it was wrong to have killed the royal family but horrible to have massacred the children.

As Thaïs was growing up, her older sisters, Fanya and Rebecca, got married, and the prettiest one, Brania, was being courted by a dashing merchant marine named Joseph. He warned Thaïs' parents that they should leave Siberia since the Whites and the Reds were now fighting for control of the Trans-Siberian Railway and that Jews were being killed by the White army soldiers in their bloody rampages from Ukraine to Siberia. Joseph managed to convince Thaïs' father Samuel that they needed to leave Novonicolaevsk before these armies reached their doorstep. Samuel agreed; having heard about the recent pogrom in Byisk, Siberia, he was understandably fearful of the arrival in Novonicolaevsk of the anti-Semitic Whites and the Reds who targeted "bourgeois" businesses and properties. Also worrisome for Samuel was the strong possibility that his six daughters would be harmed by gangs of undisciplined young soldiers. However, Samuel had a very difficult time convincing his wife Anna to leave behind their home and their business and go east to the Russian-controlled city of Harbin in Manchuria, far from the civil war on Russian soil. Anna, fearing the unknown, was also very worried about leaving her father Pavel, now aged 97. This *Nicolayevski soldat* (soldier of Czar Nicholas I) stayed behind and died at the ripe old age of 104 in 1924, the same year as the legendary revolutionary, Vladimir Ilyich Lenin. Thaïs' sister Fanya remained behind with her husband. No one ever heard from them again.

In mid-1918, Samuel managed to procure train tickets on the overcrowded Trans-Siberian Railway by bribing several local officials in Novonicolaevsk. The two days and two nights traversing Russia on wooden seats to Chita, the transfer point to Manchuria, was harrowing. The train was stopped several times by marauding White and Bolshevik soldiers and defectors who clambered aboard looking for food and money. Cossack soldiers then controlling Siberia killed several men who would not let them search their luggage and threw their bodies in the fields as a warning to the terrified train passengers. Whenever the soldiers heard people speaking Russian with a Yiddish accent they immediately accused them of hiding gold and silver and stuck their guns and sabers into suitcases and bundles to check for valuables. Like most travelers, Samuel and his family had hidden their money and jewelry in the lining and hems of their clothing. The soldiers, some of whom were barely sixteen years old, did not find the gold chains, diamonds and pearl necklaces which Samuel had purchased after selling his house and bakery. In Chita, the family transferred to the Chinese Eastern Railway for Harbin. The very long ride through Manchuria was uneventful since the civil war and the soldiers were now behind them in Russia.

In Harbin, Samuel had money from selling some of his jewelry and on impulse purchased a small rooming house to rent to the stream of refugees fleeing Russia's Far East and Siberia. Most of them, however, were poor and Samuel's business quickly failed. He was obliged to sell more jewelry to residents who had settled in Harbin before the Revolution but this was tedious work as the potential buyers bargained endlessly. Two young men leaving for Japan convinced Samuel that they could sell his remaining jewelry at much higher prices in Tokyo. They promised to return as soon as possible with the money from the sales, but Samuel never saw them again. His family was now destitute in Harbin and Samuel did not see any reason to stay in a city where he could not start a business without cash and could not find work as a clerk, as he could barely write Russian. He heard that a city further south in China, Shanghai, had become a haven for Russians fleeing the Revolution. Once again he uprooted his family and in 1920 they took a train from Harbin to the port of Dairen and embarked on a Japanese steamer bound for Shanghai.

That was the same year that Benjamin sailed to Shanghai, a city he had heard was administered by Western powers. But like Samuel and his family, Benjamin knew nothing about Shanghai, its history, its culture or its people.

Takeover by the 3 "Barbarians"

THE SHANGHAI Benjamin and Thaïs reached in 1920 already had a very colorful history. During the 18th and 19th centuries foreign merchants were forbidden to enter China except for Macao (Aomen), administered by the Portuguese, and Chinese-controlled Canton (Guangzhou). In the latter port they were allowed to live on a sliver of land set aside for them for a few months a year during the tea trading season. All contact between the Chinese people and Westerners, known as "barbarians" or "foreign devils", was strictly forbidden, except in the officially designated Chinese commercial intermediaries, the *Co-Hongs*. Since tea and spices were much in demand in Europe, foreign merchants were clamoring for the opening of Chinese ports to purchase these commodities. However, the imbalance in trade and outflow of silver from England was increasing rapidly. Ship owners and sea captains decided to fill the ballasts on their voyages to China with a very lucrative commodity: opium from British India.

For many years the English merchants ignored edicts prohibiting the sale of opium in China and in 1839 Emperor Daoguang sent Chinese authorities to confiscate the opium stock in the warehouses in Canton, burn it and prohibit any further trade in that port. Britain retaliated by declaring war on China in 1840 and sent an armada of warships to capture Shanghai. The Chinese capitulated and in August 1842 signed the treaty of Nanking (Nanjing), which stipulated that five tea-trading ports, Canton, Amoy (Xiamen), Foochow (Fuzhou), Ningpo (Ningbo) and Shanghai, were to be opened to foreign trade, with British

Seals of the International Settlement and the French Concession

consular officials in each of these ports. In addition, the port of Hongkong (Hong Kong) was handed over to the British Crown. The prize, however, was Shanghai, a very busy commercial port on the banks of the Whangpoo River (Hungpu Jiang) near the mouth of the Yangtze River (Chang Jiang), with easy access to the Grand Canal and the Pacific Ocean. There was no indication in the negotiations that enclaves would be set aside for foreign residents, nor was there any mention of extraterritorial privileges for non-diplomats in the five treaty ports, which were addressed in subsequent treaties.

This so-called "Opium War" marked the beginning of China's humiliation by the Western powers, for soon after, France and the United States negotiated treaties acquiring the same rights and privileges as Britain. Subsequently, the English Settlement of Shanghai was established in 1845, followed by the French Concession in April 1849 and an American Settlement in February 1854, both adjoining the English Settlement. Extraterritorial rights were granted in these enclaves to citizens of these three treaty powers, which meant that if they became embroiled in civil or criminal matters they would be tried according to their respective countries' laws and never by Chinese courts or laws. Later, the Americans in their small settlement in Hongkew (Hongkou) decided to join with their British counterparts and in 1863 the two entities merged with other nations eager for concessions to become the International Settlement. The French were invited to join them and initially accepted but later refused, leery of the Anglo-Saxons, especially the British, who were so heavily involved in the China trade and who would surely take a leading role in a unified settlement.

The extraterritorial city of Shanghai was born, and for the next hundred years two-thirds were controlled and administered by an international body dominated by the British and Americans and one-third by the French, while the three districts of Chapei (Zhabei), Nantao (Nanshi) and Hongkew were under the Chinese government's jurisdiction – and sometimes even controlled by a warlord.

The principal aim of these three treaty powers in the second half of the 19th century was to increase Western trade. Although the Treaty of Nanking did not lift the ban on opium, this commodity was still being smuggled into China by Westerners with the help of corrupt Chinese intermediaries and government officials. Ships stocked with opium cases arrived from British India while American ships, which could not buy opium in India because of England's fear of competition, had to sail to Smyrna – present-day Izmir – in Turkey to replenish their stock. With demand increasing and foreign merchants and their Chinese intermediaries enriching themselves, the trade could not be stopped until finally it was banned in 1917.

A second "Opium War" started after a series of incidents that incited the ire – and opportunism – of the British. In one encounter Chinese officials boarded a formerly British-registered ship, the *Arrow*, on suspicion of smuggling and piracy and removed and imprisoned its Chinese crew members. This act, so far as the British were concerned, violated the Treaty of Nanking, and, together with the murder of a French missionary, led to an Anglo-French armada sailing to Tientsin (Tianjin) in 1858, where they threatened to attack Peking unless China made further concessions. China signed the Treaty of Tientsin under humiliating conditions but it took several more battles up to 1860, and the burning of the exquisite Old Summer Palace (Yuanming Yuan), for the foreign powers to force China to comply with its one-sided conditions. It was obliged to pay war reparations, open 11 more extraterritorial treaty ports, legalize the trade of opium and allow Catholic and Protestant missionaries to proselytize in China. In addition, the British demanded that foreigners no longer be labeled "barbarians".

By the dawn of the 20th century a dozen European countries and Japan had also been granted extraterritorial rights in Shanghai and other treaty ports. Imperial China was being dismembered by the foreign powers and ruined financially by indemnity payments, civil wars and internal waste and corruption. The millennia-old imperial era came to an end when the Qing Imperial dynasty was overthrown in 1912 and China became a republic under the long-exiled Dr. Sun Yat-sen. He soon relinquished his provisional presidency to the powerful general Yuan Shi-kai, whom Sun believed could enlist the aid of the military to unite China. This did not happen. Yuan attempted to appoint himself China's new emperor, igniting a wave of revolt and leaving China a deeply divided country with several warlords vying for power upon his death in 1916.

When Thaïs and Benjamin reached Shanghai, the city was not affected economically by the continuous civil wars in the north. Whenever skirmishes occurred too close to the two foreign settlements, Western authorities declared a state of emergency and called upon the Shanghai Volunteer Corps, composed of foreign men from various nations under the command of British officers, to guard the settlements. If need be, they would be backed by the foreign soldiers, sailors and marines garrisoned in the city and by naval contingents from the warships anchored in the Whangpoo River.

The extraterritorial city of Shanghai would prove to be a most glaring example of political and cultural discrimination towards the Chinese people, first by Westerners and later by the Japanese. Benjamin and Thaïs, although stateless and subject to Chinese laws, could take advantage of most of the privileges accorded the treaty power nationals simply because they were ethnically white.

The Failed Revolution

4

BENJAMIN AND Thaïs' first impressions were similar when they arrived in Shanghai. They were shocked at the filth, the incessant street noise and the pungent odors. They were astounded by the abject poverty of beggars in rags with open sores oozing pus, yelling for coins and chanting at the sight of foreigners, "No papa, no mama, no whiskey soda," a refrain they learned from the British and American soldiers, sailors and marines. Nonetheless, new arrivals had to focus on the demanding task of finding work in a city where they had to fend for themselves as Russians without a country. They became stateless in 1921 when the Soviets denationalized all the Russians who fled the *Rodina* (Motherland) during and immediately after the Revolution. But for Russian Jews like Benjamin and Thaïs, this was the first time in their lives that they were not subjected to the vagaries of an anti-Semitic population or government. Here it was the Chinese who were being treated as second-class citizens in their own country. Once settled, stateless refugees would often act in the same discriminatory manner towards the Chinese as did the treaty powers' nationals. They were now protected by the British and French police in charge of the two settlements.

Thaïs, her parents and four of her siblings lived for the first few years in a rooming house in the French Concession. The older daughters worked as sales clerks in small stores along Avenue Joffre (Huaihai Lu) while Thaïs found a job as a seamstress in a dress shop owned by a Chinese woman who catered to foreigners. Thaïs and her siblings began to learn English from the foreign clientele who frequented their stores and also Pidgin English in their daily dealings with the Chinese.

Meanwhile Benjamin, who had also settled down in a rooming house in the French Concession, worked part-time as a bookkeeper and Russian translator of business regulations issued in English and French by the two foreign municipalities. Gifted in languages, he rapidly learned to speak proper English since, as a stickler for correct grammar, he disliked using Pidgin English. He was relieved that he had registered with the French police as a Romanian national for he quickly discovered stateless Russians in Shanghai did not command much respect from either the foreign nationals or the Chinese. Thanks to his well-groomed appearance and neat attire, Benjamin could easily pass for a Frenchman or an Englishman, an extremely important advantage in class-conscious Shanghai.

On a sultry evening in June 1924, Thaïs came down for dinner with the other lodgers and noticed a stranger in their midst. She was struck by his handsome looks, light brown hair with a streak of white in the middle, green eyes and his 5'10" height when he stood up to greet her. Despite the oppressive heat and humidity, he was wearing a well-pressed white cotton suit, white shirt, dark-colored tie and polished black leather shoes, attire that contrasted with the scruffy appearance of the other men around the dinner table. Benjamin's quiet demeanor and his excellent use of the Russian language differed from the loud and noisy young men, especially the landlady's two sons who vied for Thaïs' attention.

Benjamin seemed quite smitten with Thaïs, a petite 5"2' young woman with black hair, brown eyes, high cheekbones, very white skin and a warm smile. After dinner he invited her to a free concert in Koukaza Park (Fuxing Gongyuan) in the French Concession. The next morning Thaïs called a close friend of hers to ask whether she knew anything about this attractive stranger. The report she received was not good. She was told he always read all the newspapers at the Shanghai Jewish Club, where he was not a member, never spent any money, and never even bought himself a cup of tea or coffee. The friend warned Thaïs to stay away from this overly frugal man, who would surely be a very difficult husband, but she ignored all these negative comments and decided that Benjamin was the man she wanted to marry. She went out with him to free concerts at local clubs or to the Public Gardens in the Settlement and the Koukaza Park – weather permitting – to listen to local musicians or band music performed by the military. With its well-manicured lawns surrounding trees and flower beds, the park was an oasis for Shanghailanders, away from the filth and noise of the city. It did not surprise Thaïs that Benjamin chose this setting, after a classical concert, to ask her to marry him.

My mother told me that the Koukaza Park was open to Chinese if they purchased tickets, however the Public Garden was closed to them unless they worked there, were guests accompanied by foreign nationals or were "amahs" – the term used for Chinese nannies – taking care of the little "foreign devils". The Public Gardens at the junction of the Whangpoo River and Soochow Creek (Suzhou He), facing the British Consulate, was the first park created in 1868 for foreigners by their Municipal Council in the International Settlement. In 1917 a sign was posted indicating this private park was reserved for the foreign community. The sign stated that dogs and bicycles were not admitted. In addition, ". . . plucking flowers, climbing trees or damaging the trees, shrubs or grass is strictly prohibited . . . Amahs in charge of children are not permitted to occupy the seat chairs during band performance." The latter proscription was clearly aimed more at noisy children than at their amahs, but the Council wanted to keep out beggars who would otherwise harass people in the park or would spend the night on the park benches. My mother added, when I asked, that she never saw signs in any park with the words "Chinese" and "Dogs" juxtaposed – as claimed repeatedly by the rulers of China and writers both Chinese and foreign. Many Chinese could not enter these parks in their own country, but the sign "No Chinese OR dogs allowed" never existed. The Kuomintang and later the People's Republic of China used and still use this

Wedding picture of Benjamin and Thaïs Willens

spurious sign as a propaganda tool to illustrate the racial insensitivity of Westerners during the colonial era.

In summer 1924 civil war broke out around Shanghai when a warlord from northern China tried to wrest Chapei, the Chinese-administered city north of the Settlement, from another warlord. Their armies began fighting on the outskirts of the International Settlement and soldiers from both Chinese factions entered Chapei, looting homes and shops and terrorizing the residents, who fled by the thousands to the foreign enclaves. The foreign authorities declared they would not take sides in this local war but did warn the warlords not to enter the International Settlement or the Concession. French and English soldiers patrolled the streets with men of the multinational civilian Shanghai Volunteer Corps, while their gunboats and Japanese cruisers bristling with guns lay anchored near the Bund as a show of force. As long as the fighting did not affect the local economy these see-saw battles by weak and disorganized Chinese armies were shrugged off by the foreigners as minor nuisances. The only change my parents recalled was the increasing number of beggars and refugees squatting and sleeping in the side streets of Shanghai and begging for copper coins.

The nearby civil war did not interfere with Benjamin and Thaïs' wedding plans. They were married in October 1924 by a rabbi from the Russian community. After the ceremony a group of friends and Thaïs' relatives attended a small wedding reception at a private home. The newly married couple rented a small two-room apartment on Avenue Joffre above the Toyland Store run by two Russian ladies. Benjamin found additional work as a translator of English, French, Russian and German while Thaïs continued to work at the dress shop, also earning Chinese silver dollars by sewing clothes at home on consignment. These dollars, at a time when China was a silver-standard country, were a safer currency than the various paper money and copper coins in circulation. The extra income enabled them to attend recitals by Russian musicians and to purchase birthday and anniversary gifts for their growing circle of friends. Benjamin's sister Sonia regularly sent them packages from Harbin containing sugar, honey, halva, caviar and jam, and in the winter woolen coats, gloves and blankets to hold off the cold in the couple's damp and poorly heated apartment.

Although Benjamin and Thaïs were beginning to enjoy their social life in Shanghai, political events were occurring that worried them as well as the other stateless residents. In November 1924, the "Father of Modern China" China, Dr. Sun Yat-sen, visited Shanghai and reminded the municipal authorities that the foreigners residing in Shanghai and other treaty ports were "guests" of the Chinese people, and that all extraterritorial treaties needed to be abrogated. Dr. Sun's views pleased the Chinese – the Shanghainese – but his pronouncements were not taken seriously by the foreign nationals – the Shanghailanders – who were strongly backed by the treaty powers. They believed

Dr. Sun's views were influenced by his Bolshevik advisors, for that year China had recognized the new Soviet government and, in return, the USSR had abrogated all its extraterritorial rights in the treaty ports and in Harbin.

Chiang Kai-shek, the heir apparent to Dr. Sun as leader of the Kuomintang Party, was encouraged by his Soviet advisors to wrest Chapei from the warlord who controlled it, unite China and end the anomaly of extraterritoriality in all of China. When Sun Yat-sen died in 1925, Britain and France were concerned that Chiang and his revolutionary communist allies would try to take all the foreign settlements in China. The treaty powers' economy and prestige were, they thought, at stake.

Thaïs was frightened when Chinese university students demonstrated against Japanese and British factory owners, accusing them of exploiting Chinese workers, paying them low wages and having them work very long hours in unsafe and unsanitary conditions. Thaïs saw masses of demonstrators exhorting the population to boycott Japanese and British goods and demanding the Japanese army leave Manchuria. Thousands of workers from these factories and mills in Hongkew, Pootung (Pudong) and Yangtzepoo (Yangpu) went on strike and were joined by students, holding large demonstrations against Japanese and British imperialism and extraterritoriality.

On May 30, 1925, a group of students and workers was demonstrating in front of the small Louza police station on Nanking Road in the International Settlement. After repeatedly warning the demonstrators to leave the area, the lone British officer on duty in the station ordered his men – Chinese and Indian Sikhs – to fire on the demonstrators, killing a dozen and wounding many more. Following this bloody encounter, 50,000 students left their classes and demonstrated for two days, calling again for strikes and retribution for the killing of innocent workers. Within a week Shanghai was in a state of siege; foreign soldiers and sailors from the various garrisons and ships began patrolling the city and the Shanghai Volunteer Corps was put on standby. Workers refused to return to their mills and factories, and shops closed as the owners feared looting and riots.

All that week, Benjamin and Thaïs did not go to work or venture out of their apartment. Trade in Shanghai went into a tailspin. The students, naming their cause the May 30th Movement in honor of the men killed at the Louza station, submitted a list of seventeen demands to the foreign authorities. Among these was the better treatment of factory workers, the withdrawal of British and Japanese gunboats from the Bund, Chinese representation in the Shanghai Municipal Council and, most importantly, the end of the unjust and humiliating system of extraterritoriality. After many months of protesting, and mounting political and economic pressure, some of the conditions demanded were met, but the gunboats stayed and Shanghai remained an extraterritorial city. Workers finally went back to their factories and Shanghai was now at peace.

As these events swirled around her, Thaïs discovered she was pregnant. Uppermost in her mind was the fear that more riots could occur and, worse, that Chiang Kai-shek's army was approaching Shanghai, intent on taking the foreign settlements. Britain, France, the United States and several other foreign countries made provisions to evacuate their nationals, if need be, to the nearby warships. Benjamin, Thaïs and all stateless Russians, however, had nowhere to go.

In July 1925, Benjamin received a telegram from his sister Sonia in Harbin. Upon reading it he cried out and fainted. His father and his sister Rebecca, it said, had been killed six years ago in the 1919 pogrom in Radomyshel, instigated by the Cossacks and White Army insurgents. The rest of the family was spared because they had left earlier for the Caucasus. News could not reach the outside world while the civil war was raging in Russia.

Benjamin would never speak about this tragic event. He hid his pain, wiping out, wherever possible, all emotional links with his native land, further hiding behind his adopted Romanian nationality.

Thaïs gave birth in September 1925 to a daughter at the Hôpital Sainte Marie, a highly respected teaching hospital established in 1908, financed by the French municipality and staffed by French doctors and nuns of the Saint Vincent de Paul orders. Thaïs was attended by Dr. René Santelli, a professor of medicine at the renowned Jesuit Université Aurore. That same day, twelve babies – French, Portuguese, Italian and Chinese – were born and registered in the hospital ledger. The French religious orders did not practice racial discrimination in their hospitals or infirmaries, and the Chinese could use them if they paid the required fees. In addition, a walk-in clinic was set aside for destitute Chinese.

Benjamin and Thaïs named their baby girl Rebecca in memory of Benjamin's sister murdered in the Ukraine. The new parents were delighted with their first-born, docile and plump with green eyes and a tuft of black hair, whom they called by her Russian diminutive name, Riva. Thaïs was petrified to handle her newborn and decided to hire an amah. With the addition of a baby and an amah in the family, Benjamin made a concerted effort to find a full-time job. This seemed feasible since the economy in Shanghai was slowly recovering, but his hopes sank when, in July 1926, Chiang's Nationalist army in Canton launched an expedition against the warlords in the north. His soldiers invaded the British concessions of Hankow (Hankou) and Kiukiang (Jiujiang) on the Yangtze River, and local mobs attacked and killed some foreign residents. Britain protested but, overwhelmed by Chiang's revolutionary forces, was obliged to give up extraterritoriality in these two industrial centers. Furthermore, British goods were boycotted and anti-foreign feelings increased in all the treaty ports.

Despite this troublesome time, Benjamin was hired in February 1927 as a general office assistant in the British firm, S. Behr and Mathew, Ltd. This company was not affected by the boycott and it was still able to ship its merchandise of dried egg yolk to its branch offices in Paris, Hamburg, Berlin and Glasgow. The following month a warlike situation prevailed in Shanghai when it was learned that Chiang's army was advancing down the Yangtze Valley towards Shanghai. The foreign municipalities declared a state of emergency and 30,000 British, French, Spanish, Italian and Japanese troops landed in Shanghai from their warships to defend the International Settlement and the French Concession. In addition, 1,500 American Marines joined this international force. Barricades of sandbags and rolls of barbed wire were placed around the two foreign enclaves, busses and tramways stopped running, the big department stores closed their doors and martial law was declared with a strictly-enforced curfew. Foreigners were asked to stay indoors to avoid any altercations with the Chinese and were also told to prepare one suitcase each for a possible evacuation. However, this announcement was addressed only to holders of foreign passports.

Benjamin and Thaïs, along with all stateless Russians, had no choice but to wait and pray that the Nationalists would not be able to take over "foreign" Shanghai. Although registered as residents in the two extraterritorial enclaves, Russians could never acquire British or French citizenship since Shanghai was a settlement and not a colony. Very few of them had applied for the League of Nations' "Nansen" identity certificate, a "laissez passer" to travel and resettle in countries willing to accept them. The Russians, having fled their country, did not want to move again after adjusting to life in Shanghai. Benjamin and Thaïs would have to fend for themselves, although it was now more difficult with a one-year-old child and a second on the way.

As Chiang Kai-shek's army was advancing towards Shanghai, his allies, the communists, had infiltrated the factories and instigated massive strikes and demonstrations by workers and students. The city was at a standstill. Benjamin and Thaïs could hear the roar of gunfire and see smoke billowing from Chapei. Little did they and other foreigners know that Chiang had already assured the treaty powers and wealthy Shanghainese businessmen that he intended to settle the question of extraterritoriality by peaceful means. He informed them he had no intention of sharing power with his communist allies.

Chiang Kai-shek kept his promise. On April 12, 1927, his soldiers turned on the communist cadres, students and workers in the city, killing 5,000 of them in a two-week bloodbath. The young communist agitator, Chou En-lai (Zhou Enlai), who later became one of the leaders of the People's Republic of China, barely managed to escape from Shanghai. During that "White Terror" period, as it was subsequently labeled, Benjamin and Thaïs did not budge. Thaïs was extremely concerned, wondering whether she would be able to give birth to her second child at the Hôpital Sainte Marie, since the French doctors and nuns would be evacuated if Chiang took the foreign settlements.

Chiang's treachery and subsequent victory was a boon for the foreigners, especially the stateless Russian residents. They now could return to a normal life. The civil war around Shanghai had ended, the communists were decimated and Chiang Kai-shek seemed to be in control of China and able to unite it. Benjamin and Thaïs did not have to flee into the unknown.

"Chinese" Shanghai

ON AUGUST 5, 1927, Thaïs gave birth to her second child (me) – not at the Hôpital Sainte Marie, which was still not fully staffed after the Kuomintang bloodbath in April, but at the apartment on Avenue Joffre. A few weeks after my birth my mother hired another amah whom my parents called Old Amah because she was in her late thirties, a little older than average. She was a tall, thin and rather severe-looking Chinese woman of peasant stock, her hair tied in a bun and always impeccably dressed in her standard amah's "uniform": a white jacket with hooks on the side, black cotton pants and black canvas shoes. Amahs in Shanghai usually had their own room – often windowless – in the servants' quarters attached to the main house and received wages that enabled them to send money to their families. Along with no longer having to cook their meals outside on the pavement, squatting on low stools and fanning briquette-filled clay stoves, another luxury for the amahs was the availability of soap and hot water in their quarters, freeing them from the necessity of having to line up every morning with a large thermos bottle to purchase hot water at crowded shops. If there were no other servants in the household, the amah became the "workhorse" – not only did she take care of the children, she washed dishes and clothes and occasionally helped prepare the meals. Although amahs received a meager salary and did not have a day off for weeks on end, they often considered themselves fortunate to have roofs over their heads and to be working in foreign households, where they received higher wages and were somewhat less likely to be slapped by the *Master* or *Missee* than if they worked for wealthy

Old Amah and Lily in Koukaza Park

Chinese families.

Old Amah and I became inseparable as I was growing up. She took full charge of me ("Leelee") and of my sister Riva whom she called "Leeva". She fed, bathed and dressed us in clothes which my mother no longer sewed but now purchased. My father's income increased substantially at the end of 1927 when he was hired as a sales representative for Sun Life Assurance Company of Canada, a firm headquartered in Montreal. Soon after, we moved to a larger apartment in a small complex of rental buildings on Route Ratard (Julu Lu), where my parents got a private room for Old Amah in the servants' quarters annex. Socially, our family was moving up – Old Amah, too, in the eyes of her friends.

Old Amah insisted on getting us soft canvas shoes, explaining to my mother that leather shoes were "vely no good" for our feet since the shoelaces would untie quickly and we could fall and hurt ourselves. Thanks to these soft shoes, I easily could outrun Old Amah, who walked with a spring in her gait because her feet were very narrow for her tall build.

My sister Riva hardly ever caused any problems but by the time I was five years old I was terrorizing the little girls with whom I played in the garden, fighting with the little boys living in our complex and sticking out my tongue at the Chinese children in the streets. Old Amah often saved me from yelling and spanking, calming my mother down by saying: "When Missee Leelee big, she good like Leeva." Although I had already picked up some of the Shanghainese dialect, Old Amah always spoke to me in Pidgin English for she understood intuitively that my parents and other European parents did not want their children to learn Chinese. There was no need for the foreigners to use it since Chinese servants were obliged to speak a smattering of their masters' languages, whether it was Pidgin English, French, Russian or German.

When I was about six years old my mother let me accompany Old Amah on her shopping trips in the streets of "Chinese" Shanghai, a world that I discovered was very different from my own. I was glad to be away from my noisy baby sister Jacqueline, a crying "nuisance" who had come into my life a year earlier. This child, whom all called Jackie, was getting too much attention from my parents and their friends. They could not decide whether she resembled her mother or her father but they agreed that she did not resemble her two older sisters. Riva had my father's looks and calm disposition, while I resembled my mother in looks and temperament, which meant I was a very active child.

On the way to the market, Old Amah and I walked through several very poor neighborhoods where we would inevitably pass a man slowly pushing a wide wooden cart. He went in and out of the alleys and lanes, where the Chinese lived in tenements and hovels without flush toilets, collecting the buckets of human waste that had accumulated overnight. When this *moo dong* man announced his arrival women rushed out with wooden buckets, which he emptied with a deft arm movement into large wooden containers securely tied to his cart. When they were filled to the brim he covered them with wooden lids and then slowly pushed his overloaded cart in the direction of the nearby countryside where he sold his morning collection to farmers as fertilizer. During the very humid summer months of July and August, when the thermometer sometimes hovered near 100 degrees Fahrenheit, the putrid smell from these carts hung in the air for the entire morning.

On those trips with Old Amah I watched her bargain endlessly with the food vendors over the price of rice, noodles, vegetables and fruit. She became quite theatrical when a price was quoted – she walked away complaining loudly that the street vendor was trying to rob her. She soon returned, however, and bargained again; then after much sighing she agreed grudgingly to buy the items she had earlier examined. She watched very carefully as the seller weighed her purchases on a scale consisting of a metal tray attached to a stick with a movable weight piece. On one of our excursions to the market Old Amah became very angry with me. I did not have time to tell her that I needed to "makee doodoo", so while she was talking to a friend at the marketplace I squatted on the street and defecated in my pants. I was simply doing what small Chinese children always did when they wanted to "makee doodoo", except that my pants were not split on the backside. Old Amah began lamenting that "Big *Missee* get vely, vely angly", and that Leelee "give me *walla, walla* (trouble, trouble), *ah ya, ah ya*". My proper and demure Old Amah always yanked me away whenever she noticed a man using a wall as an open-air toilet, while I wondered why he did not go home and use his bathroom as we did in our house. In my mind, only small children had the right to relieve themselves in public!

I looked forward to these outings with Old Amah because I knew that whenever she bought cooked meat, fish or baked dough she would bite off a small piece and share it with me. While flies were swarming and buzzing around the open food stalls, I admired the vendors who tried to hit them with the straw fans they used to fan their charcoal stoves. Sometimes, when Old Amah had a few extra copper coins to spare, she bought a piece of tofu fried in sizzling oil which she blew upon before handing it to me. She would also share with me her breakfast food, the small *da bing* pancake and the *you tiao*, strings of dough fried in boiling oil and then twirled by the vendor into an elongated shape. These two oily and very hot food items were wrapped in a piece of soiled paper torn from a newspaper. When Old Amah was feeling extra generous she bought and shared with me the pyramid-shaped *zongzi* filled with glutinous rice and wrapped in palm leaves, which I munched with delight. For dessert, which she bought for me when I nagged her sufficiently, there were the sticky *yuan xiao*, balls of rice covered with sesame seeds. I especially enjoyed the Chinese Mid-Autumn Festival since Old Amah would always buy me a *dousha bao*, a cake filled with mashed sweet red beans that she knew I preferred to the cakes and sweets we ate at tea time in our home.

Old Amah could never ask to be refunded for the copper coins she spent on me because my parents would not have allowed her

Birthdays with Amahs

to buy me food made in such unsanitary conditions. Of course I did not tell my mother about eating these forbidden delicacies because my trips with Old Amah would have ended. The food I ate in the marketplace was much tastier than the meat, chicken, potatoes, vegetables and soup we ate at home, where I was always told to eat slowly and wipe my mouth with a napkin. My taste for Chinese food may have been enhanced by the fact that Old Amah and I had a secret which we hid from my parents.

Whenever I ate food in the street Old Amah had to shoo away beggar children who had gathered around me watching me intently. I yelled *"sheela, sheela"* ("go away") at them, not realizing they were hungry. I thought it was silly of them to stare at me while I was eating and wondered why their mothers did not buy them food. I was annoyed when they surrounded me and I yelled at them in the Shanghai dialect, borrowing the words they used to insult me. The fact that Chinese children swore at me – the *yang guizi* (foreign devil) with her *da bizi* (big nose) – did not bother me for I had already surmised that as a white person I was superior to them. From a very early age my friends and I looked down on the Chinese, whose main function we had observed was to serve us and all other foreigners. Little did I know then we were behaving as colonial racists did in other parts of the world.

In early spring or in the fall, whenever there was a chill in the air, Old Amah stopped at a vendor's push cart or at a small portable restaurant to buy hot roasted chestnuts or bean curd soup. We slurped the soup from the same bowl and spoon, which had been washed earlier in grayish water with a soiled rag the vendor dried on his sleeve. Old Amah always asked me, "Leelee, wanchee eatee?" ("want to eat?") to which I inevitably replied, "Wanchee more." She began to learn more and more Pidgin English words while I picked up additional Chinese words from the conversations around me and from the urchins who yelled at me. Whenever they stared at me or muttered "*nakoonin pissey*" ("dirty foreign pig") I immediately retorted with "*tzoong koonin pissey*" ("dirty Chinese pig"). I did not know what *pissey* meant but realized it must be a very bad word as Old Amah tried to stop me from using it. I relished these forbidden words because at home there was only the Russian word *svinya* (swine), which my father used in moments of anger. Nor were we allowed to call the Chinese "Chinks" or the Japanese "Japs". My parents must have felt that these derogatory terms were just as hurtful to the Asians as the word "*Yid*" they had heard while growing up in czarist Russia.

While waiting for Old Amah to end her bickering with the various street vendors, I often watched the "cigarette man" as he manufactured cigarettes from discarded butts lying on the pavement or in water-clogged gutters. With his eyes glued to the ground he walked with a long stick topped with a piece of wire, which he deftly pushed into the abundant supply of stray cigarette butts, depositing them into a cloth sack attached to his waist. When the bag was almost full he squatted on his haunches and carefully removed the remaining tobacco from the soggy butts. With a lick of his tongue he wetted a thin piece of paper, rolled it around the old tobacco and manufactured a new cigarette. Remaining on his haunches, he then waited for customers. Although his clients could only afford to buy one cigarette at a time, this entrepreneurial individual must have earned a good number of copper coins during his long day, and his overheads were practically non-existent.

I was picking up "native" habits, spitting sunflower seeds in the streets, belching loudly after gulping down my bowl of rice and yelling at the urchins begging for coins. These children seemed fascinated by my white skin, brown hair and light brown eyes, and giggled as they pointed at the round eyeglasses I started wearing at age eight. They and the illiterate adults at the marketplace may have thought I could read and write like an adult, as in their world only learned people wore glasses. There actually was one such individual in the marketplace – the highly respected street letter-writer-in-residence. He sat in front of his small folding bamboo table, which was laid out with thin writing paper, envelopes and a small ink pot that he delicately dipped a writing brush into to compose letters for his clients. He looked scholarly in his long black gown, black skull cap topped by a red glass bead perched on his shaven head, and horn-rimmed glasses – whether needed or not – to impress the clientele. Since Old Amah could not read or write, she went to this scribe several times and paid him to compose short letters to her relatives in "Ningpo mofa" ("more far", meaning further than the town of Ningpo). But in my self-centered world, Old Amah was an individual who had to cater to all my whims. Neither I nor my parents ever asked her any questions about her private life or family.

These dirty, smelly and very noisy surroundings in the marketplace seemed very natural to me. After all, wasn't this how the Chinese lived in "their" Shanghai? Most of the people I encountered wore dirty clothes, while only rags covered the beggars' emaciated bodies. But I wondered why the better-dressed Chinese men wore long robes while the women wore long pants and short jackets. I was also curious as to why Chinese men did not wear suits and ties as my father did, and why Chinese women did not wear dresses similar to the ones worn by my mother and her friends. Chinese people spoke loudly and yelled a lot in a language which was not Pidgin English, and spat and blew their noses in the street. I wanted to blow my nose as the Chinese passersby did, placing a finger on one nostril then blowing very hard to allow all the mucus to squirt out quite a distance, sometimes inadvertently on the clothes of another pedestrian. Whenever this occurred, the recipient let out an interminable list of swear words while the projectile-blower yelled back that the "stupid tortoise of a man" should not have been in his way. While Old Amah stopped me copying them, I enjoyed very much watching these altercations.

Before leaving the market I often managed to drag Old Amah to the very colorful bird section to peek at the birds in large, elaborately designed wooden cages and the grasshoppers chirping away in tiny wooden containers. I would squat in front of the birds, poking my finger into their cages and trying gingerly to stroke their feathers. Old Amah pulled me away when the vendors insisted that she buy a bird for herself or for her foreign employers. I wanted to take a bird home but Old Amah knew my father would be angry and my mother hysterical if she gave in to my wishes. My parents did not want dogs or birds or even fish in a bowl in our home. Dogs reminded my mother of wolves barking in the winter nights in Novonicolaevsk.

Before long I no longer paid attention to the barrage of street noise – the incessant honking of horns and bicycle bells, the loud swearing and the shrill cries of the stall vendors, the "click-clack" sound of their bamboo noisemakers to draw the attention of passersby and the "click-click" of the abacus balls in the stores fronting the market. I was also immune to the sight of near-starving adults and children in the streets not far from the warm and safe enclave of our home in the French Concession.

I took it for granted that beggars were a permanent fixture of Chinese life. Foreigners and wealthy Chinese usually ignored the beggars' cries but from time to time a few did throw coins into an empty rice bowl or a tin cup placed on the pavement. Most of the beggars were near starvation, especially mothers with their very thin children trying to suckle milk from their emaciated breasts.

After walking back and forth with Old Amah between the various stalls, I would eventually become tired and we would ride back in a *wampatso* (rickshaw). Before choosing one Old Amah had to bargain and haggle with the rickshaw coolie puller, exchanging with him loud and often angry words, some of which I could understand. The coolie would complain that Old Amah, in the employ of "foreign devils", should pay more and not less than his asking price. But Old Amah would not budge and finally the man, desperate for a fare, would give in. Whenever it rained the coolie lowered a canvas cover to protect us while he hauled us with only a thin oilcloth over his own body. Many Chinese and a number of foreigners had private rickshaws, which were very noticeable because of the clean jacket and pants worn by the puller and the shiny brass oil lamps on each side of the carriage.

On the street near the entrance to our apartment building I always saw rickshaw coolies sitting on their haunches, patiently waiting for foreigners to appear. Whenever they spied a potential customer they leaped like tigers to catch their prey. Foreigners, who generally could not speak sufficient Chinese to bargain at length, always paid much more than the Chinese, or paid the requested fare, perhaps out of a twinge of compassion for these skinny men. Foreign men and women were nearly always a much heavier burden than the generally slim Shanghainese of both sexes. In some instances impatient riders, especially drunken foreign soldiers, would tap their foot on the coolie's back, urging him to run faster.

The rickshaw coolies' work was backbreaking, their legs revealed thick protruding veins due to running all day and well into the evening on hot macadam in the summer and wet roads in the winter, with feet clad in very thin straw sandals. Even so, they barely sustained themselves for they had to turn over a portion of their pittance to the owner of the rickshaw company. They had to be careful not to break any rules of the road, too; if this happened the short Annamite and Tonkinese policemen directing traffic in the French Concession or the towering Indian Sikh policemen of the International Settlement would take away the detachable cushion seat of the rickshaw and in the process hit the coolie with a truncheon. The loss of the cushion meant the end of the rickshaw man's livelihood unless he could retrieve it on the spot by giving some coins to his tormentor. The Chinese traffic policemen in the two settlements did not treat the rickshaw men any better.

Later, as a teenager, I became an expert in bargaining with the rickshaw coolie and never gave a thought that the extra coppers he wanted and that I refused to give would mean some vegetables and perhaps bean curd in his bowl of rice. Rarely did my parents or their friends call for taxis, the brown-and-tan Fords from "Ford Hire" or the light green Chevrolets from "Johnson Hire", as the rickshaw coolies were often faster than motorized transportation on Shanghai's clogged and sometimes flooded streets.

Old Amah got a rare moment of relaxation when my mother would ask her to take us to see the very popular Shirley Temple and Laurel and Hardy movies playing in town. We always dressed up for these outings, wearing identical frilly dresses, big colorful bows in our hair and patent leather shoes with white socks. The Chinese children of wealthy families who attended foreign movies never failed to stare at us, for we must have seemed bizarre with our various hues of hair and eyes. If they stared too long at my eyeglasses, I glared back and stuck out my tongue at them. Before the start of the movie Riva and I would gorge ourselves on popcorn, candies and the mouth-watering "Eskimo pies", the chocolate-covered ice-cream on a stick, which inevitably trickled down the front of my dress to Old Amah's clucking sounds of distress. Old Amah somehow got the gist of these movies for she reminded me to be "likee Shelee" and not behave like Shirley Temple's nemesis, Jane Withers. I was not interested in Shirley's good behavior, but I wished I had her dimpled cheeks and curly hair. Old Amah enjoyed the Laurel and Hardy films since she could follow the action and laugh, as we did, at the continuous slapstick scenes.

On several occasions I went with our cook, Shao Wang, to a nearby market to buy vegetables, fruit and rice (but never chicken or meat since my father insisted we keep a somewhat kosher home). This meant that my mother, instead of Shao Wang, had to go to a food store where cleaning of the chicken and meat products were supervised by a rabbi. It was more relaxing but less colorful to be in the marketplace with Shao Wang since, unlike the strong-willed Old Amah, he was never confrontational when he bargained with street vendors and shopkeepers. On a couple of occasions I waited while Shao Wang had his hair cut by an ambulatory barber who carried on his back all the accoutrements of his trade. The barber had a high folding chair for his customer, a basin, a flask of steaming hot water and a towel to clean his customer's face and neck, a hand-held mirror and a leather thong on which he sharpened his scissors and razor. For an additional small fee the barber would clean his customer's ears with a long stick, on the end of which was a cotton ball, proving his dexterity by proudly showing his customer how much wax he was able to remove. Shao Wang was evidently always pleased with his haircut for he thanked the barber with many shouts of "*hao ah, hao ah*" ("good, good") and paid him the price set at the beginning of the tonsorial work without any further bargaining.

At home Shao Wang washed the apples, apricots, pears and grapes in boiling water, into which he stirred purple-colored potassium permanganate solution to cleanse them properly. He did the same for the vegetables, since all had been fertilized in the countryside with human manure. We could not drink the heavily chlorinated tap water, which needed to be boiled and then cooled in the refrigerator.

Shao Wang lived in Nantao, the nearby Chinese-administered part of the city, with his wife, who from time to time came to help him when my parents held their dinner parties. It fascinated me that one of her eyes was of a milky white color, a condition I noticed on a number of Chinese adults. I got to see Shao Wang's home when he and his wife invited Riva and me there for lunch. Old Amah warned us that Nantao was a "vely, vely detee" (dirty) city, adding, "Me no likee." She had become very class-conscious, living in the servants' quarters of our apartment in the French Concession. I was amazed to discover that Shao Wang and his wife lived in one small room on a side alley, without any indoor toilet or kitchen facilities and cooked their meals on a small portable stove. I realized that in our house Shao Wang could use all the amenities lacking in his home – a gas stove, refrigerator, flushing toilet – in a clean and quiet neighborhood. The couple may have had children but we never inquired.

To my mother, Old Amah and Shao Wang seemed to have many relatives, at least some of them imaginary. They often asked for, and were reluctantly given, a day or two to go to "Ningpo mo fa" to visit relatives or friends who suddenly were sick or getting married. My parents, their *Missee* and *Master*, treated them well. Shao Wang could relax before and after preparing our daily meals, while Old Amah, who took charge of the three girls – I was sure I was her favorite – could visit her friends in the neighborhood when we went off to school.

The Parasite Imperialists

EVEN THOUGH my family and I were stateless we fully enjoyed the social privileges of extraterritoriality extended to all Caucasians. During the 1930s more and more foreign nationals came to Shanghai, some for business, some to seek adventure and some who had to flee from upheavals in their countries. Approximately forty thousand of them and about three million Chinese lived during that era in the two foreign settlements and in the three Chinese-administered districts of the city.

Who were the foreign nationals residing in Shanghai?

The International Settlement was much larger than the French Concession, extending across Soochow Creek to Hongkew in the north, where most Chinese and generally poor foreigners lived. The only demarcation line between the two settlements was the street boundary of Avenue Foch (Yan'an Xi Lu) and Avenue Edward VII (Yan'an Dong Lu).

In the French Concession, streets and avenues were named after well-known French personalities and military heroes, including the three marshals of World War I – Avenue Foch, Avenue Joffre, Avenue Pétain (Hengshan Lu) – and famous writers such as Corneille (Gaolan Lu) and Molière (Xiangshan Lu). In the International Settlement, some deference to the Chinese was shown by the Anglo-Saxon authorities by naming most of the streets and roads in the Settlement after Chinese cities and provinces – Canton, Honan (Henan), Nanking, Soochow, Szechuen (Sichuan) – interspersed with a few English names such as Edinburgh (Jiangsu Lu), Edward VII, Keswick (Kaixuan Lu), Rubicon (Hami Lu) and Yates (Shimen Er Lu). There were many

10 and 15-story apartment complexes in the Concession designed by renowned French architects, who named their buildings after French provinces – the Bearn, the Dauphine, the Gascogne, the Normandie and the Picardie. These attractive residential buildings contrasted with the big department stores on the main thoroughfares and the gray office buildings, banks and hotels on the waterfront promenade named the Bund (Zhongshan Dong Yi Lu), a word from colonial India meaning an embankment. The International Settlement, however, did not have the liveliness or cachet of its French neighbor.

To go from one foreign settlement to another, passengers had to switch between the French-owned electric trolleys and street cars and the British-owned tramways and double-decker busses, paying another fare. Fortunately the French municipality decided not to switch to right-hand driving in Shanghai, where the British had earlier established the left-hand system in use

Lily, Riva and parents at Koukaza Park

in all their colonies. The French municipality used a 110-volt electricity supply while the British one was 220 volts, meaning if a resident moved from one foreign settlement to the other, a whole new set of electrical gadgets or transformers had to be purchased.

British police officers, generally recruited from Britain and its vast colonial empire, controlled the International Settlement with the help of Chinese traffic policemen and tall, bearded Indian Sikhs wearing bright red turbans (they were disparagingly called "red-headed devils" by the Chinese). These policemen waved their arms incessantly and yelled at the slow moving carts, wheelbarrow pushers, rickshaw coolies and cyclists, and never hesitated to use their batons on jaywalking Chinese pedestrians. In the Concession, French police officers wearing khaki uniforms and *képis*, dark blue military caps with a flat circular top and a horizontal visor, were assisted by their own recruits. They were brought to Shanghai by the French colonial army from the provinces of Annam and Tonkin in French Indochina. These men, generally short of stature and with teeth blackened from chewing betel nut, directed traffic or stood guard in front of French garrisons and military installations, wearing distinctive conical straw hats. The impassive Indochinese rarely hit a Chinese pedestrian, but they and the Sikh policemen meted justice in the street by haranguing and berating any pedestrian who did not move quickly away from an approaching car. Both were upholding their version of British and French laws on Chinese territory, which gave them a sense of power in Shanghai's rigid social class system.

In both foreign police forces, Chinese men were hired as policemen, interpreters and translators, while a number of White Russians became lower ranking detectives. The French sought former officers and men who had served with the military in Indochina or in their other colonies. Some of the French officers had graduated from the prestigious army school, Saint-Cyr, while many of the enlisted men came from Corsica seeking more lucrative assignments overseas. The uniforms in the two European police forces were quite similar to those in their home countries, which created a quasi-English and a quasi-French atmosphere in the settlements.

These forces' primary aim was to maintain social order in the city and defend it with the backing of their respective army and navy against all outside military interference, especially Chinese or Japanese. The foreign police forces – with eight police stations in the Settlement and six in the Concession – provided security, not only for their own nationals and other foreigners within the extraterritorial entities, but also for Chinese politicians, drug lords, criminals and gangsters, who could not be extradited by their own government. They were usually protected, but at a high price, by corrupt foreign police officials – especially in the French Concession.

A decade after Benjamin and Thaïs' arrival in Shanghai, the number of foreign nationals had increased to approximately 60,000, from 53 different countries. Rare was the Westerner who spoke the Shanghai dialect or who cared to learn anything about China's civilization, history, literature or art. China and the Chinese were generally irrelevant to foreigners; all that mattered was to partake in an economy that was rapidly growing and which enabled them to lead a very comfortable life. Most foreigners' daily contact with Chinese people was with their servants, who quickly learned Pidgin English, interpreters and clerks in their offices, and the waiters in their country clubs. The business leaders, the *taipans* (a Cantonese word meaning "Big Boss"), negotiated commercial deals in English with educated, upper-class Chinese businessmen, and Chinese and foreigners gambled and shouted together at *jai-alai* games played by Spanish Basque sportsmen at the Jai-Alai Auditorium, at the greyhound races at the Canidrome in the French Concession and the horse races at the Racecourse in the International Settlement. Outside these narrow spheres of contact, there was a separation not by a wall but by two radically different cultures that each looked down upon the other. On one side was the foreigners' lack of interest and compassion for all matters Chinese, and, on the other, resentment from the xenophobic Chinese of the presence of the "foreign devils" occupying their country.

The Chinese saw around them American, British and French nationals living in beautiful homes and mansions with many servants, and riding to work and social gatherings in their chauffeured cars – the American Buick, Chevrolet, Dodge, Ford and Packard; the English Austin, Morris Minor and Rolls Royce; and the French Citroën, Renault and Peugeot. These Westerners tended to lead busy social lives with their respective clubs at the center: the Americans at their Columbia Country Club, the British *taipans* at their "males only" Shanghai Club (with its famous long bar) and the French at the Cercle Sportif Français. Members played cards, mahjong, tennis, golf, swam in indoor and outdoor pools, and drank aperitifs, wine, whiskey and gin. The British Club held regular polo matches. They purchased the latest novels at the American-owned Kelly & Walsh bookstore, read the British *North-China Daily News, Shanghai Times, Herald Weekly*, the American *Shanghai Evening Post and Mercury* and *China Weekly Review,* and the French *Journal de Shanghai*. They took summer vacations in Mokanshan (Moganshan), Peitaho (Beidaihe), Tsingtao (Qingdao) and Weihaiwei (Weihai), or in Japan in Hiroshima, Nagasaki and Kobe, and every few years took lengthy home leaves to their native lands. Once there, however, they often could not wait to return to their very comfortable Shanghai life, to be pampered by their servants and be part of an elite social class to which they did not belong to in Europe or in the United States. While they protected, often fiercely, their various national traditions, they had in common their endless complaints about the lazy Chinese and China's seesawing civil wars.

In the 1930s, approximately 10,000 British, 5,000 Americans and 1,500 French resided in the two settlements. They attended Sunday religious services at their respective churches; the ladies dressed in their best finery, wearing hats and gloves and fur stoles and coats in the fall and winter, the men in white linen suits or dark woolen ones according to the seasons. Imposing houses of worship were built – the American Methodist Memorial Church and Community Church facing the Shanghai American School, the Anglican Holy Trinity Cathedral and the French St. Joseph Cathedral and St. Pierre Church. Attendance, especially by women and children, was extremely high during Christmas and Easter services.

The International Settlement, administered predominantly by the British and Americans by the elected Shanghai Municipal Council (SMC), was in reality managed more by the British, who had more business holdings than the Americans. The British owned banks, textile mills, cigarette factories and warehouses in Pootung, across the Whangpoo River, the Shanghai Power Company in the Yangtzepoo area of Hongkew District, the local transportation system, and the large shipping and commercial firms and banks. The American contingent was also involved in banking, insurance and import-export firms, but on a smaller scale. They had large holdings in the Standard Oil and Texaco companies and administered a joint venture in the British-American Tobacco Company.

While the British and Americans met socially because of their common language and rather similar Anglo-Saxon culture, the French kept to themselves. They were not interested in learning English, the *lingua franca* of foreigners in Shanghai and other treaty ports in China, for they preferred to gather in their own clubs and homes, and send their children to French-speaking schools. The number of French entrepreneurs and businessmen was minimal in comparison to their British and American counterparts. The French in their Concession, headed by the French Consul General, administered and ran several very important entities – the Compagnie Française de Tramways et d'Eclairage Electriques, which ran busses, street cars, trolleys and a small power company for the Concession; the Banque de l'Indochine; and the shipping line, the Messageries Maritimes.

To outsiders, the nationals of these three treaty powers radiated wealth, class and prestige. They were at the top of the economic and social ladder, flaunting unashamedly their artificially imposed social status, and looking down on the lesser mortals from other countries, especially those without a country and the Eurasians, referred to disdainfully in Shanghai parlance as "half-castes". Young British employees, upon their arrival in China, were warned not to marry Asian women; if they did they would be fired. Although military and civilian men cohabited with Chinese women, it was not socially acceptable to marry them – though it was quite acceptable for the men to abandon the "half-caste" children they fathered.

In the first few years after Benjamin and Thaïs' arrival there was no language barrier since they only dealt with Russians in their daily lives. They encountered a Russian-speaking community of approximately 10,000 people who had left Russia, wracked by civil war, for a more peaceful life in "foreign" Shanghai. At that time, a couple of thousand of them were of the Jewish faith, the majority of whom, like Thaïs and Benjamin, had left Russia during the Bolshevik Revolution. Earlier groups of refugees had fled the deadly pogroms in Siberia at the beginning of the 20th century and a number of Jewish soldiers and sailors, stranded in Manchuria after Russia's defeat by Japan in 1905, had drifted down to Shanghai. Jewish refugees of the Bolshevik Revolution soon managed to open businesses in the French Concession: their small grocery shops, bakeries and haberdashery stores were frequented by the Russian-speaking community and other foreigners. Some of the men even managed to find work as accountants in British and American firms, while the women found jobs as store clerks or worked in cottage industries. Only rarely did they ply the streets or cabarets as prostitutes, as was the case with many destitute White Russian women. By the mid-1930s the Jewish community had increased to about 6,000 because of the exodus from Harbin when the Japanese military became entrenched there. During the intervening years they had built two Orthodox synagogues, a hospital and a home for impoverished elderly Jews. They almost never suffered acts of anti-Semitism by foreign nationals, although anti-Semitic sentiments in the Christian community, especially the Slavs, were a given. The Chinese masses, for their part, were ignorant of the Jewish people, their religion and culture.

At the outset, Russian Jewish refugees received help from their co-religionists, the well-established Sephardic community who came to Shanghai after the Opium Wars from British India and Ottoman-controlled Aden, Iraq, Persia and Yemen. A number of them – the Sassoons, the Hardoons, the Kadoories, the Ezras and the Abrahams – had become extremely wealthy during the second half of the 19th century from their commercial endeavors in China, especially the sale of opium from India. After this commodity was banned by the British in the early 20th century they began to invest their vast fortune in real estate, office buildings and hotels in the International Settlement along the main business thoroughfares on Nanking Road (Nanjing Dong Lu), Bubbling Well Road (Nanjing Xi Lu) and on the Bund. This embankment stretched along the Whangpoo River from the Settlement to the Concession where it was called the Quai de France, a rather nondescript area of low lying houses. The Sephardim were held in awe by the foreign and Chinese communities not only for their wealth, but also for their philanthropic causes, helping Chinese orphans, Jewish survivors of pogroms in Russia and refugees from the Bolshevik Revolution. In addition to the pecuniary assistance given to the newly arrived Russian Jews, the Sephardic community established an elementary and secondary school for refugee children, the Shanghai Jewish School, where students learned English and studied courses similar to the ones in England.

Although the Baghdadi Sephardim, as they were generally called, helped the Russian Ashkenazi community, they rarely mingled socially due to their economic, cultural and linguistic differences. The Sephardim spoke English – their monthly journal the *Israel Messenger* was in that language – but at home the older generation also conversed in Ladino or Judeo-Arabic, while the Ashkenazim spoke at first only Russian and Yiddish. The co-religionists observed different rituals in their respective synagogues – the Baikal Road Cemetery (Huiming Lu) in Hongkew, the largest of the four Jewish cemeteries, had one section reserved for burials of the Sephardim, the other for the Ashkenazim. Because of their radically different lifestyles, social status and wealth, the Sephardim rarely intermarried until the mid-1930s, when Russian Jews had moved up to middle-class status and could communicate with the Sephardim in English. The fair-skinned Ashkenazim were taken aback to discover, on arriving in Shanghai, some rather dark-skinned Jews who resembled Arabs. My mother often referred to them as *Arabchik*, a Russian term of endearment, never denigrating, for she had the utmost respect for the Sephardic community.

Ironically, though not surprisingly, Russian Jews in Shanghai had more in common linguistically and culturally with their historic enemy, the Orthodox Russians, than with their Sephardic co-religionists. In Shanghai they no longer feared the White Russians, Ukrainians and other Slavs, for now they could look down on the latter's low economic and social standing in class-conscious Shanghai. While the White Russians looked back, dreaming of returning to a Czarist Russia after the overthrow of the Bolsheviks, the Russian Jewish community looked forward, albeit to the unknown, relieved to be away from violently anti-Semitic Russia.

The White Russians who came to Shanghai during the Revolution were soon joined by naval and cavalry officers and men who had fought in the civil war in Siberia, and by former employees of the railway in Manchuria who moved south to Shanghai when all the railroad assets were taken over by the new Soviet government. These refugees, who referred to themselves as émigrés, were now stateless and generally destitute. The

Russians who had settled in Shanghai before the Revolution were in no position to help them and some even resented this influx of refugees who would compete with them for scarce jobs. The émigrés could not expect help from any country or community in Shanghai. The heads of households, many from the military, the middle classes and Czarist nobility (along with some bogus aristocrats), did not speak English or Chinese and could only find menial employment. They worked as watchmen and restaurant doormen, often in full regalia as Cossack officers, or flexed their muscles as bouncers at nightclubs, acted as bodyguards for warlords or wealthy Chinese politicians and businessmen, or became policemen in the foreign settlements. These jobs offered very low salaries, though still higher than those paid to their Chinese counterparts. The more fortunate ones – mainly doctors, dentists and engineers – found work in their respective professions, though always poorly paid. Professional musicians, many graduates of the prestigious Moscow and Saint Petersburg conservatories, played in the local orchestras or gave private lessons. Other émigrés taught ballet, and former Cossack soldiers taught riding and fencing to the British and the Americans.

Although married Russian women often worked in small stores or taught piano and voice lessons, many young and attractive single émigré women found the only way to avoid starvation was prostitution or work in cabarets, bars and ballrooms frequented by foreign soldiers flush with money. In Shanghai – "the wickedest city in the East" – these women were known as "taxi dancers", since they were hired on the floor and were paid a dime a dance. In addition, they received a commission on drinks purchased by the men who spent time with them. The ladies on duty imbibed soft drinks that were billed to their partners as alcoholic drinks. Inevitably, some of them extended their services beyond the dance floor. The foreign community, especially the British and the Americans, looked askance at the White Russians – especially these "immoral" women, and the men who did menial labor, often in competition with Chinese

workers. White pauperism was a loss of face for the white
elite. If the women sold their bodies to Asians they belittled the
Caucasian race, whose prestige needed to be maintained. Such
racial intermingling debased the purity of the rigid ethnic caste
system in Shanghai. For the Chinese, too, a "half-caste" child
was the product of a shameful liaison. The Chinese of all classes,
fully aware of the *taipans'* disdain towards the émigrés, reacted
accordingly and generally looked down on the destitute *Loussou*
nin (Russians) who, as whites, had no right to be poor.

Despite high unemployment and their difficult financial
straits, the émigré community tried to relive the cultural life
they once led in Czarist Russia. To preserve their heritage they
built the Russian Orthodox Cathedral and the St. Nicholas
Military Church in memory of Czar Nicholas II and his family
killed by the Bolsheviks. At Christmas and Easter beautiful
chorus voices emanated from these two churches, overflowing
with parishioners, and strong incense permeated the air outside
whenever the church doors were opened. The White Russians
established social clubs catering to various professional interests,
published several Russian language newspapers and magazines
– for example, the *Slovo* (Word) the *Zaria* (Dawn) – and sent their
children to English and French-speaking schools to prepare them
to work, hopefully in one of the foreign municipalities. Because
of the common native language the émigrés and the Russian
Jews shared, they often performed together in plays, danced in
ballets and sang in operas and operettas, enlivening the cultural
life of Shanghai. However, the two groups rarely met socially
in their respective homes. My sisters and I, however, socialized
with our Russian émigré classmates.

Along Avenue Joffre, the mile-long main street in the
Concession, White Russian chefs and cooks worked in Greek,
Italian and Russian restaurants – surprisingly there were very
few French restaurants in the Concession – while Russian women
worked in the stores on Avenue Joffre as salesgirls, seamstresses,
hat designers, hairdressers, manicurists and masseuses, catering

to their compatriots as well as to a wealthier Western and Chinese clientele. Stores advertised their *skitka* (discounts), in Cyrillic letters, while the language spoken in the streets and stores was generally Russian, not English or Pidgin English, since many of the émigrés lived in apartment buildings close to Avenue Joffre or above the stores on that street and nearby. The impact of the Russian émigrés, whose numbers had increased to 25,000 by the end of the thirties, transformed the appearance of this very busy strip in the French Concession into a "Little Moscow".

The most numerous among the Eurasians were the Macanese – Portuguese citizens whose distant ancestors were Portuguese mariners and traders who had settled in Macao in the mid-sixteenth century and later married Chinese women. In the 1930s there were approximately 3,000 Macanese in Shanghai, whose language in their homes was English with a peculiar sing-song lilt, although some older members spoke Portuguese *patois* among themselves. They were scattered across the Settlement and the Concession and met for social and sports gatherings in their "Clube Lusitano". They belonged to several Catholic parishes and prayed at the Sacred Heart Church in the Hongkew section of the International Settlement. Their children generally attended English-speaking schools, the boys preparing themselves to follow in their fathers' footsteps as clerks and accountants in British firms, especially the Hongkong and Shanghai Bank with its attractive and secure pension plan. Ethnically the Macanese resembled Asians, but they mingled socially with the foreign community, who tolerated their mixed-breed status since they spoke English, had strong soccer teams, and were useful and loyal to the British-owned firms in low-paying jobs a few rungs above the Chinese employees. The Chinese disdainfully looked down on the mixed-blood Macanese, who did not look Chinese or white but wanted to be considered part of the Caucasian community for the status it brought. A Macanese, when mistaken for one by either Chinese or foreigners, always made it clear that he or she was not Chinese.

When several German missionaries were killed in northern China at the end of the 19th century, Germany attacked China and occupied Tsingtao in the northern province of Shantung (Shandong). After Germany's defeat in World War I, however, German nationals were considered *personae non grata* and many were repatriated from their concessions in China. Yet, once the Versailles Peace Treaty was signed in 1919, many hastily returned to Shanghai, gladly leaving behind a Germany in economic disarray. They quickly resumed the lifestyle they had always led in the treaty ports, despite the fact that as enemies of China, aligned to the Allies in World War I, they had lost their extraterritorial rights. Nevertheless, the Germans were Caucasians and made good use of this. In the mid-1930s they numbered approximately 1,000, working mainly in German trading, engineering and chemical firms – among them Siemens Company (China) and I.G. Farben – and formed a close-knit community. They met in their German Club, prayed at their Evangelical Lutheran Church and sent their children to the local German school. They were shunned generally by the British, Americans and French, especially after the establishment of the Shanghai Nazi party in 1932. Soon after, German nationals were ordered to boycott businesses owned and managed by Jews in all of China.

Another foreign community shunned by Europeans was the Japanese, who began to settle in China and Shanghai in the early 1900s after Japan's surprise attack and defeat of the Russian fleet anchored at Port Arthur (Lüshun), a naval base and fort in Dairen. At the 1905 Peace Treaty of Portsmouth, New Hampshire – mediated by President Theodore Roosevelt – all Russian concessions in southern Manchuria were handed over to Japan. More Japanese civilians came to Shanghai after World War I when Japan, which had participated on the side of the Allies, was given the German possessions in Shantung province. The Japanese were concentrated in Hongkew, which quickly became known as "Little Tokyo" since nearly all the shopkeepers, merchants and traders were Japanese who catered to their nationals. They did not bother to speak Pidgin English since they rarely dealt with Europeans, although they did learn a few words of the Shanghai dialect necessary for their daily contact with the Chinese in their midst.

By the 1930s the 20,000 Japanese civilians in "Little Tokyo" were leading a comfortable life. They sent their children to a Japanese school, and they were much freer in their movements than they would have been in Japan. They were aware, however, that their government was leery of fraternization with foreigners and Chinese alike. Hardly any social interaction occurred between them and the other communities, since Westerners avoided them as Asians and the Chinese despised them for their occupation of Manchuria. Despite the fact that Japan was made to return Shantung province to China in 1922 in an about-face by the Allies, the seething anger of the Chinese towards the Japanese presence in Manchuria did not subside. Low-paid Chinese workers in Japanese-owned factories in Hongkew and Pootung regularly went on strike, goaded by university students smarting under social and political injustice. Many anti-Japanese demonstrations were held in the foreign enclaves, and Japanese goods were frequently boycotted, whether made in China or in Japan, to protest the Japanese colonial presence in Manchuria. While the Chinese displayed their anger towards Japan – calling them *Riben guizi* (Japanese devils) – the Japanese saw the Chinese as an inferior ethnic group living under the yoke of Western imperialism. The Japanese somehow did not equate their occupation of Manchuria with the colonialism and imperialism of the treaty powers.

A smattering of other foreign nationals lived and worked in Shanghai, including, typically: Indian Sikh and Indochinese policemen; Filipino musicians, who played in hotels and cabarets; Italian, Greek and Armenian restaurant owners and tradesmen; Basque *jai-alai* players; Swiss and Swedish businessmen; and Norwegians working as river pilots to guide the large ships to the Shanghai docks and wharves.

These were the ethnic, cultural, and social strata that our family encountered, up-close or from afar, in the extraterritorial and polyglot city of Shanghai.

7
Upward Social Mobility

MY PARENTS often recalled the early 1930s as the golden years for them economically. Trade was booming as new foreign business firms established themselves, many apartment complexes were being built in the Concession by French architectural firms, while high-rise office buildings and hotels rose along the Bund. China was viewed by the foreigners as relatively stable under the leadership of Chiang Kai-shek, who ruled most of the country from Nanking.

In September 1931, the Japanese staged an explosion along the railroad tracks outside Mukden, blaming the Chinese, and using the incident as an excuse to penetrate deeper into Manchuria for its immense natural resources. This "Mukden Incident" did not greatly concern the foreigners, nor did it affect the economy in Shanghai because the northeast of China was far removed from their world. However, Aunty Riva's husband Ralph decided to emigrate with his family to Australia. This was a great surprise to his relatives and caused much consternation, especially for my mother, whose sister would live so far away. My father, on the other hand, was successful in his insurance business and did not want to leave Shanghai. Even as the Japanese set up their puppet state, Manchukuo (Manzhouguo, "Land of the Manchus"), with the last Qing Dynasty emperor on the throne, many Westerners did not imagine that the conquest of Manchuria would be the springboard for further attacks against China. It was inevitable that incidents would occur – strikes by workers in Japanese-owned factories in Shanghai – but foreigners were extremely surprised when, in January 1932, the Japanese Naval Landing

Party and their "blue jacket" marines attacked the Chinese soldiers in the city's Chinese districts, with the heaviest fighting in Chapei.

My mother remembered the terrified Chinese inhabitants streaming into the foreign enclaves, with local welfare organizations struggling to secure enough bamboo-supported tents and food supplies, and vaccinate the refugees against smallpox. The treaty powers, concerned about this "Shanghai Incident" in which thousands of civilians were killed, proclaimed a state of emergency, strengthened their garrisons and enforced a month-long curfew in Shanghai. Nevertheless, my father was able to go to work while my mother, fearing a shortage of food, went to various stores and filled the refrigerator with meat, vegetables and fruit, and the kitchen cabinets with bread, rice and beans. To everyone's relief the League of Nations was able to negotiate an armistice, and a peace agreement was signed on May 5, 1932, between the Japanese and the Chinese. Japan withdrew its forces from Chapei but they remained in Hongkew to protect their nationals in "Little Tokyo", fearing possible retaliation by the Chinese population. This did occur when outraged Chinese students in Shanghai held numerous anti-Japanese demonstrations and workers in Japanese-owned factories went on strike, urging residents to boycott Japanese products. Some Japanese civilians were spat upon and molested.

After a temporary stoppage of business and self-imposed ban on evening outings because of the fighting, Shanghailanders quickly returned to their former lifestyle of partying and making money. My father was very successful in selling insurance policies and within three years was initiated in Sun Life's prestigious Macauley Club for top salesmen. The in-house bulletin noted that "B. Willens scored big success from January to March, giving him a place among our 20 Eastern-Western leaders. Grand work, Mr. Willens!" His ability to speak French was necessary to sell policies to French officials working for the municipality, while his knowledge of Russian and English enabled him to sell insurance to stay in their hotel but they enjoyed my talkativeness. I conversed with them using words in the Shanghai dialect, but also taught them a few words in English, the emerging language of capitalism that they were most eager to learn. Every morning I went to a corner stand to buy food, to the great amusement of the vendors on duty, and had lunch, usually noodles and vegetables, in a nearby hole-in-the-wall eatery run by a cook and his wife, who reminded me eerily of Shao Wang and Old Amah. I managed to explain to them that I was born in Shanghai and lived in the city during China's civil wars, the Japanese occupation, the return of Chiang Kai-shek and his flight to Taiwan, and the establishment of the People's Republic of China. Although the Chinese shied away from political discussions, I did not hesitate to express my views on the corrupt Chiang Kai-shek regime, the barbaric decade of the Cultural Revolution, my respect for Chou En-lai, my derision of the "Gang of Four", and my admiration of Deng Xiao-ping for having opened China to private enterprise.

I was careful not to criticize Mao Tse-tung since there were posters of the late Chairman around town and his pictures dangled from the rear view mirror of many taxis, but I was surprised that I could talk at length in my limited Mandarin and Shanghainese about the events that had wreaked havoc in China. The couple listened intently to my comments and seemed to be in agreement, nodding their heads but not expressing their thoughts verbally. They refused to accept the tips that I tried to give them. Obviously, capitalism had not yet fully reached them.

I felt the need to walk around the French Concession, to look for the homes my family had lived in and, just as importantly, to see my school, which I was told by former classmates was still there. I came upon Avenue Joffre, which the older Chinese still remembered as "Yaffee Lu", but I could not recognize it. I stared in amazement, craning my neck at the skyscrapers and big department stores where once stood many small shops catering to the foreign community, and apartment buildings not generally higher than ten stories. I was surprised to see how much the plane trees, brought from France in the early 20th century to provide some shade for pedestrians and French soldiers on parade, had grown in height and girth. I remembered trying to hide behind them from Old Amah as she wheeled my sister Jackie in her carriage, never successfully since the tree trunks were much smaller at that time. These trees, a vestige of French colonialism, are now protected as national treasures and cannot be uprooted to make way for more skyscrapers along this very busy boulevard. A number of Western-style office and apartment buildings of the Thirties and Forties are now municipally protected – for the moment anyway – because of their architectural value.

I asked a pedestrian for directions to a nearby park, which he pointed out on my map and then told me in broken English that I was on a "very important street" in the city. I silently and wholeheartedly agreed; I was born in a house on this famous street. The side streets were more recognizable to me since a number of the apartment buildings, though in need of a good scrubbing or several coats of paint, had not been torn down.

The former International Settlement was covered with skyscrapers, hotels and office buildings, and, as in the former Concession, masses of people milled about in the streets while the roadways were clogged with cars, taxis, motorcycles, bicycles and jaywalkers. The odors, the noise, the pedestrians spitting and blowing noses still prevailed despite warnings and numerous advertisements by the municipality denouncing these dangerous and unhealthy habits. The Racecourse complex where I once worked had been transformed into the People's Park, a very large green expanse where people strolled about and children rode their tricycles, ate ice cream and ran holding kites aloft. How could I ever forget the imposing solid mass of buildings that still lined the Bund? The Customs House with its clock tower, the Hongkong and Shanghai Bank with its magnificent interior still intact, and the Cathay Hotel, renamed the Peace Hotel, were never erased from my memory. The 20-story Broadway Mansions apartment building, now a hotel, which for me always loomed so tall, was now dwarfed by taller buildings reaching up towards the sky. I looked with astonishment at the panorama across the Whangpoo River: the once-flat area of Pootung was now dominated by high-rise buildings, cranes and the garish Oriental Pearl TV tower with its neon-lit balls straight out of Disney World. The sampans and junks with families aboard had disappeared from the river, replaced by floating tourist restaurants in the shape of junks, a faint reminder of a distant past.

Although many of the physical aspects of my hometown were no longer familiar, vendors still crowded the streets selling the food I had always enjoyed eating, especially the crispy, oily *da bing* and *you tiao*. When I bit into the latter after so many years, the aroma lured me back in time to the voice of Old Amah reminding me to eat slowly and "no detee dless" ("don't dirty your dress"). The vendors now wore white cotton caps and clean smocks over jeans and tee-shirts and cooked food at much cleaner stalls than in the past. The hungry street urchins and beggars who used to crowd around me on those shopping trips with Old Amah, begging for coins and staring hungrily at me whenever I was eating, had disappeared completely.

Friendly gazes now replaced the disparaging comments once addressed to the foreign child, the *nakoonin*, who would yell back and show her tongue. The attitude of the Chinese in the street towards the foreigners – the one-time occupiers of their country – had changed from resentment to friendliness.

Whenever I asked for directions pedestrians went out of their way to help me, trying to say a few words in English or giggling at my attempts to speak the Shanghai dialect. Rags that once passed for clothing had also disappeared, replaced by jeans, slacks, shirts and Western-style suits for men, and simple cotton or nylon dresses for women, and jeans and short skirts for heavily made-up young girls rushing to work on overcrowded busses and subways.

I knew that the Collège Municipal Français was now used as a center for scientific research, and I easily found it on the former Route Vallon, a very familiar street as I had bicycled along it both to and from school for so many years. When I saw its façade I reacted with some trepidation as I remembered how I struggled in mathematics and science classes, and how my classmates and I regularly cheated on quizzes and tests. As I entered the building I immediately recognized the enormous crystal chandelier that hung in the wood-paneled hall but was surprised to see the addition of a sculpture of Alfred Nobel and not of Mao Tse-tung. I could not help but wonder if this was possibly a reminder and an incentive for the scientists working in the research center to earn Nobel's coveted prize? Their offices were located in our former classrooms, where posters of Maréchal Philippe Pétain once looked down sternly at us. The schoolyard where the boys and girls had played soccer or grass hockey, in separate sections, had been transformed into a well-manicured lawn, although half of its original area had disappeared under office and apartment buildings.

I walked up the large staircase, with its rich mahogany banister and Art Deco railing interspersed with the letters "CSF" – the initials for the original owner of the building, the Cercle Sportif Français. Surprisingly the colorful stained glass windows, made in the 1930s by Chinese children from Catholic orphanages, had not been destroyed during the Cultural Revolution. As I walked into the large auditorium at the top of the stairs I relived the excitement of the annual St. Charlemagne festivities and the ceremony for the distribution of prizes at the end of the school year, our "liberation". I saw myself, after all these years, climbing the steps to the dais to receive books from our principal, Putia, who would look at me with his cold blue eyes and a serious mien that seemed to imply *"tu pourrais mieux faire"* ("you could do better"). I believe he and all my teachers would be surprised that I finally did do "better", not in Shanghai but in the United States, where I obtained a doctorate in French literature. They would have been amazed – and surely pleased – that eventually most of my classmates became teachers, engineers and scientists, while three boys became ambassadors of France. Never would I have imagined that a number of us, often labeled "*bêtes comme des ânes*" ("dumb as donkeys"), would later have professional careers – especially not my female classmates, whose main goal, and mine, was to find a husband and, as in French fairy tales, "*avoir beaucoup d'enfants*" ("have many children"), which in English fairy tales is translated as "and they lived happily ever after".

I walked to the residences where my family and I once lived, and was pleased to discover that the Savoy Apartments complex on Route de Say Zoong and our house on Route Delastre had not been torn down. The entire façade of the Savoy Apartments was very poorly maintained, however, the entrances had not been swept for some time and laundry was drying from nearly every window. The other striking change was the disappearance of the very large playground where the amahs in their white jackets and long black pants had gathered daily, weather permitting, to watch over babies in their carriages and young children at play. As I looked at the small plot of greenery that now replaced the former garden, I suddenly remembered how Old Amah always kept a watchful eye over me, constantly warning me not to climb trees or tease the small children – warnings I always ignored. I located our house on Route Delastre and noticed that the wooden fence built around the complex soon after the arrival of the People's Liberation Army to enable the watchman to keep a close watch over the comings and goings of the residents, had been replaced by a stone wall. Though I was eager to go in if the present owners would allow, I was disappointed when no one answered the doorbell.

I had the opportunity, however, to see the interior of both

our residences when I returned to Shanghai three years later in 1999, flying into the city's new ultra-modern airport in Pootung. On this trip I was accompanied by my niece Renée and Marie, a Chinese-speaking Canadian friend who could converse with the people now living in our former residences. The entire façade of the Savoy Apartments was now painted gleaming white and the complex had been transformed into expensive rental units. Jutting out from many windows were air conditioners, which we could have used during those sultry and very humid summer months in Shanghai. Yet laundry still flapped from the windows and balconies. Art Deco etchings sculpted in the masonry graced the dusty entrances, where maintenance apparently was still not a high priority. Renée, Marie, and I walked up one flight of stairs to the heavy oak wooden door of "my" apartment, which still bore the original blue metal embossed number 15 and the mail slot with the English word "letters". I wondered why the Red Guards and other revolutionaries had not destroyed this reminder of foreign imperialism. No one answered our knock at number 15 so I tried the adjoining apartment, where a couple opened the door and invited us in when my friend explained that my parents, my sisters and I had once lived in the apartment next door. The husband and wife showed us their apartment, which had been sectioned off into two residences, their part consisting of a living room and a small bedroom which corresponded to Old Amah's room in "our" apartment next door. From their balcony, adjoining "ours", we could see bamboo poles from which hung towels and underwear, a sight as colorful as,but far less aesthetically pleasing than, the pots of flowers we had kept there in the spring and summer. I related to Renée and Marie how our family had been asked to leave the Savoy Apartments when, from this balcony, I inadvertently watered the bare head of a Frenchman.

I was disappointed that I could not get into our former apartment but the couple suggested that, since their neighbors were presently overseas, they could ask the building manager to open it for us, which he did. As we entered the hallway I remembered vividly the location of the two mahogany chairs inlaid with mother-of-pearl and the carved wooden *joss man* statue (all of which I still possess). I recalled Old Amah warning her two little girls, Riva and me, that if we misbehaved, the *joss man* would take us away from our parents and our home. This hallway led directly to the dining room but we could not get to the living room and the balcony since they were behind a wall, where another family now lived. French doors once separated these two rooms to offer some privacy for my parents' guests when Shao Wang and Old Amah set up or cleared the dining room table.

I thanked the couple and the superintendent profusely and left to take the elevator to the eighth-floor roof, from where the boys in the complex and I had thrown ice cubes on pedestrians and vehicles. The original elevator, with its clanging doors, had been replaced by a cab with doors painted a sickly green that clashed with the Art Deco wooden wall panels and sculptured metal railings in the hallways. The roof garden was now cluttered with crates and discarded pieces of furniture rather than pots of shrubbery and flowers tended by a gardener as when we lived there. As I related my childish pranks to Renée she was clearly shocked and asked me whether Chinese lives meant anything at that time to me and other foreigners. My answer was that we were brought up in a discriminatory colonial environment, which, I quickly added, had fortunately disappeared.

We left the Savoy Apartments to look for the residence on Route Delastre where I had lived for ten years as a teenager and young woman. As we rang the bell I remembered how we spent the war years sitting on the steps singing songs and playing tricks on each other. When no one answered the bell we walked to the back of the house and asked a woman working in the garden if we could visit the house. She let us in through the verandah,

Lily returns to her school, the CMF

now enclosed as a room, and then led us to a large room that used to be our living room. In the adjoining dining room, now a bedroom, a young boy was busy with his homework. The woman explained that the two rooms on the first floor were rented by her family who had the use of the guest toilet, but they had to share the kitchen with two other families living on the second floor. We went up to that floor, where the tiled bathroom with its bathtub, sink and toilet were still the same as when I left Shanghai in 1951. We were introduced to the couple who lived in the large bedroom where my sisters and I once slept, and I was surprised to see still existent the built-in drawers and two closets that caused many sibling arguments over space for our clothes. We met their neighbor who lived in my parents' former bedroom with its adjoining balcony, now enclosed and used as an additional room. I remembered the constant whirring sound of Lao Papa's sewing machine on the balcony and recalled vividly the day he cried when he told me his son had died. I also visualized how

Riva used to stand on this balcony to flirt with Captain Clément Ouvrard of the French colonial army, whose office was in a house facing ours. The present tenant told us she and her family had moved into the house in early 1952. I realized it must have been her parents who paid the US$2,000 "key money" to my father. She added that she remembered well the living room furniture, the sofa, the armchairs, the large cabinet with its gramophone and radio, and the piano, a most impressive piece for her at that time – and Jackie's endless practice of the scales rang in my ears. I visualized the adjoining dining room where our cook Shao Wang, in his long white frock, served us our meals, the display hutch where my mother kept her silver pieces and crystal, and the plush Chinese carpets covering the floors. The very talkative tenant explained that soon after the outbreak of the Cultural Revolution in 1966 her parents were ordered to share this "bourgeois" house with two other families, and the heavy pieces of furniture had to be removed and replaced by more utilitarian beds in every room. We learned that the piano suffered a shameful death; all musical instruments had been banned as decadent relics of Western imperialism and had to be destroyed. The tenant explained that her parents, fearing a rampage by the Red Guards, had quickly removed the piano to a nearby dump, chopping it up with an axe. The wood was salvaged; the black and white keys, on which Jackie had played classical music, were silenced forever.

As Renée, Marie and I walked downstairs I remembered how I used to rush down, never holding on to the banister, whenever the phone rang. The three families living in "our" house had never replaced the gas stove, and the sinks in their communal kitchen were still in place though understandably, after half a century, slightly cracked and badly tarnished.

I have since returned to Shanghai several times and am always surprised by the continuous modernization of the city, exemplified by the endless skyscrapers that have sprung from the muddy fields of Pootung. Shanghai is filled with elegant shops and huge department stores selling products from all around the world, nightclubs, Internet cafés and Japanese, European and Chinese-made cars clogging the narrow streets and the many wide highways now encircling Shanghai. The city is vibrant and booming economically, the inhabitants having taken to heart the adage by the late Deng Xiaoping that "to get rich is glorious" as long as it happens under "Socialism with Chinese Characteristics".

Most of the tangible aspects of the former French Concession – those physical reminders that I might gaze upon – have long since disappeared. But the new Shanghai, all confident and brimming with economic development, has grown on me, and I always feel at home.

Postscript

by Tess Johnston

WHEN I first read Liliane Willens' manuscript I was especially intrigued by the breadth of her story. It was one of the few narratives I had read that covered a Westerner's life in China, not only in the more fabled golden era of Shanghai but also during the difficult early period of the Communist rule. Liliane lived through both and her narrative covering the contrast between these two disparate eras makes for very revealing reading.

Born in Shanghai, Liliane is uniquely qualified as a "witness to history". She spent the first 25 years of her life within an encapsulated enclave of Western privilege, the city's former French Concession. Since 1863 the city had been divided into three self-governing entities, the International Settlement, the French Concession, and the Chinese-governed remainder. British, French and American administrative bodies controlled every facet of civil life. While each of these added a bit of their own culture and methodology, Shanghai itself developed its own way of life, blending all of these influences into the Chinese lifeline upon which the city depended.

Liliane has recorded the unique experience of living in Shanghai in this fascinating era, as a keen observer of the minute details of life as well as the broader political spectrum. She lived through the tumultuous Thirties, the Japanese occupation of the city from 1941-45, the economic chaos that followed, and finally a renewed civil war that saw the Communist forces achieve final victory in the spring of 1949 with their conquest of the last bastion of Western commercialism, her native city.

Perhaps the greatest value of this volume lies in this latter history. Many books have been written both about Shanghai in its hey-day and under Japanese occupation, but very few foreigners stayed on to witness the post-Communist era. Here Liliane gives the reader a day-by-day, blow-by-blow account of what it was like to live under the new regime of the People's Republic of China. As an on-site witness, Liliane has given us a rare and fascinating account of the slow demise of a once-powerful foreign city on the improbable shore of China.

Tess Johnston
Shanghai, 2009

Places Mentioned in the Book
Then and Now

Streets

Baikal Road $\cdots\cdots\cdots\cdots\cdots\cdots\cdots\cdots\cdots\cdots\cdots$ Huiming Lu
Bubbling Well Road $\cdots\cdots\cdots\cdots\cdots\cdots\cdots$ Nanjing Xi Lu
Bund, The $\cdots\cdots\cdots\cdots\cdots\cdots\cdots\cdots\cdots\cdots\cdots\cdots$ Wai Tan
Canton, Road $\cdots\cdots\cdots\cdots\cdots\cdots\cdots\cdots\cdots\cdots$ Guangdong Lu
Corneille, Rue $\cdots\cdots\cdots\cdots\cdots\cdots\cdots\cdots\cdots\cdots$ Gaolan Lu
Chu Pao San, Rue ("Blood Alley") $\cdots\cdots\cdots\cdots\cdots$ Xikou Lu
Delastre, Route $\cdots\cdots\cdots\cdots\cdots\cdots\cdots\cdots\cdots$ Taiyuan Lu
Dubail, Avenue $\cdots\cdots\cdots\cdots\cdots\cdots\cdots\cdots\cdots$ Chongqing Lu
Edinburgh, Road $\cdots\cdots\cdots\cdots\cdots\cdots\cdots\cdots\cdots$ Jiangsu Lu
Edward VII, Avenue $\cdots\cdots\cdots\cdots\cdots\cdots\cdots$ Yan'an Dong Lu
Foch, Avenue $\cdots\cdots\cdots\cdots$ Jinling Xi Lu and Yanan Zhong Lu
Joffre, Avenue $\cdots\cdots\cdots\cdots\cdots\cdots\cdots\cdots\cdots\cdots$ Huaihai Lu
Keswick, Road $\cdots\cdots\cdots\cdots\cdots\cdots\cdots\cdots\cdots\cdots$ Kaixuan Lu
Paul Henry, Route $\cdots\cdots\cdots\cdots\cdots\cdots\cdots\cdots\cdots$ Xinle Lu
Miller Road $\cdots\cdots\cdots\cdots\cdots\cdots\cdots\cdots\cdots\cdots\cdots$ Emei Lu
Mohawk Road $\cdots\cdots\cdots\cdots\cdots\cdots\cdots\cdots$ Huangpi Bei Lu
Molière, Rue $\cdots\cdots\cdots\cdots\cdots\cdots\cdots\cdots\cdots$ Xiangshan Lu
Nanking, Road $\cdots\cdots\cdots\cdots\cdots\cdots\cdots\cdots$ Nanjing Dong Lu
Pétain, Avenue $\cdots\cdots\cdots\cdots\cdots\cdots\cdots\cdots\cdots$ Hengshan Lu
Pichon, Route $\cdots\cdots\cdots\cdots\cdots\cdots\cdots\cdots\cdots$ Fenyang Lu
Quai de France $\cdots\cdots\cdots\cdots$ Zhongshan Dong Er Lu (East)
Ratard, Rue $\cdots\cdots\cdots\cdots\cdots\cdots\cdots\cdots\cdots\cdots\cdots$ Julu Lu
Rubicon Road $\cdots\cdots\cdots\cdots\cdots\cdots\cdots\cdots\cdots\cdots$ Hami Lu
Say Zoong, Route de $\cdots\cdots\cdots\cdots\cdots\cdots\cdots$ Changshu Lu
Szechuen, Road $\cdots\cdots\cdots\cdots\cdots\cdots\cdots\cdots\cdots$ Sichuan Lu
Tenant de la Tour, Rue $\cdots\cdots\cdots\cdots\cdots\cdots$ Xiangyang Lu
Vallon, Route $\cdots\cdots\cdots\cdots\cdots\cdots\cdots\cdots\cdots$ Nanchang Lu
Victor Emmanuel III, Route $\cdots\cdots\cdots\cdots\cdots$ Shaoxing Lu
Yates Road $\cdots\cdots\cdots\cdots\cdots\cdots\cdots\cdots\cdots$ Shimen Yi Lu

Districts/Sites in and around Shanghai

Chapei · Zhabei
Great World Entertainment Arcade · · · · · · · · · · · · · · · · · · Da Shijie
Koukaza Park · Fuxing Gongyuan
Hongkew · Hongkou
Hungjao · Hongqiao
Jessfield Park · Zhongshan Gongyuan
Lukawei · Lujiawan
Lunghwa · Longhua
Nantao · Nanshi
Ningpo · Ningbo
North Railway Station · Bei Zhan
Pootung · Pudong
Racecourse · Renmin Guangchang
Soochow Creek · Suzhou He
Woosung · Wusong
Whangpoo River · Huangpu Jiang
Yangtze River · · · · · · · · · · · · · · · · · · · Yangzi Jiang (Chang Jiang)
Yangtzepoo · Yangpu

Cities and Regions in China

Amoy · Xiamen
Canton · Guangzhou
Chungking · Chongqing
Dairen (Dalny) · Dalian
Foochow · Fuzhou
Hangchow · Hangzhou
Hankow · Hankou
Honan · Henan
Hongkong · Xianggang
Kiukiang · Jiujiang
Macao · Aomen
Manchuria (Manchukuo) · · · · · · · · Jilin, Heilongjiang, Liaoning
Mokanshan · Moganshan

Mukden · Shenyang
Nanking · Nanjing
Ningpo · Ningbo
Peitaiho · Beidaihe
Peking · Beijing
Port Arthur · Lushun
Shamchun · Shenzhen
Shantung · Shandong
Soochow · Suzhou
Sungari River · Songhua Jiang
Szechuan · Sichuan
Tientsin · Tianjin
Tsingtao · Qingdao
Weihaiwei · Weihai
Yenan · Yan'an

Historical Timeline

1832 First attempts, a failure, to open Shanghai to foreign trade.

1839-42 "Opium War" British retaliation over trade disputes. China defeated by Great Britain. Treaty of Nanking.

1843 Shanghai and four other southern ports, opened to foreign trade as treaty ports.

1843-44 Additional treaties with England, France and the United States established "most favored nation treatment" and "extraterritoriality"

1845 Establishment of British Settlement in Shanghai

1849 Establishment of French Concession in Shanghai

1850 Taiping Rebellion against the Manchu government

1854 Establishment of American Settlement in Shanghai

1856-58 Second Opium War – China defeated

1860 Destruction of Summer Palace by allied forces. Treaty of Peking. Opium trade legalized; Christian missionaries allowed to proselytize in China; opening of more treaty ports

1862 Taiping attacks on English Settlement in Shanghai

1863 Fusion of English and American settlements into International Settlement

1864 Taiping Rebellion crushed

1894-95 War between China and Japan. Japan agreed to regard foreign settlements of Shanghai as outside the zone of warfare.

1896 China defeated by Japan

1900 Boxer Rebellion. Edict by Peking for the extermination of all foreigners. Foreign troops arrive in Shanghai to protect their nationals. Rebellion crushed. China pays high indemnities to victorious powers

1906 US Court for China established in Shanghai by Act of Congress

1911 Outbreak of Republican Revolution led by Dr. Sun Yat-sen against (Manchu) Ching dynasty

1912 Establishment of Chinese Republic under Sun Yat-sen, founder of the nationalist Kuomintang (KMT) party

1912-16 Chinese Republic under Yuan Shikai

1916-21 Warlord civil wars in China

1921 Founding of the Chinese Communist Party (CCP) in Shanghai

1923 Alliance between KMT and CCP

1926 General Chiang Kai-shek's Northern Expedition against warlords

1927 January-March – Nationalists army advance down Yangtze valley towards Shanghai. Foreign troops from various Western nations land in Shanghai to defend it

1927 April 12 – Massacre in Shanghai of communists by KMT forces begins

1931 Japanese occupy Manchuria

1932 Japanese naval forces attack and defeat KMT forces in Chapei bordering the International Settlement

1934-35 Chinese Communists Long March (6,000 miles) led by Mao Tse-tung

1937 Japan's take-over of eastern China. Japanese forces control outskirts of foreign settlements of Shanghai

1939 September 1 – Outbreak of World War II

1941 December 7 – Japan attacks Pearl Harbor

1941 December 8 – Japanese take International Settlement. Japanese occupation of Shanghai begins

1943 End of extraterritoriality in Shanghai and in all treaty ports in China

1945 Nazi Germany defeated.

1945 August 15 – Japan surrenders

1946-49 Civil war between KMT and CCP forces

1949 May 25 – People's Liberation Army enters Shanghai

1949 October 1 – Establishment of the People's Republic of China headed by Chairman Mao Tse-tung

About the Author

Photograph by Hannah Quimby

LILIANE WILLENS was born of Russian parents and raised in the former French Concession of Shanghai where she attended a French lycée. After immigrating to the United States, she received her Ph.D. from Boston University and taught at Boston College and at the Massachusetts Institute of Technology. She has published a book on Voltaire and articles on French literature and history. When she moved to Washington, DC she worked for the Agency for International Development and for the Peace Corps. Now retired she gives lectures on China and on Old Shanghai.

to a smattering of other foreign nationals working as architects, engineers, import-export managers, shipping agents, accountants and teachers in the private sector. My father did not have many Anglo-Saxon clients, however, since they tended to take out policies from well-established American and British insurance companies in Shanghai. He had very few Chinese policy holders since life insurance was a rather strange concept in a country where relatives would take care of a family suddenly bereft of a wage earner. Although he managed to convince clients of the importance of life insurance policies, I was puzzled when I later discovered that my father never bought any for his family.

Thanks to my father's well-remunerated employment at Sun Life, our family now belonged economically to Shanghai's middle class – but not to its upper social class, the domain of citizens of the treaty powers. He was able to purchase a car when ownership was a rarity in the Russian community which relied on rickshaws, tramways and busses to move about the city. Car owners in Shanghai were mostly Americans, British and French, driving automobiles manufactured in their respective countries, or being driven around town by chauffeurs in black uniforms and caps.

On the many cold and drizzly mornings when my father could not start his English-made Morris Minor, he had to go to the front of the car and crank the engine until it turned over. He would not hire a chauffeur since he enjoyed driving his car and spent much time washing and polishing it and carefully drying the chrome without any help from our servants. My mother never learned to drive since in her group of friends only men drove cars. Also, why bother driving a car in narrow streets filled with wheelbarrows, carts and jay-walkers when it would be simpler and safer to hire a chauffeur for the ladies in the household?

After the birth of my sister Jacqueline in October 1932, our apartment in Route Ratard became too crowded for the five of us and the daily presence of Old Amah. In addition, being so close to the shopping district of the Concession, we could hear the cacophony of car horns, the singsong of the street vendors and the shouting and arguments under our windows all day and night. My parents wanted an apartment with a yard where their three girls could play with other children under the watchful eye of Old Amah. They found a spacious one – with two bedrooms and large living and dining rooms – in a complex on Route Paul Henry where the tenants included French, Swiss, Italians, a few stateless Russians and other European nationalities. I believe my father wanted to give his family the opportunity to socialize with non-Russian speaking adults and children. He also felt that my mother needed to perfect her English language skills since she spent all her afternoons speaking Russian with relatives and friends. Although my father was a strict grammarian, he never corrected her mistakes, leaving it to Riva and me to do so whenever she repeated them too often.

Many children lived in the complex; Riva played quietly with the little girls while I preferred climbing trees with the boys or running with them in the yard or adjacent streets. Our parents never worried about us since Old Amah took care of "her" little girls, and there were never any incidents of foreign children being molested by strangers. Old Amah chatted with the other amahs and never failed to remind them to ask their "*Missee*" to invite Riva and me to any child's upcoming birthday party.

For these celebratory events we wore our "party" dresses and big colorful bows in our hair and always brought a gift or two. I enjoyed seeing the birthday child rip open his or her numerous gifts, and would later gorge myself with ice cream, candies and cakes, soiling the front of my dress. I was overly excited when Riva's and my birthdays came around. Our dining room would be decorated with balloons and paper flags of various nationalities strung from the ceiling. More importantly, I knew I would receive gifts, and even a gift or two on Riva's birthday from children who complained to their parents that I glared at them when they only brought one gift. The mothers came towards the end of the afternoon to meet the hostess and other parents living in the building, and many of them became close friends.

On one occasion Old Amah told my mother that Riva and I were invited to "Looshie's" birthday, which we presumed to be a girl named Lucie. We brought a big plastic doll but Looshee turned out to be a boy named Roger. My mother called the hostess the next day to apologize and sent a more masculine gift to the birthday boy. This mix-up led to a long friendship between my mother and Aline Picciotto, who was born into a prominent Sephardic family in Egypt. Thanks to Aline, my mother met a group of Ladino and English-speaking women, one of whom was the widow of Auguste Chaplain, the French Postal Commissioner of the Chinese Post Office. In addition to these new acquaintances, my mother became close friends with Blanche Saint-Oyant and Irene Grillon, whose husbands in the French police force were my father's clients and whose children we played with. Since these French ladies barely spoke English and my mother did not speak any French, they communicated with each other in Pidgin English and sometimes used us as interpreters when we were in the house.

They spent many afternoons in each other's homes drinking tea, eating pastries prepared by their respective cooks and complaining about their children's behavior and their servants' constant requests for higher wages. When my mother invited them over to our home she prepared her mouth-watering cream cakes while Shao Wang baked his celebrated sponge cake. Dressed in his long white gown, he would roll in a small carved mahogany table on which were placed the silver teapot and sugar dispenser, cakes, biscuits and jam, and would wait for my mother to give the signal to pour the tea. When my mother indicated the guests were ready, he carefully poured tea into delicate little cups, adding a slice of lemon, and then cut the cake, which we children later ate – we did not want to sit with the grownups and they did not want us around.

My parents' social life revolved around visiting relatives

and friends or inviting them to our new apartment for *tiffin* – an Anglo-Indian word for "lunch" used in the British colonies – and dinners prepared by Shao Wang. For any of the elaborate sit-down meals in honor of my parents' wedding anniversaries or their respective birthdays, there were at least a dozen guests bearing gifts of silver platters and ashtrays (my parents did not smoke) and crystal vase bowls and decanters made in Czechoslovakia. These were usually purchased at a jewelry store on Avenue Joffre owned by Michael Sukenik, a close friend of my parents and others in the Russian Jewish community. Shao Wang played an important role at these soirées, serving dishes for which he and my mother were much complimented by all the guests, especially the women, who unfailingly asked for the recipes. My mother and Shao Wang deserved these praises for they spent several days at the market buying the food and preparing the meals before setting the table with an embroidered tablecloth and napkins and the finest china and silver.

Shao Wang became an excellent cook, learning from more experienced cooks in the neighborhood and from my mother who taught him Russian and Jewish dishes and cakes. He prepared *zakuski* (hors d'oeuvres), *pirochk*i (meat or vegetable rolled in oily dough) and *pelimeni* (small dumplings with meat or vegetable), a native dish of Siberia. Shao Wang also cooked special food for the Passover holidays and learned quickly that matzo, and not bread, was to be served for the next eight days. He and Old Amah knew they had to clean all the kitchen cupboards and replace the china, cutlery, tablecloth and napkins with the ones set aside solely for Passover week.

On the first two nights of Passover, Shao Wang, along with hired help, had to wait for the reading of the *Haggadah*, led by my father and intoned by our guests, before they could serve dinner. As the evening wore on, the guests drank more vodka, clinked their glasses repeatedly for everyone's good health, and sometimes broke into sentimental Russian and Yiddish songs. Our servants knew they would be well compensated by the 20 or so relatives and friends invited for this occasion or for the dinner on *Rosh Hashanah* (Jewish New Year). Like other domestic help in foreign households they received generous *cumshaw* (tips) from the guests, who were always in a joyous mood after these hearty meals.

It was customary that the cook and his assistants sometimes hired other servants for very special occasions. "No. 1 Boy" and "No. 2 Boy" would wait at the door to hand the departing guests their coats and hats, and receive their well-deserved *cumshaw*. Although the servants spent the next few hours clearing the table and washing dishes, they seemed very happy with the guests' largesse. Even Old Amah received her *cumshaw* for preventing me from rushing into the dining room to see what the adults were eating. But Riva and I once poured water into the felt hat of one of the guests. It belonged to my father's close friend, the person who suggested he leave Harbin for Shanghai – a bachelor very fond of our family life. He found this incident quite amusing but my mother did not, and she berated Old Amah for not keeping better watch over us.

For my parents and their stateless friends, Shanghai, and specifically the French Concession, had become their country. My country was also Shanghai, but a Shanghai populated by foreign nationals and not Chinese.

Schools for Little White Devils

WHEN IT was time for Riva and me to start school, my parents had a variety of considerations. Riva and I talked with each other in English, which we first picked up playing with the children in the yard of the Paul Henry apartment building. English, not French, was spoken by most of the children of various nationalities – many of whom were British and Americans – living in the French Concession.

Municipal, private and religious English and French language schools were established in the early 20th century in the French Concession and the International Settlement to meet the educational needs of the increasing number of foreign children born in Shanghai. The Shanghai Municipal Council's schools in the International Settlement followed faithfully the curriculum in England but enrollment in several of them was based on the pupil's nationality and ethnicity. The Shanghai Cathedral School for Boys and a similar one for girls were for British nationals whose parents had to be Caucasians from England or from the white population in its vast colonies. No exception could be made for "half-caste" children. The pupils in the Cathedral schools resembled in their social standing their counterparts in the elitist "public" schools in England. The boys wore maroon blazers with the school crest, white shirts, short gray pants, neckties and school caps, while the girls were dressed in dark blue tunics, white blouses, school ties and blue berets adorned with the school badge.

In Shanghai, parents from various nations who wanted their children to acquire an English education sent them to the municipally administered Public School for Girls and the International Thomas Hanbury School for Boys. A great number of students in both schools were Eurasians, many Portuguese nationals originally from Macao, and a sprinkling of stateless Russians. Russian Jewish children and, surprisingly, a number of White Russians – whose parents were generally anti-Semitic – attended the English-based Shanghai Jewish School established by the wealthy Sephardi Elly Kadoorie.

A school comparable to the high educational standards of the Shanghai Cathedral schools was the elementary and secondary Collège Municipal Français, established by the French municipality in the former Cercle Français building on Route Vallon (Nanchang Lu). It was regulated by the French Ministry of Education, which issued all directives on policy and curriculum, while the teachers were hired in France under contract with the Concession's municipality – not with the French government – a point of contention many years later. In 1933 the French municipality established another school, the Ecole Rémi, geared to White Russian pupils. Tuition fees were much lower than at the Collège Municipal, the courses were a watered-down version of the established French curriculum generally taught by teachers from the White Russian community. Students could graduate from this school at 16 with a "*Certificat d'Etudes*" since the baccalaureate degree was not part of their curriculum. While I attended the Collège Municipal Français I looked down on the Ecole Rémi both scholastically and socially because most White Russians were close to the bottom of the Shanghai economic order. Many of the French-speaking graduates of the Ecole Rémi eventually worked as clerks, stenographers, policemen and detectives in the various branches of the municipality in the Concession.

The Shanghai American School in the French Concession had a large campus and attractive, colonial-style buildings. It also had a boarding school for missionary children whose parents lived in the hinterlands of China. This school, which did not discriminate on national or racial grounds, was the envy of pupils in the other schools because of its vast playing fields along Avenue Pétain, its "easy" courses with less homework, and the belief that its students spent more time playing than studying. In reality, they received a classical education and even studied Chinese language and culture, subjects rarely taught in the other foreign schools in Shanghai. Nevertheless, teachers in my school did not hesitate to tell students who were struggling academically to transfer to the Shanghai American School.

The small German community in Shanghai founded the Kaiser Wilhelm Schule at the end of the 19th century, shortly after Germany's annexation of the Shantung Peninsula. Although after World War I no Kaiser reigned in Germany, the school never changed its name. An unusual sculpture was placed on the school grounds – a half-sheared mast of the ship *Iltis* – which had originally been erected on the Shanghai Bund as a memorial to German seamen who perished when their ship sank in 1898 in a storm off the Shantung Peninsula. It was removed after Germany's defeat in World War I, but reappeared soon after at the German school. In the 1930s boys of the *Hitler Jugend* (Hitler Youth) unit of the school wore red armbands with the swastika along with their brown uniforms.

In addition to these secular schools were several religious ones, whose pupils where mainly taught by American, French and Irish priests and nuns. Most prominent for foreigners were the English-speaking Saint Francis Xavier School for boys, the Sacred Heart Convent, where girls could opt for classes in English or in French, and the Sainte Jeanne d'Arc French religious school for boys. Since the nationality, race and economic background of students from all these schools varied enormously, they rarely met socially except on the playing fields to compete in soccer, volleyball and grass hockey, and at clubs for swimming and water polo matches. In addition to these secondary schools, several missionary-controlled universities taught Chinese students in the English or French language – the American Episcopal St.

John's University, the Baptist Shanghai College and the French Jesuit Université Aurore.

Thus, my parents could choose from a plethora of possible schools for their daughters. The choice of a school for my sister Riva fell on my father, since my mother had stopped attending school at 16, when the family left Novonicolaevsk. She always looked up to my father in matters of finance and education, for she was impressed with his knowledge of politics, classical music and his ability to speak many foreign languages. Since my father wanted Riva to attend a school where either French or German was the language of instruction, he could choose between two highly regarded schools, the Collège Municipal Français or the Kaiser Wilhelm Schule. He decided on the latter, influenced by the fact that the German system was highly valued in Russia and he had worked for a German firm in Vladivostok. Riva was enrolled in kindergarten in 1931 with twenty other pupils, most of whom were German nationals.

Two years later I was also enrolled in the Kaiser Wilhelm Schule despite the fact that Hitler's anti-Semitic rantings were already emanating from Germany. According to our parents, we adored our motherly kindergarten teacher, Tante Gretchen, who later died of scarlet fever when, as a Christian Scientist, she refused to call a doctor. My mother also told me I must have had some psychic negative premonition about Nazi Germany because in my second week I tried to run away from the Kaiser Wilhelm Schule, though I believe a better explanation would be that I did not want to spend a whole morning without whining to Old Amah. One morning at the entrance to the school, as she climbed down from the rickshaw I dashed down the street and tried to hide from her – but she managed to catch me and yelled for all to hear, "Missee Leelee vely, vely bad, no wanchee go school, ah ya, ah ya." I tried to run off several more times in the ensuing months but my escapades ended when my father took us out of the Kaiser Wilhelm Schule in January 1934. Adolf Hitler's shrill and obsessive speeches and actions against the Jews were bitterly confirmed by the arrival in Shanghai of a smattering of German Jewish refugees fleeing from anti-Semitic laws and incarceration in prisons and concentration camps.

Riva and I were then enrolled at the Collège Municipal Français, attended mainly by children of French nationals, a number of whom were my father's clients. Riva had to be weaned away from the German language and tutored in French while I went back to kindergarten. As a seven-year-old, I had to repeat kindergarten to learn French. Our parents had no qualms

Lily in 1st grade – Collège Municipal Français (CMF)

about transferring us to another language setting since children in Shanghai heard and spoke many languages, and a new one could be learned without any harmful consequences. Riva and I were not affected by this linguistic switch as we did not have a language we could call our own and therefore considered it quite natural to learn another one.

The aim of the Collège Municipal Français, besides teaching French, was to inculcate in the minds of all its pupils, French or otherwise, the *mission civilisatrice* of the Third French Republic, that is, the greatness and glory of France in all its colonies and territories. The curriculum in the French colonies and possessions was similar to the one in France since the teachers who taught the core subjects were trained in France. The teaching staff remained for many years in Shanghai, where their lives as colonists were far superior economically and socially to that which they could have attained in France.

Within a few months of interaction with our French-speaking classmates Riva and I could switch between English and French without any difficulty. However, my mother later told me that on my first day at school I did not know how to ask to be taken to the toilet and simply wet my pants. Until I could express myself verbally, I signaled my intention by raising my hand and pointing to the back of my dress.

I remember clearly my kindergarten teacher, the Englishwoman Miss Thompson, who taught us the English alphabet and whose class I enjoyed very much because I always understood what she was saying. She was a heavy-set woman who loomed large before me, often reprimanding me for being too disruptive in class, once noting in my first grade report card that I was "a chatterbox . . . Liliane does not know how rude it is". Obviously, at the tender age of seven, and spoiled by my Old Amah, I could not become obedient overnight. This same teacher discovered that I memorized short sentences but when I was asked to read a specific word, I was unable to do so. I had to go back to the beginning of a sentence to "read" it in its entirety.

Miss Thompson suggested to my parents that I needed a tutor to teach me how to read English one word at a time. I did not have the same problem reading French since every word was new to me.

In my elementary school there were several other non-French teachers hired locally to teach "unimportant" subjects such as drawing, sewing, singing and gymnastics. Our drawing teacher, Madame Olga Alekine, was a tall White Russian woman whom we did not respect simply because she spoke French with too many grammatical mistakes. Adults who used this language incorrectly were scorned, and I disliked Madame Alekine because she accused me of tracing a picture of a rabbit from a postcard when in fact I had drawn it. I had not yet learned, at this very young age, the art of cheating, and blamed the teacher for squelching any innate artistic talent I may have had at that time. Fortunately for me, Madame Alekine taught only in the elementary school, since different teachers were assigned to specific grades during their career at the Collège Municipal Français.

Although I was a restless child, I was also a curious one, for I often wondered why the principal of our school, Charles Grosbois, who frequently visited our first grade class, always wore only one brown leather glove. I have never forgotten this. I decided that he must have lost the other glove and never had time to buy a new pair, spending time observing classes at our school. Only much later did I find out that he had lost his right hand as a soldier in World War I and that, despite his handicap, Grosbois performed as a violinist in chamber music sessions with his friends.

From elementary school on, it was drilled into all of us that incorrect usage of the French language was a crime of *lèse majesté*! Many years later, at a reunion of classmates of the Collège Municipal Français in Paris, my former classmate Jeanine Reynaud recalled that she had asked me in elementary school whether I was French and I had replied, *"Non, Roumanienne,"* to which she had retorted haughtily that I should have said, *"Roumaine."*

Two-thirds of the 500 students at the Collège Municipal Français were French nationals, with a smattering from Francophone Belgium and Switzerland, and French-speaking pupils from Indochina and Africa whose fathers were serving in the French colonial army in Shanghai. Most of the non-French students were stateless Russians, Eurasians (usually with one French parent) and a few upper-class Chinese. The school did not adhere to any discriminatory racial or national clauses. Riva's classmate Margaret Ho and her younger sister, the daughters of a high official in the Chinese government, came often to our house to study, eat and play with us. We visited them at their home but our parents never met. My parents did not have any acquaintances among the middle or upper-class English-speaking Chinese families. A lack of interest in each other's culture, more than feelings of superiority, seemed to keep these two socially equal groups apart. My classmate in middle and high school, Claude Daroso, and his younger sister, Christiane, whose parents were of African heritage from the Antilles, were considered French to the core and "one of us" by the white student body. Their father, who had served in the French army during World War I, was a supply officer in the colonial forces in Shanghai so his family was part of the French social scene. The Chinese thought differently. Whenever Claude rode his bicycle with us from school, Chinese pedestrians stopped walking, stared and pointed at him since Africans were a rarity; foreigners were either Caucasians or Japanese. While the French held their culture in very high esteem, they were not as disdainful of other ethnic groups as the Americans and the British, especially the latter.

Despite the fact that secular education in the public schools had become French law in 1881, a Catholic priest in Shanghai, le Père Beaucé, came once a week to our school to teach catechism to pupils preparing for their religious communion. The French bureaucrats in China did not consider these weekly religious classes in a secular school a violation of France's strict laws of separation of state and church. Another priest, the Jesuit Robert Jacquinot de Bésange, was a frequent visitor to our school, presumably to meet with our principal. On several occasions he waited in the school yard, watching us play during recess. While my classmates lowered their voices and greeted him with, "*Bonjour, mon père*," I slunk away, not wishing to say the same to a representative of the Catholic Church which, I was told, criticized my faith. However, I was fascinated by the fact that one sleeve of his jacket hung loosely because his hand was missing. I wondered why high-ranking Frenchmen all seemed to only have one hand.

French and foreign pupils at the Collège Municipal were steeped in the culture and history of France, reciting in lower classes about *Nos ancêtres les Gaulois* (our ancestors the Gauls). It did not take long for us to believe that civilization and culture was the exclusive domain of France. We memorized the names of French kings and the dates of their reigns, and learned about heroic army and naval officers and their brave men who fought and conquered far-flung colonies and sacrificed their lives to "civilize" and Christianize, with missionary help, *les bons sauvages*, the good natives. In the geography classes in our early years we drew and memorized detailed maps of Indochina, North Africa, "Dark Africa", and the islands in the Antilles and the South Pacific. I was annoyed to see on maps that the British had many more red markings – colonies – than France, and was shocked that treacherous England had burned the saintly Joan of Arc at the stake.

I realized at a very early age, as did my classmates, that the particular foreign language Shanghailanders spoke instantly revealed their economic and social standing in the community. This came to the fore one day when my mother came in a rickshaw to our school instead of my father, who normally drove by in his car to pick up Riva and me. As I was approaching my mother I overheard her speaking Russian to a friend and upon seeing me she told me in her strong Russian-accented English to wait for her. At home I had never taken into account that my parents spoke English with a discernible Russian accent and now I was most embarrassed. I quickly ran off and waited until the coast was clear of my classmates since I did not want them to imagine that I could be a White Russian, a class of people I already knew was one rung above the "half-castes". I was Romanian.

It was in school when I was about ten years old that I realized I could understand some of the Russian language when it was spoken by my Russian classmates. I pretended that I did not understand, although I did eavesdrop when they were talking about me – and what I heard was never flattering. But I did not want to belong to their crowd as some of them, perhaps, would not have wanted my friendship if they knew I was Jewish.

Although I was not French, I became close friends with my French classmates Ginette Grillon and Denise Froquet, and a Belgian girl, Aline Bodson. We spent much time playing in each other's homes and talking about some of the boys in our class and decided that each of us had to choose a "secret" boyfriend. I chose a Swiss boy named Pierre Schmid, not for his intellect, although he was a very good student, but for his light blond hair and dark blue eyes, which contrasted sharply with the black hair and brown eyes of the Chinese around us.

My favorite subject became English, which was extremely easy for me since my sisters and I spoke it with each other and with our non-French-speaking friends. In the upper-level classes English was taught by one of the few teachers I liked, Madame Marguerite Egal, a very lively and excitable woman, who spoke English with a heavy French accent and could not pronounce the "th" sound. I smiled whenever she read us stories about "ze fazer and ze mazer" and their "verry, verry" good or bad children. I could accept her accent, since it was a French one, but not my mother's Russian accent. Madame Egal was probably the only teacher who could tolerate my restlessness and chattering in class, for I spoke somewhat correct English and enunciated it clearly while my French classmates massacred its grammar and pronunciation. In general they disliked anything associated with England, their perpetual enemy, who had beaten them in so many wars. Many French adults in Shanghai did not really see the need to learn English. The men spoke French at work and at their club, communicating in Pidgin English with their lowly staff, while their wives taught their servants the basic French words necessary for household chores.

I felt all our teachers were too demanding and too strict, and would never accept any excuse if I did not hand in my assignments on time. We toiled on our homework after supper, reading, writing, trying to solve arithmetic problems, and memorizing poems and stanzas from plays by the famous classical triad, Corneille, Racine, Molière, and other dramatists. Nowadays, whenever I meet an African or a Vietnamese of my generation who attended French schools during the colonial era, we reminisce about those plays where we declaimed on honor, passion and the eternal *"gloire de la France"*, and how we believed, as foreigners in the primary school, that the Gauls were our ancestors.

Scholastic Warfare

ALTHOUGH WE benefited from an excellent educational system, it was a very difficult one for the average student. In order to survive scholastically, most of us in middle school started to cheat on quizzes, devising many ways to keep from being caught. We copied poems, dates of battles, wars and the reigns of kings on scraps of paper and pinned them on the back of a willing student sitting in front of us. This of course enabled me and my classmates to recite passages flawlessly and with fervor whenever called upon by our teacher. Since I was near-sighted I had much difficulty in deciphering my own handwriting and had to practically lean on the neck of the student accomplice. However, problems arose when the teacher asked me to stand in front of the class, where I was at a loss since I had not studied the poem. I was quickly sent back to my seat and given a very low mark by the annoyed teacher. Another instructor, equally as high-strung but not as friendly as our English teacher, Madame Egal was Madame Louise Hameury, who taught French grammar in the middle school. She constantly yelled at the top of her voice, *"Tu vas sentir ma main,"* which meant, "I will slap your cheek." These were, however, merely threats, since corporal punishment was not allowed in our school. It annoyed me and some of my classmates that Madame Hameury hovered over her daughter, Paulette, who received top marks in every subject. We did not realize that Madame Hameury was concerned about her daughter's diabetes and stunted growth, and only later did we understand the seriousness of her disease when she died in her early teens. We wondered whether grief-stricken Madame

Classmates – Lily in middle of 2nd row

Hameury lost her hair at that time, for she started wearing one of two wigs which she changed intermittently.

Although our coterie of classmates was weak in mathematics, algebra, geometry, physics and chemistry, we were able to survive the rigors of quizzes and exams in these subjects because our teacher, Monsieur Camille Vergez, wore very thick-lensed glasses and could not see us cheat, even when he was close to our desks. Several of the boys even managed to sneak out of his classes while he was explaining some mathematical formula and rushed to the bathroom to smoke cigarettes. We were told that Monsieur Vergez was nearly blinded by mustard gas at the end of World War I and was still suffering from his war wounds. We believed the pain made him drink, since on several occasions he came to class reeking of alcohol. We did not have much sympathy, however, for Monsieur Vergez because he constantly reminded us that we were "*bêtes comme des ânes*" ("dumb as donkeys"), an opinion other teachers may have had about us but did not verbalize. We ignored such remarks for we had developed a thick psychological armor in this hostile environment, and cheating became our defense mechanism for educational survival.

My classmates and I started a barter cheating system where I would give them answers to English language and grammar tests and they in turn would provide me answers for the quizzes on science and mathematics. In addition, when a teacher's back was turned, we opened the lid of our desk and quickly glanced at an open book for the correct answers. We even developed a system of rolling slips of paper into a small ball and sending them through the air to the intended party. We were proud of all these methods for we were rarely caught and our educational bartering and aeronautical skills prevailed throughout high school, where the pressure became intense in preparation for the dreaded baccalaureate exams. We were not as fortunate in our classroom crimes with Madame Delga, our teacher of French grammar and composition, who watched all our moves with an eagle's eye and a stern look. She was aware of our schemes because one of her daughters was in the class and reported them to her mother. Fortunately, I was an above-average student in French; inexplicably it was often the case that non-native speakers of French were more adept in writing stylistic essays than their native French counterparts.

Two White Russian teachers were in charge of the music program for the entire school. The corpulent Madame Teliakovsky, always wearing colorful long dresses, taught us to sing, cupping her hand to her lips to draw out strange sounds while her accompanist, the tiny Madame Stelnitsky, banged irritatingly on the piano. Since we could not hold a tune she had to endlessly repeat the same songs. Our dance teacher, Madame Svetlanova, tried to teach the girls various dances in preparation for the annual school production. She had a difficult time with most of us who were not interested in performing but relished being out of class, and made fools of ourselves by jumping up and down. It must have been a pathetic sight for this professionally-trained teacher from a Saint Petersburg ballet school to see us dancing the two-step or the arabesque.

Those of us who did not study Latin, one of the rare electives in our school, had to study another foreign language besides English. German was offered but not Spanish or Italian since these romance languages were considered too close to French, while Russian, a useful language in the Concession, was not part of the baccalaureate exams. I chose German, taught by Mr. Kazatkine, a White Russian who fought the Bolsheviks during the Revolution, and whom many of us believed was a Nazi sympathizer – why else would he want to teach Hitler's guttural language? I could not master German grammar, failed the course and dropped it. Instead I was allowed, surprisingly, to take private Spanish lessons to fulfill the requirement for two foreign languages. A subject at the Collège Municipal considered useful for the body but not the mind was gymnastics and sports. It was taught by a ruddy-faced Irishman, James Kelly, who reminded us that he was from Eire and not from England. His daily function also included monitoring the rows of students as we marched in and out of our classes at the beginning and end of the day, refereeing our after-school soccer games and supervising our weekly gymnastics class. Mr. Kelly, who had worked elsewhere in the Far East before coming to Shanghai, was now reduced to monitoring rowdy students whose behavior at times must have reminded him of the fierce animals he saw when he served in Ceylon. Once a year Mr. Kelly could show his true worth as a coach when he coordinated a full day of sporting events on our school grounds, consisting of a volleyball competition, relay races and pole jumping. Officials from the French municipality and the military distributed medals and ribbons to the winners.

Whenever we were caught cheating or were too disruptive in chatting with our classmates, our teachers would send us out of the classroom as punishment, *au piquet*, where we leaned against a wall or a pillar until the end of the class session. Although we were glad to be out of class, we feared being seen by the new principal of our school, a very short man named Pierre Guillemont, who was nicknamed "Putia" by the older boys in the secondary school. This name was a distortion of the French slang word *petiot* for a short person. Putia had the habit of walking the hallways while classes were in session and if he saw a student *au piquet*, he would pounce like a panther. On many occasions he stared at me with his cold blue eyes and asked why I was *au piquet*, all the while rocking on his heels, perhaps to appear taller. He would not accept any excuse and ordered me to remain in school after hours to do extra homework. I always wondered how Putia found time to run the school.

The teachers were our enemies and had to be thwarted by whatever means possible, by cheating or complaining about them to our parents. But our criticism was always brushed aside by our parents, who held our teachers in great esteem and would never have found fault with them.

My classmates and I were always glad when we left our classes to go to the school infirmary for our obligatory annual vaccination shots against typhus, smallpox and cholera, necessary in a city beset by epidemics and diseases. In compensation, we were excused from afternoon classes. We were also released from school every Wednesday afternoon to give us time to catch up on homework, although we had to go to school Saturday mornings to make up the lost classroom time. I looked forward to these Wednesday afternoons, not to study but to ride my bicycle, and in the fall and winter to buy sweet potatoes and chestnuts that street vendors sold from large basins heated by charcoal. When the weather started getting warm we purchased sugar cane, enjoying the sweet taste of the juice and spitting out the husks as we cycled to our respective homes. I enjoyed racing my bicycle, scaring Chinese pedestrians who, as I rode very close to them, yelled at me in Chinese, "Damn foreigner!" or, "Long-nose white devil!"

Our academic progress, or lack of it, was noted in a *livret scolaire*, a booklet where grades for our class work, home assignments and conduct were recorded weekly by French-speaking Chinese clerks. Monsieur Guillemont scrutinized every middle and high-school *livret scolaire,* since he signed all of them and wrote comments if the student's marks were dangerously low. Every Saturday afternoon we brought this booklet home to show either parent, who then affixed his or her signature as proof they had seen it. We always wondered whether Putia ever found time to sleep, since every week he had to review at least two hundred *livrets scolaires.* I stopped showing mine to my father for I was tired of hearing him preach about my poor conduct in class and my failing grades in mathematics. Instead I asked my mother, who did not speak French, to sign the booklet since I could translate incorrectly Putia's negative comments on my conduct in class. I was regularly reprimanded for talking to my neighbors instead of listening to the teacher, who would then yell, "*Silence, Willens,*" the French word for "silence" rhyming quite poetically with the French pronunciation of my family name. If students failed in any two subjects during the course of the year, they had to repeat the grade, since the concept of "social passing" did not exist. When Putia recommended that I be tutored in mathematics, my father asked his client's son, Bernard Saint-Oyant, to help me during the summer vacations. He did so but to no lasting result.

From time to time my classmates and I were sent to read some assigned books at the Alliance Française library on the second floor of our school. There we spent as much time as possible reading passages of forbidden books such as the ones written by the well-known female author Colette. We did not understand why her works were banned but could understand why *Lady Chatterly's Lover*, with its vivid sexual descriptions, was not for students at the Collège Municipal Français. We wrote down the page numbers of erotic passages and gave this valuable information to our classmates who managed to read excerpts when the off-duty French librarian was replaced by a Chinese clerk. One of our classmates informed us that her older brother and his friends read about the female genitalia in the medical Larousse dictionary. We tried to get hold of this book to learn about boys' genitalia but could not locate it and did not dare ask the librarian to set it aside for us. The girls in our group were sure the boys hid this book somewhere in the library so they could read it anytime at their leisure.

Despite our dislike of the Collège Municipal Français, there were nevertheless two yearly events we looked forward to with much anticipation and excitement. One was held every February in the vast auditorium of the Collège in honor of the patron saint of French education, Emperor Charlemagne (who in reality was of German stock). Except for kindergartners and the first two grades, the student body was invited to *"La Fête de la Saint Charlemagne"* party, where we were treated to tea and cakes and later watched skits performed by the higher grades. We enjoyed ourselves, gulping down the food, talking loudly to our heart's content without being hushed by teachers relegated to the back of the auditorium. We sang along with the performers and laughed and clapped heartily, especially if our friends were in the show. In one performance my sister Jackie played Chopin's *Fantaisie Impromptu* on the piano; on another occasion I appeared on the stage with our dance group as a Russian peasant wearing a colorful blouse, wide skirt and red boots, dancing clumsily on the stage. I thoroughly enjoyed the attention and applause, which I felt was somewhat directed at me. The most pleasing aspect for the girls on that day was to show off their new dresses, while the boys looked uncomfortable in their blazers, stiff white cotton shirts, ties and short pants.

Another pleasurable event was held at the end of the scholastic year, when medals and books were distributed to students who had excelled in specific subjects. The auditorium was decorated with French flags, and along the walls palm trees were placed in large pots. As each class filed into the auditorium under Mr. Kelly's stern gaze there was always much excitement in the air as we hoped to receive at least one book as a reward for our studies during the year, and we were all looking forward to our long-awaited summer vacation. I knew I would not go home empty-handed, for I always received a book for my excellent marks in English and another one for French history. The teachers took their seats on the stage followed by officials of the French municipality, and by army and navy officers in their medal-bedecked khaki and white uniforms, which contrasted with the black cassocks worn by priests from the various French religious schools, among whom I recognized the Jesuit who had only one hand. After the arrival of the French Consul General the band of the *Garde Municipale* (the French police) would play the national hymn, *La Marseillaise*. The Consul opened the session with a short speech, which would be followed by a longer one from Putia. He would inevitably note that students around the world were becoming lax in their studies, but he nevertheless seemed proud to read the names of the students who had passed the first and second part of the baccalaureate degree. He would end his talk

CMF teachers in front of a poster of Vichy leader Maréchal Pétain during World War II

by exhorting us to read many books during our summer vacation and to study harder for the upcoming school year. We would wait impatiently for him to stop talking for we wanted to collect our prizes and leave the school as quickly as possible. When our names were called we ran to the stage to receive our books from Putia, who made an effort to smile as he handed them to us. It was interesting that the ultimate prize, the *Prix d'Excellence* for the best student in every class in the secondary school, was nearly always won by non-French nationals born in Shanghai – especially by two Russian Jewish girls, Ira and Genia, and the Lazaro sisters, fervent Catholics whose Indian parents were from Goa, the Portuguese colonial city. When the ceremony ended, the Consul General would say a few parting words, followed by music from the *Garde Municipale* as the dignitaries and the teachers slowly walked out of the auditorium. We followed them quietly but once out of their earshot we would sing, *"Vive les vacances, plus de pénitence, les cahiers au feu et les maîtres au milieu,"* ("Hurrah for our summer vacation, no more punishment, let's throw our notebooks and our teachers in the bonfire"). When I was in elementary school a shortened ceremony was held in the morning for pupils who received books from the wives of dignitaries in the Concession. These ladies in their summer silk and organdy dresses and hats and gloves, sat on the stage smiling as the children walked awkwardly up the dais to collect their books.

In November, on Armistice Day, students aged 12 years and older attended a solemn ceremony at a Catholic cemetery to commemorate the fallen heroes of World War I who fought and died for the glory of France. Our classes went to the cemetery, where wreaths of chrysanthemums were placed on the tombstones of French veterans of that war and where speeches in homage to these heroes were intoned by the Consul General and representatives from each branch of the military. All the municipal buildings and the six police stations of the French Concession were illuminated in honor of Armistice Day.

These ceremonies, with patriotic speeches on the greatness of France, its culture and civilization and colonial conquests marked me forever. I still get goose bumps whenever I hear *La Marseillaise,* with its thunderous call, "*Aux armes, citoyens*" ("take up your weapons, citizens"). These themes were emphasized every morning before class in a brief ceremony held on school grounds, where a student chosen for his or her excellent grades and conduct would be called to raise the French flag, while an Annamite soldier from the colonial army played the bugle. To my great regret I was never chosen since one needed to be a French citizen to partake in this patriotic ritual. I consoled myself that my poor marks and conduct in class would have precluded me from raising the revered tricolor anyway. But as a stateless person in Shanghai, I always wanted to be a French citizen.

The Dazzling Mid-thirties

AS MY parents' circle of friends grew, they decided in early 1935 to move to a much larger apartment in the Savoy Apartments complex on Route de Say Zoong (Changshu Lu), one of the few Chinese-named streets in the French Concession. Close to Avenue Joffre, the recently built Savoy was an eight-story Art Deco building with a very large garden.

It was not only the wealthy treaty-power nationals who led a very hectic social life: others of the middle class, including many stateless Russian Jews like my mother and father, were able to do the same, although on a lesser scale. My parents never joined the new Shanghai Jewish Club, built in 1932, where members played card games and mahjong, listened to lectures and concerts, and gossiped. Still, every year they attended charity balls and New Year's Eve festivities at this club to support the Shelter House for destitute elderly Jews, and for the German and Austrian refugees who began arriving in Shanghai in the first half of the 1930s. For these formal events my mother purchased a brocade or silk bolt at one of the four Chinese-owned department stores – Sincere, Sun, Sun Sun and Wing On – or at the more expensive English-owned Whiteaway and Laidlaw department store. She then gave the material to a Russian seamstress who deftly transformed it into two evening gowns and several dresses. On these occasions my mother was bedecked with pearl necklaces, and a diamond ring and earrings from Michael Sukenik's store. Whenever there was a chill in the air she wore her silver fox stole around her shoulders. My father accompanied her in his "smoking" – as tuxedos were called in Shanghai – although he was never too pleased to be in this stiff formal outfit. My parents' cultural life centered on

Shanghai Symphony Orchestra concerts at the Lyceum Theater under the baton of the celebrated Italian conductor Mario Paci. When they went out for the evening Old Amah warned us and perhaps tried to scare us – although Riva and I were no longer babies – that if we did not go to bed by a certain time the carved wooden statue of the *joss* man in the hallway would come into our bedroom and take us away.

Although my parents did not belong to any club, they were members of the Ashkenazi synagogue and supported it by purchasing seats for Passover and the High Holy Days of *Rosh Hashona* and *Yom Kippur*. My father was orthodox in his religious beliefs, while my mother had only received a secular upbringing in Novonicolaevsk, despite her grandfather Pavel's rigid orthodoxy. When I was about seven years old Riva and I started attending the synagogue with our mother. We sat upstairs with other ladies who participated in the services with some difficulty since they could not read Hebrew. We never understood what was said and sung in the synagogue during our twice-yearly attendance since we never studied Hebrew, which was only taught to boys to prepare them for their Bar-Mitzva. We were bored with the solemn atmosphere and spent time outside the synagogue chatting with our friends and admiring each other's new outfits. My father never talked to us about Judaism, and my sisters and I remained quite ignorant of the meaning of the rituals at Passover and the somberness of the High Holy Days. We did know that our religion forbade us to eat pork or shellfish – but we enjoyed them at lunches at the non-kosher homes of my mother's sisters Brania and Riva. My mother warned us not to tell our father about these dishes and the Chinese meals of pork or the tail of the marinated fish which Shao Wang and Old Amah cooked and often shared with us in the kitchen. We enjoyed eating these "forbidden" foods, stuffing them down our throats with rice and burping to our heart's content. We knew that our father would never enter the kitchen, a domain strictly reserved for servants, women and children.

Savoy Apartments

Eating, playing games and trying to avoid homework were my passion and my forte during these early formative years. After school I rushed to the garden in our complex to play hop-scotch or marbles, climb trees, roller-skate or ride my bicycle while the amahs, knitting and gossiping, took care of babies in their carriages. Several of my friends and I played a game called "Wearing the Green", in which we had to keep a leaf or blade of grass on us at all times. I would pounce on whoever was near me and shout "green", and if that person could not produce a plant, I was owed a cut-out of a dwarf from the wrapper of a Snow White ice cream bar. Once I had collected seven cut-outs, Old Amah took me to a nearby bakery to collect my prize, a free chocolate-covered Hazelwood ice cream bar. This treat was introduced in Shanghai after the showing of the movie "Snow White and the Seven Dwarfs".

I also enjoyed riding in my father's car on Sundays, not to school but to Jessfield Park (Zhongshan Gongyuan) beyond the boundary of the International Settlement, where we picnicked or spent the day playing games. On these trips I always wanted to sit in the front seat because I enjoyed making faces and showing my tongue to pedestrians crossing in front of our car. My mother readily acquiesced to my desire and sat in the back. She did not want to hear me whine, nor did she want to listen to my father yelling at pedestrians or any moving contraption, especially rickshaws, blocking his way. During those rides my father's swearing in Russian rapidly increased my multi-lingual vocabulary. I did not always know, however, what they meant. My insistence on sitting in the front came in useful one afternoon when my father parked his car on Avenue Joffre. I remained in the car while he went to pick up my mother, who was visiting her sister Brania and her husband Joseph in their dry goods store. A car bumped into ours and dented it slightly; I quickly looked at the license plate and later repeated the four numbers to my father. My parents were amazed that I not only thought of looking at the numbers but even remembered them. My father contacted the culprit and was reimbursed for the minor repairs while for my alertness I received a Chinese silver dollar, which I added to my collection of copper coins. I was extremely pleased to possess this "Mex dollar" – the dollar imported from Mexico that was the standard currency in China until the early thirties.

My father subscribed to the English language *North-China Daily News* and the French *Journal de Shanghai,* which were delivered to our home. I was fascinated by the captions and often asked my father questions about the countries mentioned in these newspapers. Since I seemed interested in geography he brought home for me foreign stamps from his office. I placed them carefully in my album, where I had already collected a substantial number of Chinese stamps depicting colorful sampans and the serious mien of Sun Yat-sen. I was thrilled with the variety of stamps from Egypt and the British colonies of Hongkong and Malaya where Sun Life had branch offices. However, as a budding Francophile, I was disappointed to be reminded once again that England had more colonies than France.

I learned more about the British Empire when, one evening in

May 1935, my father drove my mother, Riva and me to the Bund, where the dark sky was ablaze with electric lights and fireworks lit from barges on the Whangpoo River. These festivities were arranged by the municipality of the International Settlement in celebration of the Silver Jubilee of King George V. When I told an English boy that I had attended these festivities in honor of his king, he informed me that this ruler was called "His Majesty the King of the United Kingdom of Great Britain and Ireland and the British dominions beyond the Seas, Emperor of India". After such an exciting evening, I decided that I could forgive England for having more colonies than France and some bad monarchs who should have been guillotined. In early 1936, when I learned that the old king had died, I was disappointed as I had gotten used to his bearded face on all of my English and British Empire stamps. My father took us once again to the Bund to see fireworks lighting up the city, this time in honor of the coronation of a new King of England and Emperor of India, Edward VIII.

With these events, the headlines in the newspapers and my stamps from various countries, I was becoming more conscious of the outside world. I could easily recognize the recurring pictures of Hitler, Mussolini and Stalin, who, I was told by my mother, were "bad men", and I became politically active at the tender age of ten, when I verbally attacked two young boys in our complex, an Italian and a Soviet Russian, who bragged incessantly about their respective countries. I could not brag about Romania since I did not know anything about that country and my mother forbade me to ask my father about it, although I was aware from my stamp collection that it was ruled by a king. I told the Italian boy that Mussolini was fat and ugly and resembled a bulldog with his jutting jaw, and that his planes were bombarding defenseless Abyssinians who only had spears to throw back. I had no idea on which continent Abyssinia was located but I knew it had an emperor thanks to my collection of several triangular-shaped Abyssinian stamps adorned with images of Emperor Haile Selassie. Since the young Italian boy knew less about Abyssinia than I did, he changed the subject and bragged that he and his parents had visited the Italian ship *Conte Verde* anchored on the Whangpoo River, adding that I would never be invited on this ship. The aggressive Soviet boy, an apparatchik in the making, tried to educate me about his "Papa Stalin", whom I understood my parents despised because he was mean to his people. Since this boy was still deficient in English, he could not tell me much about the Soviet Union, and I shooed him off by telling him to go back to his Papa Stalin in my limited Russian, embellished with my fount of Russian swear words. My favorite ones were *svinya* (pig) and *tchort zabroy tibya* (the devil take you). I especially did not like "Papa Stalin" since Aunty Sonia's son Vladimir had left for the Soviet Union in 1935, heeding Stalin's call to Russians in the diaspora to return and help rebuild the motherland. Vladimir, an engineering student and the son of wealthy parents, was the epitome of the despised "bourgeoisie" and was never heard from again.

Regrettably, my disputes with the Italian and the Soviet boys would end soon. Within a year of our move to the Savoy apartments my reputation as a troublemaker grew, and several parents complained to my mother that I had made their children cry. They asked her why I was not as well-behaved as my sisters Riva and Jackie – and of course she did not have an answer. The parents in the Savoy Apartments, including my own, would have been shocked to learn about a game several boys and I played on the roof garden of our building. We stealthily climbed the eight flights of stairs, never taking the elevator in order to avoid inquisitive adults who would surely ask us why we were carrying a bucket filled with ice cubes. Our purpose was to throw these ice cubes down at people on the street who, from our perspective, resembled ants. Once our projectiles landed we waited to see the reaction of the pedestrians and cyclists, who would look around and then up but could not see us as we ducked behind the grilled railing on the roof, giggling. Fortunately for the pedestrians we were poor marksmen and no one was ever hit by these ice cubes from the skies.

During the mid-thirties the lifestyle of the foreigners – lunches, high teas, dinners, concerts, parties and balls – was in stark contrast with the dire situation of most of the Chinese living inside and outside the invisible walls of the two foreign settlements. Two radically different worlds existed in Shanghai. My parents, my sisters and I, and all of our friends considered it natural to live side-by-side with the Chinese, yet ignore them.

11
Summer Holidays

WHEN THE school year ended, the greatest excitement for my sisters and me was to escape Shanghai's oppressive summer weather for our vacation at a seaside or mountain resort. At home the open windows and the ceiling and table fans in our apartment and the numerous glasses of iced water we drank were not sufficient to alleviate the heat and humidity. The thick Chinese wool carpets were taken out of every room, hung on railings and swatted by the servants to remove the dust and lint that had accumulated during the winter months. These carpets were then rolled and wrapped in thick paper and placed in whatever enclosed space was available in our apartment or at friends' larger homes. Light cotton or sisal rugs were placed in every room, offering a semblance of coolness on the floor and in the air. In the evenings Old Amah covered us with talcum powder before we went to bed under mosquito nets with the window open. Between June and September, when the heat became unbearable in the servants' airless rooms, many slept outside on cots or simply on straw mats, while foreigners scurried far from the city.

In the 1930s during July and August, foreign mothers and their children, sometimes accompanied by their amahs, left Shanghai for the beaches and the mountains while their husbands remained at their jobs. In 1931, when I was four years old, my mother took Riva and me to Harbin to visit Aunty Sonia and her family. We went by ship to Dairen and then took a train to Harbin via Mukden. Aunty Sonia and her husband always sent us many gifts on our birthdays, unlike our parents who gave us only one; I knew that I could expect more during our stay in Harbin. We spent the entire summer in that Russified city, pampered by our two older cousins, Vladimir and Sarah, who frequently took us swimming in the Sungari River (Songhua Jiang). Old Amah remained in Shanghai taking care of my father while Aunty Sonia's Russian *nyanya* (nanny) looked after us. Every morning she took Riva and me to a children's daycare center where both of us switched without any difficulty from Pidgin English to (ungrammatical) Russian. I babbled away and sang songs with Russian-speaking children, and I believe I became proficient in that language during our stay in Harbin. As a child I thought that every adult had his or her own private language to communicate with me and in turn I automatically responded in that particular language.

Riva and I spent only one summer in Harbin because Japanese soldiers were beginning to control the city and their military police, the *Kempeitai*, were extorting money from the rich merchants and businessmen. They targeted Jewish merchants whom they believed participated in the political activities of the communist Third International, which the Japanese abhorred. The Japanese found willing collaborators among the often anti-Semitic and fascist-leaning Ukrainians in Harbin, who would harass or kidnap heads of households for large sums of money. Aunty Sonia's husband, who owned a very profitable pharmacy, feared being the next victim, and sold his business in the early thirties and moved his family to Shanghai.

In 1934 my mother, Riva, two-year-old Jackie, Old Amah and I went to Tsingtao, a seaside town popular with foreigners, especially American and English Protestant missionaries and their families, who could relax by the beach before returning to their harsh lives in the hinterlands of China. Tsingtao was always a favorite resort for Germans as they had controlled it until the outbreak of World War I, building many summer chalets that resembled the Bavarian architecture of their homeland. Their successful brewery, established in Tsingtao in 1903, produced and sold beer in all the treaty ports for consumption by Chinese and foreigners alike, especially the treaty powers' servicemen.

We sailed to Tsingtao on a Japanese passenger *maru* (ship) owned by the Yusen Kisen Kaisha maritime line, a trip which lasted two days. Our cabin was comfortable, the service impeccable and the Japanese officers and crew very friendly with the passengers, especially children. My mother, always careful with money, purchased second-class tickets since the Japanese ships had a reputation for cleanliness in all the cabins. The officers and crew members patted me on the head whenever I strayed near to their quarters and gave me candy, which I quickly ate before returning to our cabin so that I would not have to share my booty with Riva or anyone else. We spent a month in Tsingtao, where my mother, together with our relatives and friends, rented a large house with a wrap-around verandah where adults and children gathered in the evenings to talk and sing. Several families also brought their amahs to take care of the smaller children and help prepare meals. Riva, our friends and I went to the beach, where we built sand castles, collected shells and went swimming (with life belts) under the watchful eyes of our amahs, the only Chinese people allowed in a section reserved for foreigners. The boys from our cottage and I played near our beach on a series of concrete bunkers with protruding cannons that the Germans had built before World War I. Under these deep fortifications small wagons used to run on narrow tracks to carry ammunition to the harbor in case of an attack by the Japanese entrenched in Manchuria. I enjoyed straddling the cannons and scampering up and down these bunkers with the boys while playing war games – Chinese versus Japanese. Knowing that in the real world they would always win, all of us preferred to be on the Japanese side.

The following summer, when I was eight years old, Riva and I were sent to a private British school in Tsingtao for the sole purpose of improving our spoken English, which had become too interspersed with French and Pidgin English words. We attended the St. Giles boarding school where Aunty Riva

– who had recently returned from Australia with her children – enrolled her two young sons, Bruce and Harry. I was not happy at the thought of spending my vacation in a classroom instead of frolicking at a beach resort and, worse, Old Amah would not be around to bathe me, wash my hair and lay out my clothes every morning. The boarding school had numerous rules and regulations and before long I got into a number of scraps and was punished by Mr. Inge, the very strict English headmaster. He called me into his office, where he put me across his knees and spanked my backside several times with a brush, which made me cry more out of embarrassment than pain. I thought of myself as grown up, for even my mother no longer spanked me (although she did yell at me). No parent ever questioned the fact that this man lowered our pants without another adult around, and now I wonder whether this bachelor derived some sort of sexual thrill from uncovering the backsides of so many young girls and boys.

Sex was never mentioned in our home. Not having a brother, I was very curious what a boy's genitalia looked like. I got my chance in the salty waters of the Pacific, when a boy about my age and I had an innocent exchange of "show me". We did this rapidly and with much giggling. I was curious to know how babies were born because I no longer believed our parents who had told Riva and me – when we had the courage to ask – that babies appeared in cabbage patches or were delivered in the beak of a pelican. Once I had seen my first penis, I asked my classmates how it was used between a man and a woman. I was shocked at the answer and asked Riva whether this could be true, since I could not believe our parents could behave in such a dirty fashion. I was glad to uncover the mysterious world of sex but it was disappointing to discover and accept that our own parents would participate in this lurid game.

My mother intended to return to Tsingtao in 1936 for our vacation but skirmishes between the Chinese and the Japanese in northern China stymied her plans. She considered other resorts,

Riva, Lily, mother holding Jackie

Mokanshan and Peitaho in China, as well as in Japan, where her friends were planning to spend the summer in Nagasaki and Bepu. Many Shanghailanders went to Japan for the summer as they were welcomed by the Japanese tourism office, and even stateless foreigners were allowed to enter the country. My father, however, was leery about the Japanese and my mother thought it would be too expensive to go there even though my father had had a very successful year selling insurance policies. My mother never felt secure financially, always believing that she had to save money for unexpected emergencies. Her flight from Russia as a young girl always remained uppermost in her mind.

My mother eventually chose Peitaho, northeast of Tientsin. She rented a small cottage with several relatives and friends, and took along Old Amah to look after the three of us, wash our clothes and help with the communal-style cooking. My friends and I swam in the mornings in the ocean and after lunch we reluctantly took a nap, which Old Amah insisted was necessary since the sun was too hot to stay outdoors. In the late afternoon we rented bicycles and rode to a nearby lake surrounded by summer homes owned by wealthy Chinese and rented by foreigners. After supper we walked in the dimly lit streets carrying flashlights and shining them on the fireflies flitting about, or scaring each other in the dark.

When the fighting between the Chinese and the Japanese increased in northern China, the foreigners forsook Peitaho and began spending their summer vacations closer to home at the Mokanshan mountain resort about 120 miles southwest of Shanghai. Located at the top of the mountain, it was developed at the beginning of the twentieth century by English and American missionaries who came in the summer months to rest from their arduous evangelical work. My mother, my siblings and I, Old Amah and our relatives spent July and the beginning of August 1937 in a house perched high in the mountains. We had to take a five-hour bus ride over bumpy roads, then transfer to another bus for an additional two-hour ride until we reached the foot of Mokan Mountain. My mother brought along cold chicken, boiled eggs, bread, cakes and juice to sustain our hunger and irritation during this endless trek. Since there was no motor road to take us to the top of the mountain, the only mode of transportation was the sedan chair carriers, who waited for clients at the foot of the mountain. The sedan chair had two parallel bamboo poles carried by one man in front and another at the back, while a third man trotted alongside as the relief carrier. The load could be very heavy if one of the passengers was obese, which many Shanghailanders were. As the two men carried me up the narrow and slippery path, huffing and grunting, I wondered whether we would ever reach our destination – but I was not aware of the danger that one of the pole carriers, in his straw sandals, could slip on the smooth rocks.

We enjoyed the cool air of Mokanshan amidst the hissing sound of cicadas, playing Chinese checkers, shuttlecock games on the lawn, listening to records on a squeaky gramophone and fighting over the two hammocks in the garden. In the evenings we walked in the bamboo groves and later sat on the verandah,

Lily and Riva at Tsingtao beach

where I related some of Old Amah's fairy tales about the *joss* man. One day, however, a true story was told to me by my five-year-old sister Jackie and her older friends, who had encountered General Chiang Kai-shek, accompanied by many guards, taking a stroll on one of the mountain paths. Jackie mentioned that the tall Chinese man had smiled at her, said "hello" in English and she had waved at him, not realizing that she had just seen the President of China. I then suggested to several of my friends that we should find the Generalissimo's home. When we approached his big house the soldiers on guard barked at us to leave the area. We did so rapidly, scampering away at the sight of their guns.

Leaving Mokanshan I finally realized the danger of traveling by sedan chair. As my carriers were running down the steep mountain, I was pushed forward in my sedan chair and on both sides of the narrow path I could see the deep gorge leading down to the valley. I closed my eyes, gripped the bamboo chair and tried not to think of tumbling down the mountain. I opened my eyes only when I felt we were on level ground.

Our leisurely, uneventful summer vacation in Mokanshan was the last our family was able to take in China. While at our summer resort we learned that on July 7, 1937, shots were fired between Chinese and Japanese soldiers at Marco Polo Bridge near Peking. Very soon after, when a Japanese naval officer was shot and killed in Hungjao, the Japanese bombed Chapei, Hongkew and Pootung. The Anti-Japanese War of Resistance had begun; it would last eight years and 20 million Chinese would die.

12
The Gathering Storm Clouds

UNTIL THE "undeclared war" broke out, my parents believed Japan was satisfied with its conquest of Manchuria and the prize city of Harbin. They and other foreigners in Shanghai had not been concerned about the Sino-Japanese squabbles in 1932 or the skirmishes in the hinterland in the mid-thirties between the Nationalist government forces and the communist rebels. Generally, the various foreign communities continued to lead a very pleasant life, especially the treaty-power nationals who wined and dined at cocktail and dinner parties, balls, and at their clubs and hotels.

British nationals celebrated with gusto the coronation of King George VI in May 1937, setting aside mixed emotions over the abdication of the former King Edward VIII. Bamboo arches covered with garlands of paper flowers were erected at major intersections in the International Settlement, and in the evening my father drove us to the Bund, lit up with spotlights, to watch the fireworks in honor of this festive occasion. I overheard my parents say that the English king had had to abandon his throne because he wanted to marry an American woman who was twice divorced.

But two events in 1937 made the reality of death frighteningly clear. My maternal grandmother Anna died of pneumonia and Riva and I attended her funeral with our parents. I shuddered when the coffin was lowered into the ground, while around me my mother and her sisters were crying as the rabbi chanted his prayers. I had never seen my mother cry and was shocked to see Aunty Brania throw herself on the coffin, sobbing hysterically, until she was dragged away from the open grave.

The other event was the Sino-Japanese War. I saw Japanese warships bristling with cannons and their planes bombard Chapei. Chinese planes appeared on August 14 over Shanghai with the intention of bombing the *Idzumo,* the Japanese flagship anchored close to the Japanese Consulate. That day I was playing with my classmate Alla Rabinovich in her garden in the French Concession when we heard the muffled sound of anti-aircraft fire and extremely loud explosions. I was very scared, and, feeling that I needed the security of my family, I quickly jumped on my bicycle and sped home, accompanied by the boom of detonating bombs. That evening I heard from my parents, who did not know that I had ridden my bicycle during the bombardment, that many people had been killed in the International Settlement.

Over the next few days I learned that Chinese pilots had been flying over the city when bombs on two of their planes were dislodged from their racks by anti-aircraft fire and fell in the business center of the International Settlement. The bombs from one plane landed on Nanking Road between the Palace Hotel (Peace Hotel, South Buidling) and the Cathay Hotel (Peace Hotel, North Building), killing many Chinese pedestrians, rickshaw coolies, motorists and some foreigners. The bombs from the second plane fell on the crowded Great World Amusement Center (Da Shijie) at the edge of the French Concession. Approximately 1,000 Chinese refugees, who had assembled there to pick up their rice allotments, were killed instantly. On that "Black Saturday", as it became known, 2,000 people lost their lives and 2,500 were wounded in downtown Shanghai.

A few days later the tall Wing On department store received a direct hit from Japanese planes, killing and wounding customers in the building as well as pedestrians on Nanking Road and nearby streets. I saw pictures in the English and French newspapers of wounded civilians and dead bodies in the street. Fighting immediately broke out between the Japanese in Hongkew and the Chinese army in the Chapei and Nantao Districts. The Japanese

Shanghai Volunteer Corps (top and middle) and the Japanese marines guarding Chapei after defeating the Chinese army (bottom)

soldiers took over the American Seventh Day Adventist mission in nearby Yangtzepoo, ordering the foreign missionaries living there and in Hongkew to leave their homes. They were warned that their churches, schools and a hospital in the Chinese sector would be demolished if they harbored Chinese soldiers.

I was terrified by the artillery fire from Chapei but nevertheless took the elevator to the roof of our apartment building and saw in the distance dark grey smoke floating skywards. My father witnessed the destruction of houses in Chapei from the rooftop of his office building along the Bund. Members of the Shanghai Volunteer Corps were ordered to return to active duty and quickly erected barbed-wire barricades, complete with sandbags and protruding machine guns, along the main thoroughfares of the International Settlement. The French Concession was guarded by Chinese and Indochinese policemen and French officers and Indochinese soldiers from the colonial army.

In late August I learned from a classmate, whose father was in the French police, about a very serious incident between the Japanese and the Americans. Several men from the American Company of the Shanghai Volunteer Corps, who were riding in their personnel carrier at the southern boundary of Hongkew, encountered a column of Japanese soldiers armed with rifles and bayonets marching towards the Settlement. The American driver was ordered by his officer to stop in front of the Japanese soldiers and block them from advancing any further. The Americans then dismounted from their truck and formed a line across the road, facing the Japanese soldiers who began threatening them with their bayonets. Nevertheless, the poorly armed civilians of the Volunteer Corps held their ground. This encounter would have had dire consequences but for the intervention of several men from the 4th Marine Regiment who came to their rescue. Their commandant berated in very forceful language the Japanese officer in charge for trespassing, and ordered him and his men to immediately leave the International Settlement which, he bellowed, was under the jurisdiction of the Americans and the

World War I War Memorial

British. He then allowed two of his tall and brawny Marines to grab the rifles of two of the Japanese soldiers who had been threatening the Volunteers, dangle them in the air and then throw them back to the soldiers. Although the well-armed Japanese column outnumbered the Volunteers Corps and the American Marines, the Japanese officer did not retaliate; obviously he had not been ordered to start a war with the United States. He turned on his heels and they marched off.

Despite the nearby fighting between the Japanese and the Chinese, which lasted until mid-November, the treaty powers held a commemoration ceremony on Armistice Day – with prayers and wreath-laying – at the Angel of Victory War Memorial, erected on the Bund in 1924 to honor the Allied soldiers killed during World War I. It was a six-foot bronze statue of an angel with very large wings and one hand resting on the head of a small child, perched on a high column. This monument, facing the entrance of Avenue Edward VII, was an imposing sight greeting ships entering Shanghai's harbor. On this day the solemn speeches by representatives of the Western powers were accompanied by the deafening noise of artillery shells exploding at the nearby boundaries of the International Settlement. As this was simply a war between Asians, the fighting did not seem to concern the officials in attendance. (Earlier, the treaty powers had declared their neutrality in the skirmish being fought around them.)

The battles in Chapei, north of the Settlement, lasted three months and over 100,000 Chinese soldiers and civilians were killed, wounded, or died of diseases. The Chinese army, overwhelmed by the well-armed Japanese infantrymen, sailors and marines, evacuated Chapei, burning what remained of the town. Many of the Kuomintang soldiers discarded their uniforms and disappeared into the foreign enclaves alongside thousands of terrified refugees. Once again, as in 1931, the police and foreign charitable organizations were overwhelmed, and, despite vaccinations in the streets and in temporary camps, the refugees and their small children died by the hundreds every day, unable to fight off the prevailing epidemics of smallpox, dysentery and malaria.

In November 1937 the Japanese declared victory and took full control of Chapei and the industrial Yangtzepoo district in the northern part of the International Settlement. The fighting was over but the Japanese erected more army barracks, signaling to the foreign authorities that they intended to remain on a permanent basis. The British authorities, with backing from their armed forces and the Shanghai Volunteer Corps, drew up their defense lines at Soochow Creek facing Hongkew, unofficially giving up Hongkew. Our cook, Shao Wang, told our family he had heard that, in early December, the Japanese held a victory parade in Hongkew with armored vehicles and soldiers carrying guns and the Rising Sun flags, led by their commanding general on horseback. A small crowd of sullen Chinese and stunned foreigners watched in disbelief the column of Japanese soldiers marching, singing and playing martial tunes along the main thoroughfares of Hongkew.

I heard from several of my French classmates whose fathers

were high-ranking officers in the French police and colonial army that the Japanese were not as successful the following day, when they intended to hold a similar parade in Nantao, adjacent to the French Concession. They needed to cross one of the Concession streets to reach their destination but had not asked permission from the French authorities. As they approached one of the avenues, they were stopped by tanks, French officers and soldiers from the colonial army. The officer in charge showed both his disdain for the Japanese and also his courage by sitting calmly on a chair in front of a Japanese tank poised to enter the Concession. After much negotiation and loss of face for the Japanese, only one unarmed food supply convoy without any flags or chanting was permitted to enter the Concession to reach Nantao, escorted by a detachment of French colonial soldiers. My classmates and I were very excited to hear that the French were able to thwart the Japanese army from holding a full-dress victory parade.

Shanghailanders did not fully realize that the Japanese arrival and entrenchment in Hongkew in 1937 was the beginning of the end of the military superiority of the white man, who had ruled the extraterritorial settlements in Shanghai and other treaty ports for close to a century. Japan had shown the treaty powers that it was militarily their equal. Japan's army, backed by its navy, now controlled the formerly Chinese-administered districts of Chapei and Nantao, and the Hongkew district of the International Settlement. The Japanese demanded extra seats in the Shanghai Municipal Council and sought to replace the British Chief of Police with a Japanese national, but their request was turned down.

When calm returned in the fall, my father wanted to go to Chapei to assess the damage and upon my insistence he took me along. The devastation from fire caused by the Japanese artillery shocked me and I suddenly understood that wars meant the killing of real people, not death toll statistics printed in newspapers and mentioned on the radio. There were only a few buildings standing in Chapei and the deserted streets were strewn with pieces of plywood from the former hovels, twisted metal and blocks of concrete. I saw a gleaming new bicycle in a bombed-out shop and told my father that I wanted to put it in the back seat of our car, but he said that I would be stealing from a shop owner who had fled Chapei or might even have died in the bombardment.

I saw another aspect of the war in the vast numbers of homeless refugees in the foreign enclaves. The foreign municipalities had established open-air camps, with straw mats for covering, where refugees received their daily bowl of rice from charitable organizations headed by American and English missionaries and French religious orders. Many years later I learned that Jacquinot de Bésange, the one-handed Jesuit who was well known in our school, had managed to persuade the Japanese military to set aside a one-square-mile "safety zone" in Nantao for the 250,000 homeless refugees who had been barred by the foreign authorities from entering the overcrowded refugee camps in the International Settlement and the French Concession.

Trade and commerce came to a standstill when the defeated Nationalists blocked all river traffic to and from the interior of the country. Shanghai began to suffer economically; that year my father sold only two life insurance policies to his foreign clientele. Our lifestyle did not change, however, because he was regularly receiving commissions on the many policies he had sold in the last few years. My mother's two brothers-in-law, who were business partners in a leather goods store on Avenue Joffre, saw a steep decline in sales. Aunty Brania's husband applied for and received Chinese citizenship in preparation of going to another country if need be. They applied to immigrate to the United States and suggested my parents do the same. My father, who was not interested in going to America, did not see the need to acquire a Chinese passport since he felt that the Japanese presence was temporary and that normalcy would soon return. He was wrong.

The attacks by the Japanese military in China continued,

including one against the American navy and a ferocious one against the Chinese army. The USS *Panay*, a gunboat of the US Yangtze River Patrol, was anchored in the Yangtze 25 miles above Nanking when, on December 12, 1937, Japanese planes swooped down, strafed and sank it. A nearby British river boat suffered the same fate. Japanese patrols on the shore machine-gunned these sinking ships and killed several of the survivors who tried to crawl aboard the ship's few lifeboats. The attacks were deliberate – the decks of these boats were painted with very large American and British flags and could not have been mistaken for Chinese gunboats (as later claimed by the Japanese). The Japanese government apologized and offered to make reparations, which the United States accepted, and the outrage felt by the public in America soon subsided. In Shanghai, however, Americans and other foreigners witnessed in anger the arrival of the wounded survivors.

Another tragedy of much larger and more murderous scope was the capture of the city of Nanking by the Japanese army on December 13, 1937. Flush with victory as they entered the then capital of China, the soldiers went on a rampage, killing and raping indiscriminately. This was done with the consent of their commanders, who may have followed a so-called military tradition that gave the conquering soldiers a three-day "holiday" to do as they wished. The killings, however, continued for another six weeks. The International Military Tribunal of the Far East has estimated that during the first six weeks of the Japanese occupation 260,000 Nanking residents and captured Kuomintang soldiers were massacred and more than 20,000 women and girls were raped – though the exact numbers have never been authenticated.

Although I had heard on the radio that the Japanese army had taken Nanking, my parents and others were horrified when they read in the newspapers about the massacre. Understandably they did not tell Riva and me, aged 12 and 10, about the carnage, although we overheard them speaking in hushed tones about the brutality of the Japanese army. I listened to the radio, read the headlines about the killings and saw pictures of dead bodies in the *North-China Daily News* and the *Journal de Shanghai*, but I did not fully comprehend the enormity of this tragedy. For its part, the foreign community of Shanghai soon put aside this massacre of Chinese people as their attention turned to Europe, where there now loomed a strong possibility of war with Nazi Germany.

Old Amah told me many times that the Japanese, whom she disdainfully called the *xiao riben* (Japanese dwarfs), were "vely, vely bad" and that she "no savee" (did not know) why they bombed cities and killed people in the countryside. She explained to me by showing on her fingers how wars had broken out in China every five years – 1927, 1932 and 1937 – and that in five years' time Japan would attack again. Old Amah's prediction would prove just about right, only this time the attack would be against the United States of America.

13
European Refugees

BY EARLY 1938 the barricades of barbed wire and sandbags disappeared, the curfew was lifted and the streets were no longer patrolled by the Shanghai Volunteer Corps or foreign soldiers. The residents were relieved that the hostilities had ended, but there was a certain malaise in the city. The Japanese were governing Shanghai from their stronghold in Hongkew and had an armada of gunboats anchored in the Whangpoo River. The International Settlement and the French Concession were surrounded by ever-increasing numbers of heavily armed Japanese troops, anti-aircraft guns and tanks. The Japanese, and not the authorities in the settlements, were now the real power players in Shanghai. Their army also controlled the ports and rail lines in the major cities of Nanking, Peking and Tientsin. China was now ruled by three governmental entities: the Japanese in Nanking, Chiang Kai-shek in Chungking (Chongqing) and Mao Tse-tung in Yenan (Yan'an).

Nevertheless, in Shanghai the Western and Chinese factories resumed their pre-1937 levels of production and cargo ships sailed in and out of the port without any hindrance. Once the Sino-Japanese hostilities around Shanghai ended, my father sold many insurance policies to heads of households, who must have been concerned about the threat of war not only in China but also in Europe. Since he was now meeting potential clients in the evening at their homes, he was no longer able to help Riva and me with our school assignments. My parents decided to hire a French-speaking governess, Maria Stepanova, to speak to us exclusively in French, supervise our homework and, just as importantly, inculcate in Riva, and especially in me, good manners and a proper deportment acceptable for young girls. Maria Stepanovna was a White Russian with bright red hair and aristocratic demeanor who before the Russian revolution was a tutor to children of Russian nobility in St. Petersburg. Although my mother was filled with pride to hear us speak French with our governess, friction soon arose in our household: three determined women – my mother, Old Amah and Maria Stepanovna – each had their respective philosophy on bringing up children. Within six months the governess left our household in a huff because, as a professional educator, she resented the constant interference from my mother and Old Amah's sullen attitude at no longer being in charge of "her" girls. I also watched Maria Stepanovna's departure with relief, since the governess was too strict for my liking – and she had not succeeded in making me less combative or better-mannered either.

Despite the increasing number of Japanese soldiers in Hongkew and the presence of their warships on the river, wealthy foreigners and Chinese still dined in the best restaurants, attended weekend tea-dances at elegant hotels, and crowded the movie theaters for the latest films. Bright night lights reappeared all over the city and it was reassuring to see once again on Bubbling Well Road the neon "Bee Hive Wool" advertisement with bees flying in and out of their hive. In our home, Shao Wang prepared many dinners for my parents' guests, starting with a New Year's Eve gathering before they went out dancing, and for my father's birthday in January.

Amidst this social frenzy, Riva and I heard more Jewish refugees from Austria and Germany were disembarking in Shanghai because of increasing anti-Semitic violence in their home countries. No visas or permits were required to enter Shanghai and the refugees were let in by the authorities without any hindrance, not out of compassion but out of indifference. The refugees were immediately taken care of by the Sephardic and Ashkenazi organizations. Among the new arrivals were many professionals – doctors, dentists, lawyers, architects and engineers – a number of whom, having managed to bring money and valuables, soon left the squalor of Hongkew for the foreign residential enclaves. Qualified to work in medicine, banking, insurance, engineering and import-export firms, they still had to quickly learn English. A small number of musicians, who had once played in orchestras and symphonies in Europe, joined the Shanghai Symphony Orchestra and other ensembles, or taught private lessons.

It was reassuring to Shanghailanders to hear Neville Chamberlain proclaim there would be "peace in our time" after meeting with Hitler in Berlin. My parents seemed worried, however, about Hitler's *Anschluss* of Austria in March of 1938, which my father explained to me was an annexation of the country, albeit in this instance with the general consent of its leaders and population. That summer President Roosevelt initiated a conference in Evian-les-Bains, France, to discuss the resettlement of Jews leaving or being expelled from Germany and Austria. Nearly all the 33 countries in attendance, including the United States, voted not to increase their immigration quotas for Jewish refugees. One surprising exception was the Dominican Republic, headed by the dictator Rafael Trujillo, which offered to take in 100,000 German and Austrian Jews. By that time, however, it was extremely difficult for Jews to leave Europe, and only 700 refugees managed to reach that Caribbean island by the beginning of World War II.

At the tea gatherings in our apartment my mother bemoaned the fact that more and more anti-Semitic laws were being decreed against the Jewish population in Germany. I heard my parents talk to each other and their friends about Hitler but could not fully comprehend the danger in far off Europe because I only understood some of their conversations in Russian. I did, however, grasp that in Germany and Austria Jews were forbidden to attend schools and universities and even had to wear a yellow Star of David on their clothing, identifying them as targets for insults and beatings by ruffians and the local police. Their properties were seized under the latest Nazi decree to remove Jews from the German economy, and thousands were arrested and sent to prisons and internment camps. I overheard my mother lamenting on the phone to her sister Brania that the dire situation for Jews in Germany reminded her of the pogroms in Czarist Russia.

Even more refugees streamed into Shanghai a few months after *Kristallnacht* (Night of the Broken Glass) on November 9-10, 1938, when German and Austrian Jewish businesses, stores, homes and synagogues were set on fire and Jews were attacked or killed by Nazi storm troopers. In the early spring of 1939 Riva and I saw bedraggled and penniless German and Austrian refugees disembarking on the Bund from the Italian-owned Lloyd Triestino passenger ships at a rate of about 1,000 a month. Most of them had had to bribe European travel agents and pay exorbitantly high fares for the five-week voyage to Shanghai with stops at Port Said, Colombo and Hongkong. The British, who controlled all these ports of call, would not allow any of the refugee passengers to disembark, not even to stretch their sea legs, fearing some would try to remain on land and leave for Palestine. When these ships tied up at the Shanghai wharf they were met by representatives of the Ashkenazi community, who took the refugees in trucks to temporary dormitory-style shelters at the *Heime* center in Hongkew. Funds for housing were provided by the wealthy Sephardim, while soup kitchens and meals were staffed by volunteers from the Russian Ashkenazi community, which also donated money to alleviate the desperate situation of the latest wave of refugees. Although rumors were rampant in 1939 that war would break out in Europe, the refugees still believed they would quickly leave Shanghai for a new life in another country. Various Jewish organizations provided financial and spiritual assistance with the same expectation. The Sephardic community funded the Shanghai Jewish School for refugee children, where they quickly learned English. The

American Jewish Joint Distribution Committee gave funds to house and feed the new arrivals, while the Russian Ashkenazi community brought clothing and furniture, and invited the refugees to attend their social functions or participate in religious services at their synagogues. Some of the young refugees joined the militant Betar and Trumpeldor Zionist organizations and proudly marched in brown uniforms holding aloft a Star of David flag while belting out songs in German and Yiddish. They shared the streets of Shanghai with another militant group, the *Hitler Jugend* unit from the Kaiser Wilhelm Schule, who paraded in their brown uniforms with red, black and white swastika flags and banners, lustily singing militant Nazi songs.

Eventually the ever-increasing number of refugees became a financial burden for the Sephardic and Ashkenazi communities. The influx also raised concerns among members of the Shanghai Municipal Council, who feared the refugees would soon overburden the resources of the International Settlement and even affect their comfortable upper-class lifestyle. In 1939 there seemed to be limited understanding of the situation of Jews in Germany and Austria, even among the Jewish Relief organizations in Shanghai. All felt that immigration to Shanghai needed to end. The Shanghai Municipal Council passed an edict that no more refugees could enter Shanghai unless they had relatives there, had some financial resources or had offers of jobs. In addition, the Council made a concerted effort to restrict future refugee arrivals by asking the German government not to send any more refugees to Shanghai and to stop all ships *en route* to China. The Council, however, was not successful because, during the first half of 1939, the Japanese authorities in charge of most of the city allowed the ships to dock after the German government had asked them help rid Germany and Austria of all Jews. Eager to please their new ally, the Japanese had raised no objections.

Riva and I overheard many conversations at home about how shocked the refugees were to see the poverty, filth, squalor and misery of the Chinese in Hongkew, but now Europeans who once belonged to the middle and upper classes had to live in the narrow lanes too, often sharing very small apartments with their compatriots. Their newly acquired living quarters often lacked toilet facilities, meaning they were obliged to use wooden buckets, as their Chinese neighbors did, and place them on the sidewalk early in the morning for the *moo doong* man. The refugees' immediate concern was not to fall prey to cholera, tuberculosis, dysentery and the other diseases prevalent in these unsanitary surroundings. The only consolation was their strong and tenacious belief that they would receive immigration visas to the United States or other countries and would not have to remain too long in Shanghai. Despite all their problems and concerns they were, at least, far from Nazi Germany and Austria.

In Shanghai the refugees discovered they did not have much in common with their benefactors, the very wealthy Sephardim and the Ashkenazi Russians. From the outset there was hardly any social interaction between the refugees and the non-German or non-Yiddish speaking Sephardim; there was more contact with the Ashkenazi community, which was able to communicate with a number of refugees in Yiddish. There was a feeling, however, among the Russian Jewish community of shopkeepers and merchants that many of the highly educated German professionals looked down on them. It annoyed my mother that the assimilated Germans who came to our house to sell their meager possessions, spoke glowingly, usually in Yiddish or Pidgin English, about their German upbringing and refined culture. She testily told them, after buying an item or two, that they were no longer Germans but Jews who were being helped by their Shanghai *landsman* (co-religionist). She reminded them that when her family and other Russians fled to Shanghai during the Bolshevik revolution they received very little assistance and had managed to elevate their lifestyle through hard work. Despite my mother's irritation, she collected clothes, household gadgets and utensils for the refugees, while my father translated their German-language documents into English and French for submission to the Shanghai municipal authorities. He also drove my mother to the refugee-processing centers to donate foodstuffs and clothing, and later told Riva and me how shocked and despondent they were to see Caucasians living in rooms in the narrow and dirty lanes of Hongkew. Riva and I simply could not imagine whites living in tenements next to the wretchedly poor Chinese.

These living conditions, however, were made somewhat bearable, emotionally at least, when the refugees discovered that the Chinese did not harbor any anti-Semitic feelings. They learned that they had an advocate in Sun Yat-sen's widow, Soong Ching-ling, who headed the China League for Civil Rights. In 1933 she had led a delegation of this organization to meet with the German Consul General in Shanghai to protest Nazi Germany's treatment of its Jewish citizens. Not surprisingly, this plea by a group of Chinese intellectuals fell on deaf ears. There was minimal social interaction between the Chinese and the refugees, despite living in such close quarters, separated as they were by language and culture. The poor and illiterate Chinese crowded in Hongkew by the influx of refugees, did not display any resentment towards them.

It was clear in the summer of 1939 that war was imminent in Europe and in Asia. American families sailed to Manila or the United States and British families left for Hongkong, Singapore and England, the "home" country that many had never seen. French nationals did not see the need, as yet, to leave Shanghai. One afternoon my father drove us to the Racecourse to see a farewell parade by the Inniskillen Fusiliers from Ulster and the Seaforth Highlanders as they prepared to leave for England, marching in their kilts and playing their bagpipes. We were fascinated by their colorful ceremonial uniforms. The Chinese, too, gawked at these men in skirts but seemed to enjoy the Scottish tunes, which sounded somewhat similar to their own music.

After the withdrawal of the British forces, the American military and the Shanghai Volunteer Corps patrolled the

International Settlement under the watchful eyes of the Japanese authorities and the *Kempeitai* in Hongkew. At home my father told my mother on several occasions that he had noticed fewer American and British naval ships anchored in the Whangpoo River, and that presumably they had sailed home because of Hitler's increasingly bellicose statements.

World War II broke out when Germany attacked Poland on September 3, 1939, and, in response, Great Britain and France declared war on Germany. In Shanghai the students from the Kaiser Wilhelm Schule held a parade, this time in honor of Germany's rapid and successful invasion of Poland. The 18,000 Jewish refugees in Shanghai – approximately 8,000 Germans, 4,000 Austrians and 6,000 Poles, Lithuanians and Czechoslovakians – were safe from the Nazis but they were extremely concerned about their relatives and friends in Nazi-occupied Europe. By early 1940 only a trickle of refugees was able to reach Shanghai.

Like everyone else, I was shocked when Belgium, the Netherlands, Denmark and Norway fell in the spring of 1940 and France's "impenetrable" Maginot Line was overrun by German tanks. A pall fell over our school; we simply could not accept the reality that the French were defeated by the Germans – and so swiftly. The announcer on the French radio station cried when she read the news of this defeat and ended her program with a stirring recording of *La Marseillaise*. There was more bad news in June when Italy declared war on England. Italian passenger ships could no longer safely leave the Mediterranean ports, meaning all sailings with Jewish refugee passengers came to a standstill. Shanghai, this port of last resort, was now closed to them. In July of the same year Japan officially joined the Axis powers by signing the Tripartite Pact, a military alliance with Germany and Italy.

Despite the worrisome news about the war, the refugees in Hongkew rebuilt and refurbished some of the buildings destroyed during the Sino-Japanese hostilities of 1932 and 1937. They began to recreate a pale semblance of their former social life in Europe, performing in plays and participating in chess tournaments and reading clubs. In the spring and during the hot summer months they sat in outdoor cafes and, according to my German-speaking father, reminisced about their "normal" life before Hitler came to power. The highlight of all conversations was learning whether families and friends had been able to procure visas and leave Europe. Some of the refugees in Shanghai managed to acquire, for a hefty fee, Portuguese passports indicating Macao as their place of birth from the corrupt Portuguese Consul General. As newly anointed Portuguese nationals the refugees believed they could obtain transit visas from other countries and wait there for their immigration quota number for the United States – the dream destination of nearly all the refugees.

I was very curious about these European refugees living among the Chinese. On one occasion a couple of friends and I decided to bicycle to Hongkew, which none of us had ever seen, where we knew a smattering of poor White Russians and some Portuguese families who wanted to be close to their Catholic church and lived among the Chinese. We crossed the Garden Bridge spanning the Soochow Creek and swore under our breath at the scowling Japanese soldiers guarding it. We did not have to dismount from our bicycles, as the Chinese were obliged to do, nor did we have to bow or remove our hats. When we reached Hongkew we saw the European refugees sitting in outdoor cafés drinking coffee, smoking cigarettes, cigars and pipes, and conversing in languages we did not understand. We were ill at ease, however, when we passed a marketplace and saw refugees selling their possessions to Shanghailanders who had come to Hongkew to see what bargains they could get. We were shocked at the dilapidated state of the two and three-story buildings where, we were told, many of the refugees had rented small apartments or single rooms.

I decided I would not go back to Hongkew, an alien world to me where white people lived in such squalor.

Return to "Normalcy"?

14

FOR SEVERAL years I had my doubts that we were Romanians because my father always brushed off my questions about Romania. My suspicion was confirmed when Aunty Riva's daughter, Julie, told my sisters and me that my father was born in Russia, but did not want to be known as a Russian. I could appreciate this in class-conscious Shanghai.

Since I realized now that I was stateless, the French Concession became my country. I was not interested in Chinese Shanghai, the adjacent districts of Chapei and Nantao controlled first by the Chinese government and then by the Japanese. Except for the one trip to Chapei with my father after the 1937 bombardment and another to visit Shao Wang's home in Nantao, I did not want to return to these towns teeming with poor people. Nor did I have any desire to cross the muddy Whangpoo River on rickety ferry boats to Pootung, which was dotted with British and Japanese-owned factories where thousands of men, women and children worked very long hours in deplorable conditions.

To me, the French Concession was France. I had French playmates and attended a French school steeped in French history, literature, culture and belief in the greatness of France. Whenever my classmates and I saved some money we dashed over to the "Marcel" bakery or to one of the six "Tchakalian" stores in the Concession to purchase croissants, baguettes and chocolate. I believed that the ambience in the residential sectors of the Concession, with its French-named streets, was similar to France.

If we were still in town for Bastille Day we would watch the very exciting *Quatorze Juillet* parade, where the *Garde Municipale*, the fire brigade, French army and navy officers and their troops, followed by an Annamite and Tonkinese detachment, would march and play martial music. The main thoroughfares of the Concession were bedecked with French flags on buildings and on the plane trees. A smaller ceremony with a brass band was held at Koukaza Park, with officials from the municipality and French boy scouts and girl scouts in attendance. The festivities continued in the evening when various colored lights shone from French cruisers anchored in the Whangpoo River, and in Koukaza Park, where candles in bright red paper lanterns floated on the artificial lake or hung from surrounding trees. French sailors in flat hats topped with red pompons, wildly celebrated this special day in their history at cabarets, where the sing-song girls, the "taxi dancers" and the ladies of the night eagerly awaited them. Inevitably brawls broke out in the narrow Rue Chu Pao San (Xikou Lu), which was crowded with bars and aptly nicknamed "Blood Alley"; brawls between drunken French sailors and other sailors, soldiers and marines, and especially the British and the Americans.

The only times we cared to enter the International Settlement was to window-shop or watch parades by the remaining British and American armed forces. My friends and I went into one or two of the major department stores to see the latest fashions from France and the gadgets from America. Even though we were already in our early teens, my mother still chose and bought our coats, dresses, underwear and shoes in the small stores of the French Concession.

Our favorite parades were those held by the United States 4th Marine Regiment on the Fourth of July. While their band played catchy tunes the Marines marched stiffly, but still managed to ogle the pretty Russian girls. We were in awe of the Marine officers who strutted in the streets of Shanghai in their khaki uniforms, rounded campaign hats, riding breeches and boots, clutching their swagger sticks. We agreed that these tall American men, who sometimes looked in our direction and whistled, were strikingly handsome in their uniforms and quite dashing in comparison to our scrawny upper-class schoolmates. However, we admired the Marines and all soldiers and sailors from afar as they were known to imbibe too much, pick up "taxi dancers" in cabarets and inevitably get drunk and fight. The lowest-ranked American Marine, thanks to his US dollars, led a very comfortable life in Shanghai, where he could hire a Chinese "boy" to wash and iron his uniform and shine his boots and shoes.

My parents never allowed us to go to the Settlement on nights when cruisers sailed into port and hundreds of sailors on shore-leave converged on the areas where bar girls and prostitutes would welcome them. Their favorite ship was the USS *Augusta*, the flagship of the US Asiatic Fleet, which disgorged sailors eager to spend their money on women and alcohol. No European woman from a "proper" family would ever consider marrying an American serviceman since it was feared that once he returned to the United States he would quickly forget his wife, and perhaps a child or two, back in Shanghai.

This had happened in the early 1930s to Aunty Riva's oldest daughter Julie and my mother's youngest sister Bessie, whose Marine husbands left them soon after the birth of their respective sons. My sisters and I knew my father was very displeased that they had married such men because he grumbled whenever he had to attend gatherings at the apartment Julie and Bessie shared. It was risky for any stateless woman to marry an American but they could claim and acquire his citizenship even when abandoned. When mothers, generally White Russians or Chinese, did not have the means to support their offspring, an orphanage maintained by American missionaries would take in the children.

Another daytime entertainment, when we were not in school, was to watch Chinese wedding parties passing in the street, with the bride hidden in a sedan chair, accompanied by men in dark business suits, women dressed mainly in red and

Riva, Jackie and Lily at the Route Delastre home

musicians playing their trumpets or banging loudly on cymbals and drums. This contrasted with the solemn funeral processions, where people dressed in white carried the picture of the deceased and musicians played mournful tunes, sometimes discordant Western ones.

The most exciting pastime for my friends and me was going to the movies. There were about 40 movie theaters in Shanghai, all built by the mid-thirties, among which were the Cathay – where only American films were shown – the Carlton, the Lyceum, the Nanking, the Odeon, the Paris, the Rialto, the Ritz and the Roxy – all showing first-run American, English and French films – and the Grand, which deserved its name because of its ultra-modern and luxurious interior. It even had seats fitted with headphones for translations into Chinese. It was in this theater that the 4th Marines band played a concert every Sunday. Riva and I were thrilled when American friends of my parents invited us to one of these concerts and bragged to our friends about this musical performance by the Marines.

During the stifling summer months we luxuriated in the more

expensive Roxy Cinema, since it was one of the few that was air-conditioned. In the damp winter season we disappeared into the movie houses and watched the beautiful young women on the screen, who sang, misbehaved and suffered but in the process got their man and lived happily after. We collected pictures of leading men and ladies, especially the handsome threesome, Clark Gable, Errol Flynn and Tyrone Power, and as Francophiles were enamored with Charles Boyer's French accent. My favorite comedy was the very popular "The Great Dictator", where both Chinese and foreign audiences guffawed at Hitler's antics, superbly imitated by Charlie Chaplin. The German consul in Shanghai had demanded, to no avail, that this film be banned.

Chinese patrons who could afford the price of a ticket rushed to see foreign films without any Chinese subtitles, especially American musicals that showed people living in big homes and driving big cars. They apparently preferred this to the stilted acting of Chinese stars, and it never occurred to us to see a Chinese movie. On Saturday night after the movie we usually had dinner at the Chinese restaurant Sun Ya, much frequented by foreigners because of its clean interior and succulent meals. We would talk about the film and how we wished we could go to America to live in penthouses like all the unmarried secretaries in the movies. We often ended our summer evenings with a dish of ice cream by the soda fountain at the American "Chocolate Shop" on Nanking Road, and then took a rickshaw home.

The heavy presence of the Japanese military in Shanghai and the news about the victories by the German army on all European fronts were not conducive to New Year celebrations in 1941. My parents spent a quiet New Year's Eve at their friends' home where, according to my mother, the main topic of conversation was the fate of the Jews in the Nazi-occupied countries. That evening my sisters and I invited a dozen boys and girls to our apartment, and spent the evening dancing to music on our gramophone, flirting and sometimes disappearing on the verandah to steal a kiss or two. I was not successful in that regard.

The Ashkenazi Russian Jews must have felt reasonably safe – protected, ironically, by Vichy France, an ally of the Axis powers – because in the spring of 1941 the community broke ground on Rue Tenant de la Tour (Xiangyang Lu) for a large synagogue, called simply the New Synagogue. That summer, the Sephardic and Ashkenazi communities were taken aback when a Japanese ship, the *Asama Maru*, docked near the Whangpoo River with approximately 1,500 Polish Jewish refugees aboard. These passengers had been among 6,000 Lithuanian and Polish refugees who had found their way to Kobe, Japan, after crossing the USSR on the Trans-Siberian train to Vladivostok. Eventually 4,500 of the refugees received visas to other countries and left Japan. However, the Japanese authorities, anticipating war with the United States, did not allow the remaining 1,500 refugees to stay any longer in Kobe, an important naval base, and decided to send these refugees to Shanghai, where the Jewish community would take care of them.

Among the passengers on the *Asama Maru* was the entire 300-strong student body, and their rabbis, of Mir Yeshiva, a Polish seminary of advanced Talmudic learning. These bearded young men with side locks, long black coats and felt hats were a strange sight in Shanghai to Chinese and foreigner alike. I thought so too, whenever I saw them walking in groups, talking in Yiddish and never glancing at anyone. I was extremely surprised, given my secular upbringing, that Jews could be so religious. My mother grumbled that these men, who lived and studied at the Beth Aharon Sephardi synagogue in Hongkew did not seek employment and so it fell on the Shanghai Jewish communities to pay for their upkeep.

A few months before the outbreak of World War II, I was responsible for an incident that obliged our family to move out of the Savoy Apartments. One afternoon I was watering the pots of gardenias on our balcony when I decided, as a lark, to pour some water onto friends below. I missed them, however, and instead drenched the head of a hatless Frenchman who was walking towards the entrance of our building. All hell broke loose because he saw me before I had time to disappear from the balcony. The French police came by and politely suggested to my parents that they find another apartment, since the head I had watered belonged to a high official of the Concession. My parents apologized profusely and later yelled at me, but I overheard my mother tell a friend over the phone that the Frenchman in question had been looking for an apartment for his White Russian mistress and ours would be an excellent hideaway. My parents decided to rent a house rather than live in a big apartment complex, where I would surely continue to cause trouble.

Within a month we moved into a two-story town house with a small garden in a very quiet residential area on Route Delastre (Taiyuan Lu). My parents could afford the higher rent because in 1938 and 1939 my father had sold many policies to wage earners who wanted to protect the financial future of their families in case they were called to serve their country. Our new neighbors were French, Germans, Italians and several wealthy Chinese families with children our age. Next door were two couples who had left Hungary in the mid-thirties because the husbands were Jewish. This foursome soon became close friends with my parents.

The excitement of living in a new location and making friends with other teenagers living in the townhouses on Route Delastre was tempered by a very great loss for me. Old Amah decided that since the three of us were now young *missees* – Riva had turned 16, I was 14 and Jackie 9 – it was time for her to return to her family "somewhere" in China. I cried for several days, missing her very much, but within a few months I calmed down, busy with schoolwork and weekend gatherings with my friends. I never forgot Old Amah, although she was soon replaced in our household by a new amah who took care of Jackie and helped with the household chores.

Another loss that fell not only on me but on all the foreigners still in Shanghai (more American and British families were leaving for Hongkong and Manila because of the real threat of war with Japan) was the news that the 4th Marines were going to the Philippines, leaving the city they had been stationed in for the last 14 years. Several friends and I intended to see them off on November 27, 1941, but their parade was cancelled because of inclement weather and the first group of Marines rode in double-decker busses to the wharf to embark on the SS *President Madison*. The following day, however, was a crisp one and the second group marched down Nanking Road, accompanied by their band playing the Marine hymn. Crowds of Chinese lined the streets – parades attracted them too, especially with a band

The Lyceum and Nanking movie theaters

playing – but some young women among them were crying: their boyfriends were leaving and who would support them now? We shouted our goodbyes happily – surely they would be back – as we followed them to the Bund, where they embarked on tenders taking them to the SS *President Harrison* anchored further down the Whangpoo River. Many of the Marines who disembarked in Subic Bay in the Philippines a week before Pearl Harbor would soon lose their lives on the island of Corregidor and during the

Bataan "Death March".

The departure of the American Marines, along with the earlier departure of the British soldiers, made me realize that we Shanghailanders, especially those without a country, were now vulnerable to the vagaries of the Imperial Japanese Army in Shanghai. The French police and the small colonial army could not protect us.

The year 1941 was a difficult one psychologically for the Shanghailanders. The Germans were winning on all fronts in Europe while British and American families were advised by their government to leave Shanghai. My parents and the other stateless residents of Shanghai could only hope that the threat of war between Japan and the United States would never materialize.

15
Japanese Military Takeover

ONE MORNING in early December, 1941, my sisters and I had just finished eating breakfast and were ready to leave for school when the phone rang. My mother picked up the receiver and then screamed that Japan had declared war on the United States. I could not believe that those puny Japanese soldiers I had seen in the streets of Shanghai could fight the strong American Marines who had just sailed to Manila.

Although most of the British and American cruisers and gunboats, and their contingent of soldiers, sailors and marines had already left for war in Europe or had been reassigned to the Pacific islands, several of their ships were still anchored in Shanghai and Tsingtao. News spread fast that the SS *President Harrison*, which had sailed back to Shanghai after transporting the Marines to the Philippines, had been taken over by the Japanese and its crew detained. In addition, the USS *Wake,* anchored in the Whangpoo River with a skeleton crew and stripped of all its armaments, had been overpowered at 3 a.m. by Japanese marines who climbed stealthily aboard. The British commander of the HMS *Peterel* had already begun preparations to scuttle his ship when the Japanese cruiser *Idzumo,* anchored half a mile away, fired its powerful guns, sinking the *Peterel* within minutes.

That afternoon I heard on the radio that Japanese planes had bombed American military installations and sunk a number of battleships in Hawaii. In the evening my father received a disturbing phone call from one of his insurance policy holders, Leon Grillon, a police superintendent who lived with his family at the Poste de l'Est police station fronting the Quai de France (the French Bund). Very early that morning they had witnessed a number of British sailors from the *Peterel*, who had managed to leave in launches before the ship sank or swim towards the shore, being machine-gunned by Japanese marines from the deck of the captured *Wake*. Perhaps because Mr. Grillon had helped several of the wounded sailors, but more likely because they wanted to commandeer the Poste de l'Est's excellent vantage point, Japanese soldiers had ordered the Grillon family to leave their home within twenty-four hours.

My sisters and I were aghast when we heard that sailors had been killed close to the Bund. Not too long ago, sailors from the *USS Augusta* had been strutting in the streets of Shanghai in their bell bottom trousers, their caps jauntily placed on their head and, as usual, whistling at women, especially when they saw my sister Riva. At 16 she was strikingly beautiful, with her slim body, long brown hair and green eyes. Men always stared at her as she walked by on high heels wearing a tight fitting dress or skirt, and a blouse revealing her ample bosom. I was always proud to be with Riva for I enjoyed hearing comments about her good looks. At 14, I was a skinny and a rather flat-chested teenager who wore thick lensed eyeglasses, although I never felt any envy when they looked at her and later at Jackie when she blossomed into an attractive teenager.

Except for the attack on the two American and British ships, the Japanese takeover of Shanghai was swift and quiet. Their soldiers marched into the International Settlement from their garrisons north of the Soochow Creek in Hongkew, where they had been billeted since 1937. They did not meet any resistance, as British and American troops had already been withdrawn from Shanghai. The Japanese army took control of the two foreign concessions and disbanded the British police force but they did not interfere with the administration in the French Concession, which received its directives from Vichy officials in Indochina. France was presently the lone treaty power in Shanghai – and a very weak one. The "Rising Sun" flag now fluttered from many

Lily at 13

buildings and grim-faced troops in rumpled military uniforms replaced the jaunty Americans who used to whistle and stare at Riva.

Most of the high-ranking French officials working for the municipality declared themselves pro-Vichy, an action which spared harassment not only for themselves but also for French nationals and other "non-enemy" foreigners living in the Concession. The French Ambassador in Nanking, Henri Cosmé, showed his allegiance to Vichy by removing from the consular and judiciary offices all Jews and others deemed to be Gaullists or Masons. Although the French municipality and police were officially in charge of the Concession, they had to work with the Japanese gendarmerie and report on Kuomintang activities against Japan and the puppet government of Wang Ching-wei (Wang Jingwei), whom they had installed in 1940 as the leader

New Amah

of China. That fall, Roland de Margerie, chief of staff in Paul Reynaud's Third Republic cabinet, was nominated by the Vichy government to serve as the new Consul General in Shanghai. His three children were enrolled in our school, where we heard from their friends that their parents were anglophiles and despised Nazi Germany. However, my non-French classmates and I considered this Consul General a collaborator since he was representing the Vichy Government and taking orders from them.

In Paris in 2004 I interviewed the daughter of a diplomat who had worked for Consul de Margerie, and learned that he disliked de Gaulle's arrogant personality and wanted to distance himself from him. De Margerie opted to "exile" himself to Shanghai, away from the turmoil in his country and Europe. Although he was a representative of the Vichy government in Shanghai, he did not dismiss my interviewee's father, who was married to a

Polish Jew. In addition de Margerie did not demand, as he could have, that Jewish students at the Collège Municipal Français be dismissed from the school. De Margerie was never accused after World War II of collaboration with the Japanese and remained in the diplomatic corps, where he was named ambassador to Spain and the Vatican – by none other than General de Gaulle!

Although the Frenchmen in the municipality and the police were nominally pro-Vichy, a small core of Gaullists founded the "*France Quand Même*" (France Nevertheless) organization. Some of them tried, unsuccessfully, to leave Shanghai to join the Free French Forces. Among them were the former principal of my elementary school, Charles Grosbois, and a number of his comrades-in-arms from World War I, including Roderick Egal, the husband of my English teacher. The anti-Vichy contingent among my classmates learned, with great admiration and surprise, that a student in the upper grade of our school was an active Gaullist. In early 1942 Jacques Lebas told his friends that he planned to go to Chungking to join the Allies but was immediately denounced, probably by pro-Vichy Frenchmen, and subsequently incarcerated in the Shanghai Bridge House prison administered by the *Kempeitai*, the dreaded Japanese secret police. Lebas remained there for three months and was harshly interrogated like the other prisoners, many of whom never left the prison alive.

At the beginning of their occupation, the Japanese authorities had no intention of disrupting any ongoing business concerns or banning religious services in the various churches and synagogues. In the French Concession the Russian Ashkenazi community opened a new hospital, the Shanghai Jewish Hospital, staffed by European refugee doctors and nurses to meet the health needs of the thousands of refugees now living in Shanghai. The prevailing infrastructure and economy needed to be sustained and inflation needed to be stopped since, at the time of the Japanese takeover, the exchange rate for one US dollar was one million Chinese Reserve Bank (CRB) yuan. To lower this runaway inflation, the occupation authorities introduced a new *yuan* that was worth five US cents, but within a few months it too deteriorated rapidly.

Japanese military vehicles rumbled through the streets of Shanghai while Japanese soldiers, with guns and bayonets glistening, guarded all commercial buildings owned by Allied citizens in the International Settlement, Hongkew and Pootung. The Americans, British, Belgians and Dutch were branded enemy nationals, their bank accounts frozen and their clubs and homes, especially the large ones on the outskirts of the city in Hungjao, requisitioned by the Japanese authorities.

Japanese military enter Shanghai

Uncle Ralph, Aunty Riva's husband, had acquired British citizenship during his stay in Australia and was now an "enemy national" too. Before the outbreak of World War II he had sent his family back to Sydney but he remained behind to manage his small leather goods factory that churned out clothing for his store on Avenue Joffre. The Japanese soon confiscated both. Nationals from Nazi-occupied Greece, France and Norway were considered "neutral enemies" and generally spared indignities and incarceration. Initially the Norwegians were considered "enemy nationals" too, but they were placed in the "neutral enemy" category when Germany installed the pro-Nazi Vidkun Quisling as nominal head of Norway. The Macanese holding Portuguese passports and the Spanish Basque *jai-alai* players, whose countries were ruled by the pro-Axis dictators Antonio Salazar and Francisco Franco, declared their neutrality, as did the perennially neutral Swiss. All "enemy aliens" and other foreign residents had to re-register with the Japanese authorities and carry a photo identity card listing their nationality – or lack of it. My father had registered us with the Japanese authorities as Romanian nationals. No proof of his citizenship was asked for because he was listed with the French police as a Romanian. This falsehood offered protection to our family because Romania was allied with the Axis powers.

To their fellow Asians – the Indochinese, Malayans, Indian Sikhs and Filipinos – the Japanese stated that British and American colonialism would disappear from their countries and be replaced by a Greater East Asia Co-Prosperity Sphere headed, of course, by Japan. They wooed the Sikh traffic policemen to join in a fight against the British for a "Free India" but they were not as successful in Shanghai as in Hongkong, where the Indian nationalist Chandra Bose collaborated with the Japanese occupiers in his agitations for Indian independence.

But the 30,000 stateless Russians and 18,000 European Jewish refugees were, for the time being, ignored by the Japanese authorities. The Russian Jews hoped the Japanese would remember that before the outbreak of the war their community had garnered the necessary votes to install Japanese representatives in the British-dominated Municipal Council. The Japanese had never shown any sign of anti-Semitism – on the contrary, in the 1920s they had supported the Balfour Declaration for the establishment of a Jewish homeland in Palestine when it was being debated at the League of Nations. In addition, Japan, which had signed the Neutrality Pact with the USSR in April of 1941, did not want to antagonize their powerful neighbor by taking measures against Russians in Shanghai, whether they were Soviet citizens or stateless.

Shanghailanders believed the United States would quickly defeat Japan, then known for producing shoddy goods and, surely, inferior armaments. My parents and their friends' disdain for the Japanese led them to believe the war would be over within six months, at the most. When the British-owned *North-China Daily News* ceased publication on December 8, 1941, few realized the Japanese aerial attack had caught the United States off guard and that its fleet had been decimated in Hawaii. It was a shock, in the first months of 1942, to hear from people who owned short-wave radios that British, Dutch and American forces had sustained one defeat after another in their colonies. I was disgusted to learn that Vichy-controlled Indochina had enabled the Japanese army to rush down to Thailand and invade British colonies in East Asia. Soon after Pearl Harbor, the Japanese captured Hongkong, Manila, Singapore, Rangoon, Mandalay and the Dutch East Indies in the space of three months, leaving stunned Shanghailanders to ponder how Asians were suddenly able to defeat Westerners. And while the Chinese, especially since the massacre in Nanking, feared and despised the Japanese, they must have felt a grudging sense of awe towards the enemy who had so rapidly toppled the white man from his pedestal in Asia.

However, while proclaiming unity among Asians under their leadership, the Japanese exploited and generally brutalized the Chinese. I could not understand why, since they could have vented their anger and rage on the Allied nationals in Shanghai or other Caucasians whom they knew had always looked down on them. While foreigners generally gave wide berth to the military occupiers, our family was very friendly with a Japanese woman, Madame Vergez, the wife of my mathematics teacher. They lived in our complex of townhouses and their daughter Hélène, a classmate of Riva's, often came by our home. The Vergez house was so close to ours that we repeatedly heard Hélène scream in

French at her mother, "Why did you marry my father?" blaming her for the taunts she was subjected to in the streets as a "half-caste" child.

Assets of Allied companies, the large oil, shipping and trading firms, the banks – the National City Bank of New York, Chase Bank, Hongkong & Shanghai Bank, Chartered Bank of Australia – the US-owned Shanghai Power & Telephone Company, and the British-owned Shanghai Waterworks and Tramway Company, were all confiscated. The English Cathedral School and the Shanghai American School were requisitioned as billets and headquarters for the Japanese army, and the American Community Church was transformed into a stable for their horses.

My father sold his last life insurance policy on December 14, 1941, to a Norwegian who worked for the Shanghai Municipal Police before it was disbanded. Within two months the Japanese took over the premises of the Sun Life Assurance Company and he was out of a job. But we were not in desperate financial straits because my parents held their savings in several gold bars, which they could sell easily whenever they needed funds. Because of inflation and the precarious situation of the Chinese currency it became necessary for wealthy Chinese and foreigners to purchase gold and silver bullion, which they kept in their homes rather than at the bank.

Around Chinese New Year, 1942, however, my mother had to let our cook Shao Wang go when he justifiably requested a hefty wage increase. My sisters and I were very fond of him and were sorry that he would be leaving us, but my mother said she had found him a better paying job with another family and Shao Wang promised he would come by whenever necessary to help her with tea and dinner parties. My spoiled childhood had come to an end, though an amah still washed and ironed our clothes and a young houseboy was hired for half day's work to clean the home and polish the silver. My mother, however, never seemed fully satisfied with his work.

The war years drew out my mother's entrepreneurial skills and she became the sole support of our family. She hired a Chinese tailor to sew clothes for our family – dresses for us, shirts for my father – and also for her friends and acquaintances, who would pay my mother for his work. My mother gave him half of all sums received, which generated a steady income for our household and for the tailor. He was a tall, quiet man we called Lao Papa, a name indicating he was an "old" man although he was only in his early forties. In the summer he worked on the second floor balcony next to my parents' bedroom, pedaling rapidly on a Singer sewing machine that made a whirring sound that never seemed to stop. He took a break only to eat his lunch of rice, vegetables, fish and sometimes meat, which he often shared with me since he had quickly learned I would always ask to taste his food. He was an extremely skilled tailor who could copy various sketches from American magazines. Lao Papa's presence was very soothing as he got along with all of us, including my mother, who was most demanding about the quality of his work. When the Japanese, fearing American air raids, imposed a night curfew in the summer, Lao Papa sewed blackout curtains to cover our windows.

Lao Papa and I spoke to each other in Pidgin English and I asked him to teach me swear words in the Shanghai dialect to use under my breath whenever I saw the fierce-looking Japanese soldiers. But he refused, telling me, "Missee no speak bad fashion. No nice." One afternoon I saw tears streaming down Lao Papa's face as he was pedaling his sewing machine. I asked him what had happened and he said his son had died. I was very surprised to learn he had a family, for no one had ever inquired about his life, his real name or where he was born. The work provided by the servants was the foreign masters' only concern.

16
Life under the Japanese

IN THE first months of 1942 Shanghai residents started receiving ration cards and had to line up on a daily basis to purchase bread, rice, beans and cooking oil, whenever available. The monetary currency the Japanese introduced was becoming worthless as inflation increased, and my mother had to pay close attention to our household expenses since she did not want to sell off our gold bars too quickly. When electricity use was curtailed to only a few hours a day and we could no longer use the refrigerator, my parents ordered blocks of ice, which cyclists delivered and unloaded into a big wooden ice box in our pantry. Cooking gas was also restricted, which forced my mother to purchase a *hibachi* charcoal stove, on which she and the houseboy cooked our meals. In the spring and early summer they prepared the meals in our garden. In the winter they cooked in the kitchen but had to open the window to allow the acrid smoke to dissipate.

By the end of the summer my father had sold his Morris Minor, since private vehicular traffic was now limited to Japanese military personnel and high ranking Chinese, German and Italian officials, and some officers in the French police. A new type of fuel was being used for busses because of a shortage of gasoline, so now busses were equipped with large drums at the back, filled with charcoal, that spewed dark black smoke out as they lumbered along the pot-holed streets. I preferred the trams with overhead electric lines but they often stopped running when the electricity was suddenly cut off, leaving me to take rickshaws or ride my shoddily made Japanese bicycle, the only brand sold in the stores. My sisters and I found it very amusing to see our parents ride bicycles, which to date had mostly been limited to children and teenagers. Despite its Japanese origin, I was very proud of my bicycle, painted white with shiny chrome handlebars.

After my classmates attached French flags to their bicycles' handlebars, I wanted Lao Papa to sew a Romanian flag for me – even though I knew we were not Romanians. I did not know the flag's design or colors and asked my father to draw one for me but he squelched my plan immediately, explaining that Romania was allied with the Axis powers. I was somewhat confused since we were registered as Romanians and the Japanese authorities had issued our family's identity cards with diagonal red lines through them that indicated we were in league with the Axis powers. We did not remain long with the favored Nazi and Fascist nationals, however, as my father could not produce any documentation showing that he was a Romanian citizen during a routine house-to-house check. Our Axis identity cards were then replaced with ones listing us as stateless residents of Shanghai.

In October 1942 the Japanese authorities in Shanghai issued an edict requiring all enemy nationals over 13 years of age to wear a bright red cotton armband with the first letter of their nationality and a registration number printed in black. My Uncle Ralph, the newly minted Australian citizen, considered his armband a badge of honor and had his picture taken with the letter "B" – for British subjects – prominently displayed around the sleeve of his suit jacket. The Americans, Belgians, Dutch and British had to turn in their short-wave radios, revolvers, hunting guns, telescopes and cameras. They were strictly forbidden to go to restaurants, movie theaters, the Racecourse, the "neutral" French and Portuguese clubs, and other places of entertainment. They were not much affected by this latest order, however, since their cash savings were depleted.

I no longer went to the movies because American and British films were banned, replaced by Japanese and German movies and newsreels proclaiming victory after victory in Europe and the

Pacific. However, on the recommendation of our school monitor and gymnastics teacher, James Kelly (not incarcerated because he was a citizen of neutral Ireland), several of my classmates and I saw a documentary on the 1936 Olympics in Berlin that we were told was directed by a very talented woman photographer. I was fascinated by the opening ceremony and the handsome athletes but whenever Hitler appeared on the screen a stream of invectives came loudly from my mouth – *"sale Boche!" "salaud!"* *"con!" "grand fasciste merdeux!"* ("damn Kraut", "bastard", "cretin", "shitty fascist"). I assured my friends who told me to lower my voice that I had nothing to fear since the people in the theatre were all Chinese and no Nazi was lurking in the wings. I wondered how the Nazis could justify the inclusion of short Japanese men as part of the Aryan race. This film, "Olympia", was repeatedly shown in Shanghai during the Japanese occupation.

The Japanese Rising Sun over the Bund

I did not care to go out in the late afternoon since I had to return home before curfew and, more importantly, I was ill at ease seeing so many Japanese soldiers carrying guns that seemed oversized in comparison to their generally small stature. For diversion on weekends I often rode my bicycle to the Bund to look at the families living in their sampans, their floating homes, the sailing junks bobbing on the waters of the Whangpoo River, and the two passenger ships stranded in Shanghai, the Italian *Conte Verde* and the American *President Harrison*.

My friends and I, now teenagers, spent more and more time in our respective homes, gossiping about our classmates, learning how to dance and assuring each other that the Japanese would soon be defeated. Whenever our parents were out we played "spin the bottle" kissing games, pecking the boys on their cheeks and sometimes kissing them on the lips, a very daring feat for me. After school I read the heavily censored *Shanghai Times* and now pro-Vichy *Journal de Shanghai*, which were simply propaganda sheets proclaiming the glory of the Axis powers' victories over the Allies. While my mother took care of household chores, checked Lao Papa's work or visited her friends at tea time, my father kept himself busy in the garden, taking care of the mulberry trees and the corn he had planted (which somehow was never edible). Every morning he read the English and French newspapers, even though he was disgusted with the content, and calmed himself by listening to his small collection of classical records on the gramophone installed in a large cabinet. My parents, my sisters and I listened to Verdi and Puccini operas. Our favorite was "La Traviata" since Riva and I were familiar with the story based on Alexandre Dumas' "La Dame aux Camelias", as well as the drama of Bizet's "Carmen". We also listened to marches by John Philip Sousa whose music was available in stores thanks to the American Marines, who appreciated the fact that he was once their band leader. My sister Jackie, the budding pianist, was enraptured by our collection of classical music but more often than not had to spend time pounding angrily on the piano to practice scales instead of playing with her friends. She took revenge on her teacher, Maria Tubiansky, by placing on the piano a small vase of freshly cut gardenias from our garden which quickly nauseated her teacher, and subsequently many lessons had to be cut short, to Jackie's great relief. Riva and I, at 17 and 15, also took piano lessons with Madame Tubiansky, but she decided that I was not musically inclined and I gladly stopped playing; Riva persisted for another year. Jackie, however, had to continue taking piano lessons since her teacher and my mother believed she was a talented pianist.

Life was becoming increasingly difficult for the foreigners, but the poor Chinese suffered from various diseases and died by the thousands of starvation during the Japanese occupation. Riding my bicycle to school I would come across bundles of straw on the pavement or near doorways. Wrapped inside them were the bodies of babies, many newborn, who had died during the night and whose parents did not have the means to bury them. When I rode home in the afternoons the bundles had disappeared, picked up by street cleaners from the French municipality's sanitation division or by the Chinese Benevolent Burying Association. It was estimated that about 300 people, mainly very young children and infants, died every day from the cold, illnesses and starvation. At first I was terribly shocked to learn that these bundles contained dead bodies but after seeing them regularly my initial reaction of horror turned slowly to the acceptance that no one could have fed these infants. The missionaries, for example, were no longer around to save them.

Out of deference to the Vichy government the Japanese did not take over our large school building or other French municipal buildings in the Concession. The Collège Municipal Français and the Ecole Rémi were the only schools that did not have to teach Japanese, which was fortunate for me as I was already doing poorly. I had to repeat two grades, at 13 and 15, when I failed mathematics and science exams. I had excellent marks in French and English compositions, history, and geography but one had to pass every subject. I did not mind repeating these grades but I did miss several of my classmates with whom I had been in school since kindergarten.

The teachers and administrative staff at our school were left alone by the Japanese authorities since the majority were French and most of the rest stateless Russians. My kindergarten teacher, Miss Thompson, had left Shanghai before the war to retire in England. Because of the shortage of English-speaking instructors, James Kelly was elevated to the rank of English teacher for the upper grades. A pro-Axis atmosphere now reigned in our school, with large color posters of Maréchal Philippe Pétain adorning the walls of every classroom. The school's instructions no longer came from the Ministry of Education in Paris but from Vichy representatives in Saigon. Diplomas issued from French Indochina were embossed with the Vichy slogan "*Travail, Famille, Patrie*" ("Work, Family, Country") and we learned songs praising Marshal Pétain, bellowing "*Maréchal, nous voilà devant toi, le sauveur de la France*" ("Marshall, here we are facing you, the savior of France") although several of us muttered "*merde*" ("shit") at the end of these songfests. Since records were never kept on the students' religion, no Jewish student was ever barred from attending. Many believed that our principal, Putia, was a closet Gaullist.

Officially, our instructors sided with Vichy, otherwise they would have been fired, so we never knew if there were any de Gaulle sympathizers among them. While the instructors did not reveal their political views – they were for Marshal Pétain by default – Vichy sentiments prevailed in the classroom among a number of my classmates whose parents served in the police force or in the colonial army. Because they disliked England, their hereditary enemy, many showed no compassion as London was bombed by waves of German planes. These same classmates seemed pleased that Hitler's army was defeating the Allies on all fronts, especially the Bolsheviks in the Soviet Union. They no longer used the term "*sales Boches*" ("damn Krauts") when speaking about the Germans but now called them *"nos alliés"* ("our allies").

In my class a boy named Michel Guillemin not only spouted pro-Pétain and violently anti-British statements but also anti-Semitic comments, which he had obviously heard at home – his father was head of a group of pro-Nazi Frenchmen who collaborated openly with the Japanese authorities. Michel addressed his favorite expression of *"sale juif"* ("dirty Jew") to anyone he thought might be Jewish. When I became his target I reported him to Putia, not realizing that I would be complaining to a representative of the Vichy government. I did not know that in October 1940, the Vichy government passed laws – *le statut des juifs* – against French, foreign and stateless Jews residing in non-occupied France and in several of its colonies. They were dismissed from all professions and their children forbidden to attend schools. Putia listened to me with his usual cold stare, then told me that he would take care of this matter, which he did by immediately ordering Michel to stop slandering his classmates. Michel obeyed reluctantly but whenever he had a chance he whispered to me in a low voice, *"Sale juive,"* to which I retorted loudly, *"Sale Boche et sale collaborateur fasciste."* In my naiveté, I did not think that my classmate Michel might report my insults to his father and that possibly I could be dismissed from my school for insulting Vichy, the Germans and the Japanese.

It still puzzles me that the Collège Municipal Français, which adhered to Vichy's anti-Semitic policies, allowed its Jewish students to remain integrated in the school.

17
White Man's Downfall

DURING THE occupation of Shanghai the Japanese military requisitioned rice from the nearby countryside and from Japanese-occupied Indochina, and then distributed it to holders of ration cards. The priority for all residents was to purchase rationed food before it disappeared from the specially designated stores. Rice, oil and sugar could be purchased illegally on the black market but at much higher prices and by the "squeeze" method, the Shanghai parlance for bribery. In addition to the difficulty in procuring food, people dreaded the sight of Japanese soldiers patrolling the streets or riding bicycles with wide handlebars on which they placed their rifles with protruding bayonets. They barked at the Chinese pedestrians to get out of their way and when they did not they slapped them across the face or hit their heads with rifle butts.

My classmates and I avoided all eye contact and looked straight ahead whenever we encountered these soldiers but once out of earshot we would call them *petits singes* ("small monkeys"). We laughed at their bow-legged posture as they rode their bicycles and giggled about their surely minuscule genitalia. But while my classmates and I tried to make fun of the Japanese, my parents and other adults feared that any encounter with them, however innocuous, could lead to arrest and imprisonment. This happened to a friend of our family, Boris Topas, whose daughter Laura was a classmate and close friend of my sister Jackie. Topas, the president of the Russian Ashkenazi community, had been incarcerated in the Bridge House prison following a meeting he attended where the half-dozen participants discussed the disturbing rumors that the occupation authorities planned to kill all the stateless Jews in Shanghai. This had been relayed in secrecy to the group by a concerned Japanese official, but when news of the meeting leaked out, all the participants were arrested and sent to Bridge House for spreading false rumors, a crime under occupation laws. The men were eventually released, but not Boris Topas, who was accused of harboring ties with the Kuomintang, and for having written many articles in praise of Chiang Kai-shek and his political party. In addition, Soong Ching-ling, the widow of Sun Yat-sen, had often frequented the Topas household when she lived in Shanghai before the Japanese occupation.

The fundamental reason, however, for Topas' six months of incarceration and torture in Bridge House was the role he had played ten years earlier in Harbin, when he led a delegation to the city government to protest the Japanese secret police's blackmailing of wealthy Jews, and the kidnapping and murder of the French Jewish pianist Simon Karpé. Topas wrote a very derogatory report on the Japanese authorities' involvement in this murder, carried out by their collaborators in the All-Russian Fascist Union in Harbin. Unfortunately, one of the officials Topas criticized was now a high-level officer at Bridge House. One evening Mrs. Topas received a call from a Chinese jailer at the prison informing her that her husband had just been thrown out into the street to die. Boris Topas was found barely alive; he suffered a stroke and never recovered from his tortures, and at age 50 remained in a vegetative state until the end of his life. It was extremely sad and frightening for Jackie and me when we visited Laura and saw her father, known in the community as a compassionate and brilliant man, sitting in a wheelchair and unable to speak anymore.

Laura Topas, then nine years old, spent more and more time in our home, playing with Jackie or talking with my mother when Jackie had to practice her piano scales. Although I did not want to associate with Laura, who was five years younger than me, she tried to befriend me by reporting to me that my mother complained about my brazen behavior, especially my "loud mouth", which could antagonize the Japanese authorities when I rode my bicycle yelling and scaring pedestrians. She told Laura I was too "wild" for a girl and feared I would never marry. My mother was very concerned with marrying off her three daughters, and often lamented to her friends that Riva and Jackie – and especially I – would never find a "nice" man to marry in our limited social circles. My mother was one of the few Shanghailanders who believed that once the war was over there would be no future for foreigners in Shanghai, and that immigration to America would solve her concern about finding suitable husbands for her three daughters. While she dreamed about our future married bliss in America, life was becoming more difficult and more worrisome regarding possible actions by the Japanese towards stateless Shanghailanders.

In February 1943 a "Proclamation" was issued ordering all stateless refugees who had arrived in Shanghai after January 1, 1937, to move to a designated area in Hongkew within two months. This was immediately followed by one demanding all Allied nationals turn in the keys of their residences to the Japanese authorities and register for internment in one of approximately twenty civilian prisoner-of-war camps around Shanghai.

The 9,000 enemy nationals in Shanghai included approximately 8,000 citizens from Britain, Canada, Australia and New Zealand, and 400 Americans, the remainder being mostly Dutch and Belgians. Interestingly, this proclamation was issued after the US government, in mid-1942, had sent 120,000 men, women and children of Japanese ancestry – of whom two-thirds were American citizens – to various internment camps in the United States. President Franklin Roosevelt's Executive Order reinforced Japan's strong belief in America's racism towards Asians, knowing that Americans of German and Italian descent were not subjected to this presidential edict.

It was shocking and eerie for me to see Western enemy

nationals, especially the *taipans,* those once-wealthy and powerful British and American businessmen, standing in line outside the Anglican Cathedral in the International Settlement, waiting to register for their incarceration at internment camps. They waited patiently, some with an air of bravado, others dejected, holding onto two suitcases each, cloth bags and thermos flasks, having left behind their beautifully furnished homes, private clubs, cars and servants. When the paperwork was done these enemy nationals were taken to the camps in trucks. Our Australian Uncle Ralph, his daughter Julie and her young son Ronald were sent to the nearby Lunghwa camp. A few days before their departure my mother held a party to celebrate Ronald's eighth birthday. She managed to get ingredients to bake a sponge cake and serve homemade ice cream, and we decorated our dining room with balloons and paper streamers. My mother repeatedly reassured them that the Americans would swiftly defeat the Japanese and their stay in the internment camp would be brief. My mother's sister Bessie had earlier divorced her husband, the American Marine, and had married a French policeman. Never having acquired American citizenship, she and her young son were spared internment. My father's boss, Ernest Harris, the manager of Sun Life Assurance Company, a symbol of the English elite, was incarcerated while my father, a person without a country, remained free.

Six months later my mother and I saw Julie at the Shanghai General Hospital in Hongkew, where she had been sent from her internment camp for a minor operation. Surprisingly, we were allowed to visit her, and my mother took me along instead of my father who, cautious by nature, did not want to fill out the probing questionnaire required for any meeting with enemy nationals. We met Julie in the hospital grounds, far from the Japanese guards and the Chinese nurses and doctors, which enabled us to ask her many questions. I inquired about my Belgian classmate and neighbor on Route Delastre, Aline Bodson, who was interned with her parents in the same camp. Aline, nicknamed Poupée (Dolly), for she resembled a beautiful china doll, had sent me several brief messages from Lunghwa Camp – read by Japanese censors – asking that I share them with several of our classmates. Poupée could not, of course, write about the difficulties of camp life, especially the lack of food, so she penned gushing notes about the 20-year-old English and American men, especially the crew members from the SS *President Harrison* with whom she flirted and fell in love on a weekly basis. Our close-knit group at the Collège Municipal was actually jealous that Poupée could meet these men while we were stuck with the generally uninteresting boys in our class. Several of us agreed that we would not mind exchanging places with her – but only for a day or two – so we too could meet those dashing men she raved about. I was disappointed that Julie did not know Poupée but not too surprised since the internees were often segregated by nationality and slept in different barracks.

Julie told us life in the camp was psychologically very difficult as the inmates became bored and restless, cut off from the outside world and from news about the war. Julie's main complaint was that the internees were perpetually hungry, their meals being limited to a bowl of gruel, a piece of brown bread, rice with cabbage or beans, and tea brewed from overused leaves. However, they came to appreciate these meals as occasionally they had nothing to eat for lunch or dinner.

She told us of her anger at the Swiss International Red Cross and representatives of the Swiss consulate who had visited internment camps (not theirs), where they would surely have heard about the food problem. She believed the Red Cross was aware that many of their food parcels were not being distributed to the internees but taken by the Japanese guards for their own consumption. Julie was adamant that the Swiss Red Cross was profiting financially as a "neutral" intermediary between the Japanese and the internees, despite the organization's excuses about difficulties in receiving funds from the Allies at war.

Julie said that whenever the Red Cross handed over hard currency to the Japanese to purchase supplemental food for the internees, the camp authorities would exchange it on the black market at high rates but calculate the internees' food allocation at the very low official rate. The commandant and his acolytes at the camp, meanwhile, pocketed the difference. Julie felt the Swiss Red Cross should have been supervising the distribution of food, not seeming to appreciate the fact that the Japanese military, not the Red Cross, made all the decisions. She became very despondent when she learned that my mother had been sending her monthly food and clothing parcels, each weighing ten pounds, through the local Swiss Red Cross Office. She had received to date only two of them. The guards, nearly as hungry as the internees, had kept the canned food and the sweaters and gloves my mother had knitted for Uncle Ralph, Julie and her son.

Besides the shortage of food, Julie told us of the internees' damp, unheated dormitories, where they shivered during the winter months and suffered the intense heat of the humid summer. She and Ronald shared a small room with a woman, and her small girl lived in one of the buildings set aside for single women and their children. It was next to the barracks for the Japanese guards, who could be heard many nights shouting and singing after having drunk alcohol, presumably homemade.

Families slept in large barracks where they were allotted a living space of about 40 square feet, separated from their neighbors by sheets and blankets hung over ropes. This afforded them some semblance of privacy from prying eyes but not from the noise around their new "home". Rats, bugs, the stench from chamber pots and lack of medication, combined with malnutrition, led to various sicknesses and death. Attempts to escape were rare but those who tried were caught and severely beaten in front of the entire camp, then thrown into solitary confinement and often nearly starved to death.

The internees avoided the Japanese guards as much as possible since any infraction was met with a slap in the face or, worse, imprisonment in a very narrow cell with no windows. Beyond this, however, the internees were mostly left to run the camp themselves, with British management and efficiency coming to the fore. Every physically able adult was assigned a task in the kitchen, bakery, school, infirmary or supervising sports activities. Some directed plays, and internees who had brought their violins and harmonicas performed concerts. Men who had never washed a plate in their lives were now scrubbing floors, washing their clothes in cold water and lining up dejectedly with their tin plates for their meals. Many must have recalled the scene in 1937 of starving Chinese refugees from the bombardment in Chapei lining up in the International Settlement for rice being doled out by the British municipal authorities.

Rumors about the war were rampant in the camp and Julie wanted to know what was happening in Shanghai and the world. My mother told her that purchasing food was a daily struggle but she could not give her much news about the war since the local English-language newspaper was replete with Japanese propaganda. She did tell Julie, however, that everyone felt the war would soon end for, according to rumors, the tide was turning in favor of the Americans in the Pacific Islands. Julie returned the next day to Lunghwa Camp.

Many years later I questioned Julie about J.G. Ballard's book *Empire of the Sun,* set in Lunghwa Camp, where Ballard and his parents were interned. Julie remembered the young boy Jamie Ballard, who sometimes played with her son of the same age, Ronnie, but described his novel as "such fantasy". She insisted that there was never a food riot, as depicted in the novel, since internees always queued up at meal time. What disturbed me most in the novel (and in Stephen Spielberg's movie based on the story) was the scene where the young protagonist was slapped across the face by his amah. All of us brought up by amahs knew that even under the most difficult circumstances no amah would hit us since the emotional bond between the amah and "her" foreign child was extremely strong. Coming from a Chinese society where women were often considered and treated as inferior, amahs did not rebel against any exploitation by their white "Missees" and "Masters". Employment as an amah kept one from prostitution or possible starvation.

Our encounter at the hospital with Julie, a camp internee in wartime Shanghai, was a very exciting adventure for me. I described the meeting to my friend Ginette Grillon and she – as imaginative and daring as I – suggested we hire a sampan to take us as close as possible to the Pootung internment camp across the Whangpoo River. We plotted our scheme without telling any of our classmates or our parents, and a few days later hired a sampan man to take us across the river to the old factory building where we were told the internees were incarcerated. We discovered, however, that the camp was some distance from the shore and decided not to go any further. We returned to our terrified sampan man who had not realized that we intended to look at an internment camp. Fortunately for him – and for us – no Japanese soldier appeared on the scene and our brave sailor quickly rowed us back to the Bund, grumbling all the way and demanding extra fare, which we readily gave.

Of course Ginette and I did not think about any of the dire consequences we might have suffered had we been caught.

The "Designated Area"

NINETEEN FORTY-THREE was a very difficult year for Chinese and foreign residents in Shanghai as the Japanese military occupation grew increasingly oppressive.

By late 1942 the Japanese authorities had started interning Allied nationals in camps around Shanghai, euphemistically named "Civilian Assembly Centers". The first group sent were single men, but they were soon followed by entire families. Stateless Jewish refugees from Austria, Czechoslovakia, Germany, Poland and the Baltic states who had arrived in Shanghai after January 1, 1937, were ordered to move into the *Shitei Shiku*, the Japanese name for the Designated Area, by May 1943. The Imperial Japanese Army and Navy claimed the measure was "motivated by military necessity". Refugees still living outside of the Designated Area had to obtain permission from the Japanese authorities for all "transfer sale, purchase or lease of the rooms, houses, shops or any other establishments . . . now being occupied or used by the stateless refugees". This meant that the Japanese could requisition any property for "military necessity". The order was directed at "stateless" not "Jewish" refugees, but nearly all the refugees who arrived in Shanghai after January 1, 1937, were Jews or were married to Jews. Nine thousand of the 18,000 refugees were already living in Hongkew where rent, food and daily necessities were much cheaper than in the foreign enclaves.

The Designated Area sent tremors of fear throughout the stateless Russian communities. On several occasions I overheard my mother discuss with her friends whether they would be in the next group sent to an internment camp. My father tried to calm her by explaining that the Neutrality Act Japan had signed with the USSR in 1941 was a deterrent to incarcerating Russians, whether they were Soviets or stateless, since the latter group would have immediately applied for Soviet citizenship – as approximately 1,000 of them had done in the 1930s. My father pointed out that the USSR and Japan would not quibble about these Russians in China because the two countries could not afford to open a second front along the Manchurian border: the Soviets were still battling the Nazis in Russia and Japan was sustaining heavy losses in the Pacific.

Rumors were rife, however, that the Japanese were under pressure from the Nazis to exterminate all the Jews in Shanghai. The Ashkenazi and the Sephardic communities knew that the head of the Gestapo in the Far East, Colonel Josef Meisinger, the "Butcher of Warsaw", had come from Tokyo to Shanghai in July 1942 to meet with the Japanese authorities – surely he must have discussed the fate of the denationalized and stateless Jews in Shanghai and surely he had proposed a solution to exterminate them. Rumors in circulation included that the Japanese were planning to put Jews on barges on the Whangpoo River and sink them in the open sea, or that they would send them to a nearby island to starve. In addition, German Nazis expelled from the United States and several Latin American countries had come to Shanghai in the early days of World War II, and could be expected to be plotting with anti-Semitic Ukrainians to kill the denationalized German and Austrian refugees and eventually all Jews.

These were wild rumors, however, they were spread out of fear. No document to date has come to light indicating the Japanese were pressured by Berlin to take such actions against the Jews in China. In all probability, discussions were held between Japan and Germany but the Japanese must have taken all suggestions with a grain of salt. At the beginning of World War II the Japanese, flush with victories in Asia and in full control of their "New Order" policy, did not need to take orders from anyone, even their powerful German ally. They considered themselves equals in the war against the United States and Great Britain. The Japanese were innately uncomfortable with the Nazis' racist views that exalted the tall, blond, blue-eyed Aryans, and they mistrusted Caucasians more generally. The Japanese government had requested at the Paris Peace Conference in 1919 that a "racial equality clause" be included in the charter of the League of Nations, and this had been rejected by the United States, Britain and Australia.

The Japanese government never instituted any anti-Semitic laws in their country, and xenophobic mid-19th century Japan even permitted small groups of Jewish traders to settle in Kobe and Nagasaki. High-ranking Japanese military and civilian leaders were fully aware that it was an American Jewish financier, Jacob Schiff, who had helped float bonds to finance Japan's war against Czarist Russia in 1904-1905. He was later invited to an audience with the Emperor who honored him with a medal for his vital role in Japan's victory. In the mid-1930s, the Japanese had even toyed with the idea of resettling in Manchukuo thousands of Jewish refugees fleeing Nazi Germany. Most importantly for Jews living in Japan, China and Manchukuo, the Japanese government adopted a policy at the end of 1938 that required Jews to be treated in the same manner as all other foreigners. This was enacted despite the signing of the anti-Comintern Pact with Nazi Germany two years earlier and the virulent anti-Semitic publications and admiration of Hitler of the Japanese ultra-nationalists. The latter's beliefs were based on myths and lies about an international Jewish conspiracy to dominate the world as described in *The Protocols of the Learned Elders of Zion*, a violently anti-Semitic book compiled by a Czarist secret police official in the early 20th century.

The Japanese government did, however, believe in the stereotypical image of Jewish people as intelligent, hard-working and eager to make money. More importantly, they believed Jews had very close ties with President Franklin Roosevelt; perhaps American Jews could prevail upon the President not to interfere with Japan's plan of conquering Asia. But after Pearl Harbor, with communications with the United States cut off, Jews in Shanghai were no longer useful as pawns for Japan. In confining so many stateless refugees to Hongkew the Japanese authorities counted on these Europeans sprucing up and setting up businesses in an area heavily damaged during the 1932 and 1937 Sino-Japanese hostilities. The Japanese did not take into consideration that thousands of refugees moving to Hongkew would inevitably dislodge some of the 100,000 very poor Chinese living there in lane housing.

The one-square-mile internment camp for stateless refugees was never referred to as a "ghetto", a term used by present-day writers and journalists when describing the Designated Area. My friends and I simply called it "Hongkew" since it was understood that it was the area where the refugees lived side-by-side with the Chinese residents. This camp was not surrounded by walls or guarded by Japanese soldiers as were the internment camps for the Allied nationals. The latter were the enemies of Japan, the Jewish refugees were not. Boundary signs marked the Designated Area, and a refugee civil patrol checked the passes that allowed a refugee to go out for the day and return before the 11 p.m. curfew. In addition to the passes the refugees had to wear metal badges on their clothing with the Chinese characters for "May Pass", and carry a yellow striped identity card whenever they left the Designated Area. The Chinese residents did not need passes to leave or enter.

Several refugees, who had befriended my parents before their internment in the Designated Area, often came to our home when they were able to get a day pass. My mother served them lunch and gave them clothes they could use themselves, or sell or barter for other items in the Hongkew market. These refugees told us of the grim housing situation for refugee families, who lived mostly in single rooms of rundown tenements in narrow lanes. In the kitchens, shared by several families, they cooked their meals on charcoal burners, and the so-called toilet facilities were more often than not the ubiquitous wooden buckets. The hygiene-conscious washed in the communal public baths where, for a few cents, they could use hot water. Running water was often turned off in their living quarters so the refugees, armed with large thermos bottles, purchased their supply of hot water from shops selling exclusively this necessity. Our guests added they had to contend with the strange behavior of the Japanese commandant of the Designated Area, Kanoh Ghoya. Unquestionably a psychopath, he designated himself the "King of Jews" – and generally mistreated his "subjects". Refugees who needed a day pass to leave the camp for special medical care had to request it personally from Ghoya at his office. Barely five feet tall, Ghoya would fly into sudden rages and sometimes climb onto his desk to hit the refugees, especially if they were tall. The refugees never knew whether they would receive the permit from Ghoya. It depended on his mood; word would spread around quickly in the camp as to whether to ask for a permit or wait for another day.

Fortunately for the refugees, the Russian Ashkenazi community was able to help them with food, clothing and basic medicine for the sick, who were generally taken care by the large number of doctors confined in the Designated Area. The Ashkenazi were joined in this charitable endeavor by stateless Iraqi Sephardim, who were never able to acquire British citizenship and therefore not sent to the civilian detention camps for Allied nationals. These Iraqis were registered by the bureaucratic-minded Japanese authorities as "second-class enemy nationals" since they were from a British mandate country. However, the economic situation worsened for the refugees when assistance from the American Joint Distribution Center in Shanghai and other organizations in the United States ended in 1943 because funds could no longer be transmitted to Shanghai. Consequently, the Japanese authorities taxed the Russian Ashkenazi community to help defray some of the expenses in the Designated Area.

Despite their wretched condition, many refugees worked in their living quarters as tailors, seamstresses and hat makers, while others opened beauty parlors, delicatessens, restaurants and even nightclubs. The most popular places to meet and spend time with friends during the summer months were the open air cafés. People could drink tea and coffee (although of very poor quality) or simply hot water, and eat the delectable Viennese *Sachertorte* (chocolate cake filled with marmalade) prepared by professional bakers in Hongkew. Writers wrote plays, artists performed in them; academics gave lectures on various subjects; others penned newsletters in German, Polish and Yiddish while journalists wrote articles for the German-language newspaper with its English name, the *Shanghai Jewish Chronicle*. This newspaper was published during the entire Japanese occupation without any interference from the authorities.

On Friday nights many refugees gathered for prayers in private homes and during the High Holy Days went to religious services at the Ohel Moishe synagogue in Hongkew. Children in the Designated Area were permitted to leave for the day to attend classes at the Kadoorie School in the former International Settlement. Smaller children who could not walk the distance studied in makeshift classes in Hongkew run by the teachers and parents in the community. Permission was also granted during the first year of internment to another group of refugees, the 300 students and their rabbis of the Mir Yeshiva, to leave the camp every morning for their usual 15-hour religious studies and eat their meals at the Beth Aharon synagogue located in a non-restricted sector of Hongkew.

However, in this semblance of normalcy, there was always the lurking fear, fanned by fertile imagination, that the Nazis would convince the Japanese to kill the refugees in Hongkew. The internees did not know during their incarceration that their relatives and friends – men, women and children – were being killed, gassed and burned in the concentration camps. During their two-and-a-half years of confinement in the Designated Areas approximately 1,500 elderly and very young children died from malnutrition, lack of medication, cold and damp winters in unheated rooms and tropical diseases unknown to Europeans.

By now, when my mother and her friends gathered for high tea, frivolous gossip had long been set aside. Instead they relayed to each other the latest information they had gathered about the war raging in Europe and Asia. They were shocked to learn that in 1942, on the Republic of China's national day, October 10, England and the United States, the two former treaty powers, had announced the abrogation of their extraterritorial rights in China. Shanghailanders considered this act as a gesture of gratitude from President Franklin Roosevelt and Prime Minister Winston Churchill towards their Chinese ally fighting the common Nipponese enemy. In reality, the soldiers of the emerging Chinese communist army were the ones who systematically harassed the Japanese more than the Kuomintang Nationalist troops.

This relinquishment of privileges, however, did not change the status of the foreigners in Shanghai. After Pearl Harbor the International Settlement was no longer an extraterritorial enclave, while the French Concession was in fact controlled by the Japanese. For my parents and me, and the "Old China Hands", it was difficult to accept the new reality that once the Japanese occupation ended, Shanghai would never revert to its former privileged status for whites.

Another blow to extraterritoriality occurred soon afterwards when the Vichy government renounced its extraterritorial rights in Canton, Hankow, Shanghai and Tientsin. On July 30, 1943, Consul General Roland de Margerie was ordered to hand over the French Concession to the puppet government of Wang Ching-wei. "Our" Concession existed no more. The Japanese were losing the war in the Pacific but needed to show more than ever that they were in full control of Shanghai. They confiscated the French police stations, municipal buildings, utility companies and transportation facilities without any financial compensation.

Nevertheless, high-ranking officials in the French police managed to convince the Japanese gendarmerie that, for security reasons and administrative continuity, a third of the French employees needed be retained to help manage the former French Concession and handle matters dealing with their nationals. The Japanese acquiesced but continued to show their disdain towards the Chinese by paying them much less than their French counterparts. The French were allowed to keep their garrison, which included approximately 1,000 Annamite and Tonkinese policemen and low-ranking soldiers attached to the army. One of my father's insurance policy holders, Roland Sarly, the former deputy chief of the erstwhile French municipal police, was now named Inspector General of the Chinese police in the former French Concession, now called the 8th District. Several of my classmates – whose fathers were now unemployed – told me their families were receiving some financial assistance from the French consulate and food packages of rice, beans, cereals and jam from the International Red Cross. These officials from the police force, business firms, banks and utility companies had never imagined that one day they would be in need of food donations.

The street signs in French, which had for so long symbolized France's glorious past, were replaced with new signs written in Chinese characters that Shanghailanders could not read. The Chinese and foreigners alike continued, however, to use the former French names whenever asking for or giving directions.

In the fall of 1943 my friends and I heard the Italian army had capitulated to the Allies in September, and the following month the provisory Italian government declared war on Germany. I was not surprised at Italy's defeat, for my classmates and I always joked about an incident we were told occurred during World War I in the town of Caporetto, where Italian soldiers refused to fight and turned their backs on the advancing Austrian soldiers. We often used the word "Caporetto" as a synonym for cowardice. This could not be applied, however, to the Italian crewmen of the *Conte Verde* passenger liner anchored in the Whangpoo River. When news reached the sailors that Italy had declared war against Germany, they hurriedly opened the valves in the hull of their ship, which then turned over on its side in the shallow waters of the harbor. The crew was immediately arrested for sabotage by the Japanese authorities and sent to an internment camp near Shanghai. There, the Italian sailors were greeted and applauded by the Allied internees for their courageous act, which could have resulted in their incarceration at Bridge House and possible execution. Although the remainder of the small Italian community in Shanghai was ordered to register as enemy nationals and list all their properties, they were not sent to any internment camp. On the other hand they were obliged to wear arm bands made from the dark velvet drapes of the Shanghai Italian Club, which turned out to be quite decorative. My parents were extremely worried when their close Italian friends, Jacques and Aline Picciotto, were called in for interrogation by the Japanese authorities. Jacques was fluent in Japanese, which could be taken as evidence he was a spy for the Allies. The couple, however, was quickly released, and my father was convinced that Jacques' knowledge of Japanese culture must have astonished his interrogators, and that he managed to convince them in their own language that he was simply a businessman.

The local events in Shanghai in 1943 – the incarceration of Allied nationals, the forced relocation of Jewish refugees in Hongkew, and the end of extraterritoriality in the French Concession – made many Shanghailanders realize that there would be no future for "Master" and "Missee" in post-war Shanghai. Legally the Concession was no longer French. It had become Chinese. It was difficult for me to accept that Western colonialism in Shanghai, with its many privileges, had come to an end.

Ironically, Japanese colonialism now replaced it.

19
Curfew, Rations and Fear

THERE WAS a glimmer of hope at the beginning of 1944 with the news that the Axis forces were sustaining heavy losses – despite continued claims of victory in the Japanese-controlled *Shanghai Times* and on the English-language radio station XMHA. But it seemed that in retaliation for their ships being sunk and their islands in the Pacific being captured by the Americans, the Japanese became harsher towards both Chinese and foreign residents in Shanghai. Pedestrians scampered away whenever they saw soldiers with guns and bayonets, who yelled incomprehensible orders at anyone who came too close to them or the buildings they were guarding.

Despite news from clandestine short-wave radios that the Allies were winning on all fronts – their troops had landed in France in June, and American and British planes were bombing Germany and Japan relentlessly – a pall hung over the stateless Shanghailanders throughout the year. We were fearful that the Japanese, because of their continued heavy losses, would intern us. It became clear that the Japanese were in desperate straits when they started removing radiators and pipes from many buildings to be sent to Japan for melting and subsequent use in the manufacture of armaments. Daily life was getting more and more difficult; food rations were reduced and people with spare income bought their daily necessities from hoarders and black marketeers. My sisters and I were tired of the meals we ate at home so we often bought on the street sweet potatoes and bowls of *mian tiao* (noodles) cooked on small charcoal stoves or chestnuts roasting in large vats. The dearth of private cars, and the presence of crowded trams and busses churning out heavy black smoke, led ingenious Chinese entrepreneurs to design a new mode of transportation. The combination of the front of a bicycle and the back seat of a rickshaw gave birth in Shanghai to the pedicab, a three-wheeled vehicle pedaled by a driver who could often overtake busses trying to maneuver around other vehicles and jaywalkers in the crowded, narrow streets.

The Japanese, worried about the possibility of American planes bombing Shanghai, ordered store owners to cover their windows with crisscross strips of paper to prevent the panes from falling down, and residents to cover their windows at night with blackout material. In our home we hovered behind darkened windows and were very scared when we heard Japanese patrols marching nearby to enforce this order. If any glimmer of light was visible in the street, the soldiers began shouting and pounding on doors with their guns. The terrified inhabitants quickly turned off all the lights, blew out the candles and remained in the dark until the soldiers' heavy footsteps could no longer be heard.

Air-raid practice drills were held by so-called "rescue" teams of Chinese men who, under Japanese orders, rushed around looking ridiculous, in my eyes, with their helmets, buckets of sand, rope and empty stretchers. During these drills all vehicular and foot traffic was stopped and I had to wait for the all-clear whistle before continuing on my way. Streets were also blocked when high-ranking Japanese and Chinese officials drove by, and if President Wang Ching-wei was in town, all shops had to be shuttered. These street closures happened quite often and my classmates and I, who rode our bicycles, were forced to dismount and wait until the all-clear signal. As we stood by our bicycles we swore under our breath at the Japanese soldiers and commented on the uselessness of these drills since we were sure the Americans would not bomb residential Shanghai, where no factories existed. The Japanese, who were more sophisticated militarily than us, thought differently, and they placed anti-aircraft guns on the roofs of hotels and high-rise office buildings.

We suffered from the cold in our apartment, where at times the temperature dropped to 30 degrees Fahrenheit and all the windows became covered with ice whenever an inch or two of snow fell during January and February. Our rooms were heated by kerosene stoves, which were turned off at night for fear of asphyxiation or fire. The fire brigade was no longer run by professionally trained French and Chinese firemen but by underpaid men in the Chinese municipality who would not come to extinguish a fire unless the homeowner agreed to pay for their services. Our amah told us of instances of bargaining between residents and the firemen while fires raged.

Use of electricity, gas and water was rationed to a few hours daily – but we never knew when they would be turned on or off. All our rooms were now lit by low-wattage lamp bulbs and when electricity was suddenly cut we had to finish our homework by candlelight. Candles and matches were strewn everywhere in our home, ready for these emergencies. In the evening we usually washed by candlelight with hot water our amah had heated in many pots on the gas stove while it was functioning, or on the two *hibachis* in the kitchen. We could not use our bathtub since it was filled to the brim with lumps of coal needed for cooking and boiling water. As the dampness increased, my sisters and I developed chapped skin and chilblains on our fingers and toes that took on a dark blue and purple hue and turned puffy, making it painful to wear our thick woolen stockings and hand-knitted gloves. We went to bed wearing layers of warm clothing and placed hot water bottles at our pillow and feet. If it was too cold and damp to ride our bicycles or take rickshaws, we squeezed in the lumbering and overcrowded busses.

Food was more tightly rationed when rice and flour were in short supply, and sugar was replaced by glucose that gave a faintly sweet taste when we poured it into our tea. My mother stored bags of rice and flour and jars of glucose she had purchased at controlled prices with ration cards or on the black market at drastically higher prices. While foreigners scrambled for food on the black market more and more beggars appeared on the streets, and many sick and starving Chinese died during the recurring epidemics of cholera, typhoid and smallpox. Inoculated against these diseases, we sat in our unheated classrooms wrapped in our coats, scarves and knitted caps, reluctantly taking off our gloves whenever we had to write in our notebooks.

For diversion from our boring classes, we often went to the school's library to read forbidden books that our teachers considered too provocative for us. We regularly returned to our favorite novel, "Lady's Chatterley's Lover", re-reading the passages describing passionate sexual encounters. To our great surprise and excitement a real sexual encounter did occur in our school when Thérèse, a French girl of fifteen, became pregnant, but we never found out who was responsible for her "downfall". We wondered if she would have an abortion but doubted it, for she was brought up in a very devout Catholic family. We were right, because she disappeared from school for several months and returned after giving birth to a girl who was immediately adopted. Our close-knit group talked for months about the scandal; we could not believe that someone our age had dared to have intercourse. Riva and I heard my mother whisper to a friend on the phone that the baby girl was adopted by her close Russian Jewish friends but we did not hear their name.

While we went off to school hoping that our route would be blocked by air raid drills before classes started, my mother stayed at home preparing meals with Amah, nagging the houseboy and supervising Lao Papa as he pedaled diligently to keep up with the many alteration requests from my mother's friends and acquaintances – the profitable cottage industry that helped sustain our family. My father preferred staying home reading the heavily censored *Shanghai Times* in his comfortable armchair or listening to music on the radio or to his records on the gramophone. This was set in a large cabinet with a compartment for our non-functioning short-wave radio which had not been repaired because of the ban on overseas news.

The short-wave radio ban was strictly enforced by the Japanese militia, who paid unannounced visits to private homes in search of any clandestine wireless equipment. My parents, although worried, were hardly surprised when two Japanese men in uniform came one morning to inspect our home. They went straight to the cabinet in the living room and asked why we kept a broken short-wave radio that could easily be repaired. As they started questioning my father, my mother called our Japanese neighbor Madame Vergez, the wife of my science teacher, to help us out of the predicament. She quickly came over and explained to the men that the radio had been broken for several years and was never removed. They accepted her explanation and, after bowing to her and to my parents, they left, to everyone's great relief. Madame Vergez had told these two men that our family was from Romania, an ally of the Axis powers. The consequences could have been drastic if they had not accepted her explanation, for they would have inevitably searched the entire house for other forbidden items. These men might have found, for example, a large American flag that was in a suitcase an American couple had asked my parents to keep for them when they were sent to an internment camp. The suitcase was filled with jade and ivory and evening clothes – useless items in a prisoner-of-war camp – but if the flag had been discovered my parents would have been accused of harboring the despised symbol of Japan's enemy and possibly of being spies for the Allies.

The nightly curfew and blackouts relegated my social life to gatherings and sleepovers at my friends' homes where we danced to music played on a gramophone that needed to be cranked regularly. My sister Riva spent much time on the phone telling her friends about the young men who wanted to date her or discussing whom to invite to our home for our next party. At 18, she was the most popular girl on the dance floor while I was the proverbial wallflower, waiting to be asked to dance by any short or pimply boy rejected by my friends. Jackie continued her piano lessons and practiced daily after school, and was always willing to play for anyone who asked – but she was never asked by me since I was bored of hearing the same pieces over and over again. American songs, which I enjoyed very much, were banned by the authorities who had gone on a rampage in stores, smashing records and tearing up sheet music composed by American artists. During the Japanese occupation Jackie never parted with her copy of *"God Bless America"*.

I played Chinese checkers with my friends, winning most of the time, and exchanged foreign stamps with them since my regular supply had ended with the demise of Sun Life Assurance Company. At 16 I still enjoyed riding my bicycle around our neighborhood and scaring pedestrians, who jumped and swore at me as I whizzed by very close to them. My favorite targets were two young Germans living in our complex, Muschie and her brother Hans, who strutted around whenever he wore his *Hitler Jugend* uniform. I taunted him, mimicking the Nazi salute and yelling "Hell to Hitler". Hans never complained about me to his father, who was a high-ranking Nazi bureaucrat at the German Siemens Company. He wanted to be part of our gatherings so he could brag about his boxing prowess as a lightweight champion in the Kaiser Wilhelm Schule. The boys in our group called him "Max Schmeling" after the German boxer who had been beaten in the ring by a non-Aryan, the black American Joe Louis. We allowed his sister Muschie to join us, feeling somewhat sorry for her because she had had contracted polio as a child and now walked with a slight limp. We agreed that it was not her fault that she was German. My friends and I gathered regularly on the stoops of our respective houses, singing French songs accompanied by Muschie on her accordion – until we were told to stop by irate neighbors. Before curfew, my classmates and I would ride our bicycles to noodle stands frequented by rickshaw coolies and sit beside them slurping our hot bowls of noodles. Our parents would have been shocked to discover we ate food in such unsanitary conditions, that these people were our dinner companions, and that we rode around in a city crawling with

Japanese soldiers.

My parents had to reluctantly acknowledge my misbehavior had been a blessing in disguise when the Japanese requisitioned the Savoy Apartments building, the building we had been obliged to vacate because of my pranks. It would have been extremely difficult, if not impossible, to find another suitable apartment during the war.

20
Bombs and More Bombs

THE WAR in Europe and the Pacific became a reality in Shanghai on a clear morning in June 1944. The air-raid alarm sounded, but this time it was not for a practice drill. American B-29 planes from their base near Chungking appeared in the skies over Shanghai, apparently surveying the city since they did not bomb it. However, when they returned at night in mid-August we could hear explosions intermingled with the sound of anti-aircraft guns and the wailing of sirens. My parents, my sisters and I rushed down from our bedrooms and huddled, terrified, in our living room until the all-clear signal sounded. Radio station XMHA claimed the American planes had only bombed the outskirts of Shanghai, but the city was abuzz. We spent the day calling each other and wondering when these planes would return. Although we hoped it would be very soon, we were nevertheless worried the American pilots could mistakenly bomb residential sectors, and not the Japanese armament factories and warehouses in the far-off corners of Hongkew and Pootung.

During the next few months B-29 planes returned regularly on their nightly bombing missions outside the city and in the fall they started coming in the daytime. Whenever these daylight raids occurred and I was still in the street I had to find an air-raid shelter in the basement of a building, but before going in I always stopped to look up at the puffs of smoke from the anti-aircraft batteries and wave my arms jubilantly at the planes bombing the outskirts of my city. After these bombardments the announcer on the Japanese-controlled radio station never failed to claim that several enemy planes had been shot down by Japanese anti-aircraft guns on the perimeter of the city.

Electricity, gas and water were cut off for hours following these attacks. My friends and I accepted these inconveniences since we wanted the American pilots to destroy the Japanese military gasoline and oil facilities to hasten the end of the war. In order not to be short of water in our household my mother, Amah and the houseboy removed the coal from the bathtub, scrubbed it thoroughly and filled it with water.

These daytime air raids continued unabated and whenever my classmates and I were riding to and from school and the piercing sound of air-raid sirens rent the air, we dismounted quickly from our bicycles and rushed towards a shelter – though we would have preferred to remain in the streets to cheer the American planes, and to hear the booming sound of bombs exploding and the staccato reply of anti-aircraft gunfire. When the raids happened while we were at home, we would go out to the garden to see the plumes of smoke rising in the distance, oblivious to the danger that we could be hit by anti-aircraft shrapnel. To my great shock one afternoon, I found pieces of shrapnel embedded on the wall of the balcony adjacent to my parents' bedroom.

Americans planes flying over Shanghai did not encounter much resistance after they had bombed the nearby Lunghwa (Longhua) airport and destroyed a number of Japanese planes lined up for take-off. When the all-clear signal sounded one or two Japanese planes would appear in the sky, obviously trying to save face. After these air raids I would often ride my bicycle to Jessfield Park not to pick flowers, as many people did, but to gather stray shrapnel. Later I exchanged my finds for stamps from "exotic" countries with several young boys eager to add shrapnel to their collections of tin soldiers. My entrepreneurship and bartering continued quite successfully since I refused to reveal where I got my supply.

On the rare occasions that low-flying American planes were hit by anti-aircraft fire, the crew would abandon their burning plane and parachute to the ground near Shanghai. If captured or turned in by fearful Chinese villagers, who had been warned not to hide enemies, they would likely be taken to Bridge House, interrogated, tortured and possibly executed. One American plane shot down in Shanghai was displayed at the Racecourse and naturally I wanted to see it. My parents would not allow me to go, fearing the reaction of the Japanese soldiers guarding this trophy and the crowd of Chinese who, they feared, could be hostile towards foreigners in their midst. The announcer on XMHA gleefully stated that many more enemy planes similar to the P-51 displayed at the Racecourse had been downed by the powerful Japanese anti-aircraft guns, and that more of them would be hit on their next raid on Shanghai. The announcer added that the Americans had been unsuccessful in their attempts to take the Pacific Islands, where brave Japanese soldiers were withstanding the enemy's relentless bombardment.

Our family continued its social engagements, although they were often interrupted by air-raid alarms that sent us rushing for cover; Jackie presented a piano recital at the Russian Club, I went to parties and Riva went out dancing the night away at her friends' homes, often returning in the morning after the curfew was lifted.

My mother baked cakes whenever she had enough flour and eggs for her tea get-togethers, and she still managed to buy gifts for our and her friends' endless birthdays and wedding anniversary parties. On one occasion she went out to run some errands before the expected start of "enemy" air raids that now were a daily occurrence. Soon after she left American planes appeared and when the bombing started my father, my sisters and I became extremely worried, wondering whether she had had time to find a shelter. To our great relief she finally returned home, telling us she had been very scared because she could not find a shelter until a Chinese cyclist led her to one. Pedestrians caught in the streets during these air raids had to find cover on their own since the locations of dugouts were not always clearly marked. I smiled, however, when alarms sounded during our math and science classes, for then we had to go to the back of the room and lie down on the floor. During these interruptions I hoped that the all clear-signal would not ring until the period was over.

In the midst of the continuous raids our spirits were lifted when we heard, in July 1944, that Paris had been liberated by the Allies. Upon hearing this stunning news a handful of my French classmates and I celebrated the occasion at my home. All summer long we continued to hear that the Germans and the Japanese were sustaining heavy losses on all fronts.

When I returned to school that fall, my pro-Vichy classmates did not seem pleased that France had been freed by the Allies. Our yearly trek to the cemetery to honor Armistice Day and its heroes was cancelled, with no explanation given. I smirked, for I had just learned that "our" Maréchal Pétain, the World War I hero of Verdun, had fled to Germany. I whispered to a couple of classmates that "*ce grand lâche, ce traître*" ("that big coward, that traitor") was no longer in France. I was delighted that we did not go back to school for an entire week because the Japanese ordered the closure of all schools, stores and businesses to mourn the sudden death of the Chinese President, Wang Ching-wei, in Tokyo, where he had been meeting with Japanese leaders. The passing of the puppet leader of Japanese-controlled China was not mourned by the Chinese, although they did wonder who would be named the new head of the Japanese-ordained government in Nanking. In 1944 Japan had more pressing concerns than choosing Wang's replacement, since they were sustaining enormous losses of men and materiel in the Pacific Islands, and Japan itself was being heavily bombed by American planes.

At the end of the year American planes damaged the Shanghai Power Company in the former International Settlement, leaving us without electricity for several days as the small French power company did not have sufficient output for the entire former

Concession. Every night Shanghai remained dark until the first light of dawn. When electricity was finally restored it was nevertheless automatically turned off at curfew time, while water and gas, always turned off during the air raids, were rationed to only a few hours following the all-clear signal. My mother and Amah then quickly cooked the meals while the houseboy filled the bathtub with water. After dusk no one dared venture outside. Despite the presence of Japanese soldiers patrolling the streets with their guns and bayonets, purse snatching and hold-ups with knives continued and burglaries of homes became rampant. It was useless to call the police for help for they were too busy issuing edicts to the local populace to refrain from spreading rumors about the war, which they attested were lies originating with the Allies and Chiang Kai-shek's Chungking government.

New Year 1945 was greeted in darkened homes with high hopes after we heard that American troops had landed in the Philippines and the Germans were losing the war; unquestionably the Japanese occupation of Shanghai was nearing its end. In January the Japanese removed the five-ton bronze World War I memorial from the cenotaph on the Bund and sent it to the Sino-Japanese Metal Recovery Office in Nantao to be melted. Foreigners remarked on the irony of this action, which desecrated the memory of Japan's own soldiers who fought and died on the side of the Allies during World War I. When I cycled on the Bund it was very strange to no longer see the large angel perched on the column with her enormous wings.

One very cold morning in March of 1945, Amah rushed in warning us to stay indoors because Japanese soldiers, heavily armed and riding tanks, had surrounded the Bernez-Cambot and Marcaire garrisons where the French colonial army was billeted. My father wondered why the Japanese had not disarmed the French soldiers a year ago when the Vichy government had collapsed and Free French forces were fighting against Germany. My parents telephoned their friends to find out what was happening but no one had an answer. We later learned that

Japanese soldiers had encircled the French garrisons at night and ordered the commander to surrender with all armaments intact, otherwise the two garrisons would be destroyed and reprisals taken against French nationals. Capitulation was the only option for the 300 inadequately armed French officers and 1,000 Indochinese soldiers. The Japanese general and his staff entered the Bernez-Cambot garrison followed by photographers who filmed the peaceful surrender by the French officers. When the trucks carrying captured military equipment rumbled out of the garrison Chinese bystanders applauded, not for the despised Japanese but for the downfall of the French. These two French garrisons in Shanghai got off lightly, however, in comparison to their comrades-in-arms in Japanese-occupied Indochina, where French officers who refused to surrender were imprisoned or beheaded. A few months later the French colonial army suffered another blow in Shanghai when the Annamite and Tonkinese soldiers revolted against their French officers by declaring their solidarity with a revolutionary party in French Indochina led by Ho Chi Minh. They declared their solidarity with the Japanese military and were allowed to display the red and yellow flag of a free Indochina.

My sisters and I believed that only the garrison was surrounded so we rode our bicycles to school later that morning. When we arrived, however, we saw Japanese soldiers in the school yard and milling around the building. We quickly pedaled home and excitedly phoned our classmates, speculating on whether the school year would now end in March instead of late June. Our hopes were dashed within a week's time though, when the student body and instructors of the Collège Français – the word "Municipal" had been officially removed from all documents by fall 1943 – were transferred to the Ecole Rémi. We attended classes in the afternoon while the Rémi students went to school in the morning. We met at sporting events, where we spoke to them in English as we did not want to hear them speak "our" French with grammatical mistakes or tainted by a Russian accent.

As promised by the Japanese authorities, French nationals were not harmed, although those still in the employ of the Japanese-controlled 8th District municipality – the successor to the Concession – were eventually fired and many French-owned buildings and businesses were expropriated without any monetary compensation to the owners. The Cercle Sportif Français closed its doors and became the headquarters for the Japanese army. Following these measures more and more unemployed French nationals had to rely on basic foodstuffs distributed at nominal prices or free from charities for those who no longer had the means to pay.

In the following months we learned that British, American and Soviet troops had overpowered the German army in Europe, the American navy had destroyed the bulk of the Japanese fleet, and American Marines had captured more Japanese-held islands in the Pacific. We also heard that Manila had been liberated in March 1945, and that a strategically located island named Okinawa was taken by the Americans, but at the cost of thousands of lives. Long-range American fighter planes – the P38, P51 and B17 – flew from the newly conquered islands in the Pacific and joined the B-29s in their assault on the districts surrounding Shanghai. As these raids increased to twice a week, I saw planes tracing the letter "V" in the sky.

XMHA continued to spout farcical lies about German and Japanese victories. In April, however, one piece of triumphant Japanese propaganda turned out to be true, namely that President Franklin D. Roosevelt, the "cowardly" enemy of Japan and Germany, had died. This very sad news was soon overshadowed by more good news though: the Italian fascist dictator Benito Mussolini was found by partisans, shot and hung by his heels; Hitler committed suicide in his bunker; Germany surrendered unconditionally and Roosevelt's successor, Harry S. Truman, and the Allied leaders had accepted Germany's surrender. The staff of the German consulate in Shanghai, faithful to the end to their Nazi ideology and to their Fuehrer, held a memorial service for Hitler attended by "neutral" diplomats and representatives of countries in Asia still controlled by the Japanese.

After Germany's surrender in Berlin, the Japanese in Shanghai ordered the confiscation of all German-owned buildings and enterprises and we wondered whether German nationals would also be sent to internment camps; but this did not occur. I could appreciate the irony that my German acquaintances Muschie and her brother Hans were now considered enemy nationals while the French and the stateless Russians were still not placed in any category – neutral or enemy – by the Japanese military. In early May I celebrated with my friends the capitulation of Nazi Germany and later VE Day at both the Russian and Jewish clubs, which had been allowed to remain open throughout the entire Japanese occupation. Phones were ringing off the hook as we repeatedly shared the unbelievable news that Nazi Germany no longer existed. People began wearing red paper flowers on the lapels of their suits or jackets. Our outbursts of joy were tempered, however, by the fact that Japan was still at war with the Allies, while the refugees in Hongkew still feared American planes targeting warehouses could inadvertently drop bombs on the Designated Area where they lived. Their prediction became a reality when in late July bombs aimed at a fuel storage tank in Hongkew fell instead in an area adjacent to the Designated Area. Over 200 Chinese and 34 Jewish refugees were killed in their homes and in the streets, and nearly 1,000 Chinese residents were wounded. Rescuers, Chinese and refugees who seldom associated with each other, worked tirelessly together to extricate the dead and rush the wounded to a hospital.

Although there were still no indications that Japan was ready to surrender, Shanghailanders celebrated at parties – albeit without much food or drink – the end of Nazism and fascism, and the inevitable demise of Japan. On August 5, 1945, I invited many of my classmates to my eighteenth birthday party at our home, where we sang "God Save the King" and "La Marseillaise" instead of the ode to Maréchal Pétain we had sung for the last four years. We could carry the tune of the American national anthem but very few of us knew the words. We drank many toasts of ice water and tea to the Allies and to the end of the Japanese occupation. Despite empty shelves in the department stores, my guests brought me perfume, handkerchiefs, scarves and flowers from their garden, for even during the war years it was impolite to come empty-handed to a party. A few days after my birthday we heard that a city in Japan – Hiroshima – had been devastated on August 6 by a very powerful American bomb which killed thousands upon thousands of inhabitants.

Two events occurred simultaneously that we hoped would force Japan to capitulate. On August 9, the United States obliterated another Japanese city – Nagasaki – with a bomb as destructive as the first one, and on that morning the Soviet Union declared war on Japan and attacked Manchukuo. The Japanese authorities in Shanghai, as meticulous as ever despite their dire situation, immediately took action against Soviet citizens, several of whom were arrested as spies for the Allies, while the Soviet Club, and other buildings and assets owned by their nationals were immediately confiscated. My father's sister Sonia, her husband, daughter and son-in-law had all become Soviet citizens at the beginning of the Japanese occupation, believing it was safer to have a passport than to be stateless. (They had tried to convince my father to apply for Soviet citizenship but he had adamantly refused, as he had earlier the suggestion to acquire a Chinese passport.) Aunty Sonia's daughter Sarah, who was playing mahjong at the Soviet Club on the day the USSR attacked Japan, was arrested and interrogated but released within a couple of hours. The Japanese did not seem to know how to handle this new group of enemy nationals and neither they nor the Germans were sent to internment camps. Our relatives, fearing their large apartment would be taken by the Japanese, asked us to store their personal effects in our home. They arrived with several rickshaws piled with suitcases containing gold bars, silver artifacts, jewelry, clothing and family documents.

A week later my French classmates Ginette Grillon, Bernard Saint-Oyant and his sister Huguette rushed into our house shouting that Japan had capitulated and that Maréchal Philippe Pétain had been sentenced to death by a French tribunal. We wanted to celebrate by sneaking into the Ecole Rémi to tear down all the posters of the Maréchal but curfew was approaching and there was still no official confirmation that Japan had capitulated. We spent the night on the phone relaying or receiving news about Japanese soldiers leaving the city. My family went to bed in the early hours of the morning and when we woke up we were disappointed to hear on the radio that rumors about Japan's capitulation were false. Chinese residents, however, had surreptitiously and fearlessly placed Kuomintang national flags on some street corners. These were quickly removed by the still-efficient Japanese authorities.

On August 15 Shanghailanders with shortwave radios heard Emperor Hirohito announce on the airwaves in his very squeaky voice that Japan had lost the war. This was confirmed the following day when I heard the announcer on XMHA read in very gloomy tones that Japan had surrendered unilaterally to the Allies, and that a peace treaty between Japan and the United States would be signed by the end of the month.

Although the occupation of Shanghai had ended, Japanese soldiers and marines had not disappeared, and were still guarding buildings and patrolling the streets with their guns and bayonets. They did not react or even move when they were spat upon by the Chinese – who surely would have been more vengeful if they had owned guns. We later learned that the Japanese had received orders from the Allies to safeguard Shanghai from looting, demonstrations and other disturbances, and to wait for the arrival of Chiang Kai-shek's soldiers to replace them.

The conclusion to World War II ended Japan's thirteen-year occupation of China and its three-and-a-half year occupation of Shanghai. Many Shanghailanders believed their former comfortable lifestyle would return, even without the benefit of extraterritoriality. The economy would surely be stabilized and inflation brought under control.

In August of 1945 I exchanged one US dollar on the black market for 100,000 Chinese yuan.

21
Victory and Euphoria

AFTER JAPAN'S capitulation, American B-29s airdropped food packages into the various civilian internment camps, and a few days later about 20 American officers and men of the Prisoners of War and Internees Recovery Team came to Shanghai to arrange for the release of the Allied internees from their camps and the return of their former properties in Shanghai. This team also inspected the Designated Area, and arranged for supplies and medicine to be distributed to the Jewish refugees. Members of this mission were invited by the very wealthy Sephardic couple, Lawrence and Muriel Kadoorie, to reside in their beautiful mansion, "Marble Hall", in the former International Settlement. This luxurious home was still in good condition because Lawrence Kadoorie's elderly and sickly father, Sir Elly Kadoorie, a British citizen, had been allowed to live there during the war years, albeit under house arrest. It was not his advanced age which kept him out of the internment camp but the financial help he had provided the Japanese government at the time of the devastating earthquake in Tokyo in 1921. The Japanese authorities did remember past acts, some good and some bad, and reciprocated accordingly.

With the victory of the Allies, all Shanghai was euphoric. Years of stress, anxiety and fear under the Japanese occupation had disappeared, replaced by smiles and tears of joy. While the Americans were flying Chinese troops to Peking, Shanghai and Canton to help the Nationalist government re-establish its authority over liberated China, the Chinese communists had their own agenda, rushing to occupy Manchuria before Chiang Kai-shek's army could reach it. The communists discovered, however, that many of the factories and warehouses built by the Japanese had been dismantled by the Soviet army when it invaded this northern province and had sent all of the equipment and machinery to Siberia.

Our social life was hectic, with *tiffins* (luncheons), teas and dinners to celebrate our regained freedom and our positive outlooks towards a prosperous future in Shanghai. The Allied civilian internees stayed in their camps until housing could be found for them but they were able to leave for the day to visit friends in Shanghai. Uncle Ralph, Julie and her son Ronnie came to spend a day with us and we were surprised to note that despite the severe shortage of food during their two-and-a-half years' incarceration in Lunghwa Camp, Uncle Ralph and Julie had put on weight and both had a healthy tan from their work in the camp's vegetable garden. They were bitter about their incarceration, though Ronnie claimed he was happy because he did not have to go to school on a regular basis, and had enjoyed playing tricks on the Japanese guards. Uncle Ralph and Julie remarked how strange it was to sit at a table covered with a crisp linen tablecloth and laden with food, and to use silverware and attractive china instead of scraping the last morsel of food from tin plates and mugs. They told us some internees had become too weak to move about while others had lost all interest in life, no longer cared about their demeanor and stopped washing themselves. Internees too slow to obey orders had been brutally mistreated by the guards, while some who tried to escape did not survive the beatings and torture that followed. The only things that were plentiful were the endless rumors.

On one occasion my mother invited my Belgian classmate Poupée Bodson and her sister for lunch, who had also been in the Lunghwa camp, and a young British family from the Chapei camp. The British couple complained that although they were enemy nationals they should never have been incarcerated as they were born in Shanghai and had never been to England. I, as a person without a country, could not understand their bizarre reasoning and felt they should have been proud to be citizens of the British Empire. While this couple tried to talk about their miserable lives in their camp, Poupée steered the conversation towards the exciting life she had led during her incarceration with the young American internees from the SS *President Harrison*.

My father, who had returned to work at Sun Life Assurance Company when it reopened soon after the end of the war, was told by his manager Ernest Harris that the worst news at his Chapei internment camp was learning in April of the death of President Roosevelt. All the internees from the various Allied countries had held memorial services for the American President after permission was surprisingly granted by their camp commandant. Mr. Harris found it amazing to see the Japanese camp guards stand at attention during the solemn proceedings in honor of an Allied head of state, a despised enemy whose country was bringing Japan to its knees. When Emperor Hirohito announced Japan's capitulation and unconditional surrender to the Allies, the same commandant assembled all the internees in front of one of the buildings and informed them of Japan's defeat and that the war was over. He complimented them on their obedience to the rules and regulations during their incarceration, expressed his regret about the constant shortage of food and ended his brief speech stating, "You go to your freedom while I go to an internment camp." Ernest Harris added that after this strange gathering, American, Belgian, British, Canadian and Dutch flags, which had been smuggled into the camps, were raised atop the camp buildings.

The Jewish refugees in their Designated Area in Hongkew were interviewed by representatives of the United Nations Relief and Rehabilitation Agency (UNRRA) regarding immigration procedures to the United States, Canada, Australia and Latin America, countries that during the Nazi era had refused to increase their quotas.

Chinese soldiers were being flown in on American planes from the interior of China to replace the Japanese sentries, who were still stoically guarding buildings and deserted factories against looters. The newly arrived 6th Marine Regiment was sent to Tsingtao to disarm the Japanese forces still there and to control the city until the arrival of Chiang Kai-shek's troops. In Shanghai workmen began to erect large bamboo arches in anticipation of the victory parades for the Kuomintang army and the American and British forces. Protocol dictated that the Chinese soldiers would arrive first in the city and parade alone, followed at a later date by the Americans and the British. There would be no military parade by the French because of Vichy's wartime collaboration with the Nazis.

On August 26, 1945, Chiang Kai-shek's troops, who had lost nearly all their battles against the Japanese, arrived in Shanghai to a tumultuous welcome. They marched in the streets of the former foreign enclaves under arches covered with colorful bunting, paper flowers, Kuomintang flags and portraits of Chiang. The entire city was in a festive mood, and the European community started holding galas and grand balls, wearing once again their evening gowns and tuxedos, which had to be sent to dry cleaners to remove the smell of moth balls.

Businessmen and shop owners were anxiously anticipating the arrival of the Allied troops, especially the American soldiers and airmen who had served in the Philippines, Okinawa and the China-India-Burma theater of operations. These men were flush with dollars they had not been able to spend during the war years. Within a week of the Kuomintang parade British and American soldiers, sailors and marines held their own parades, marching in the streets or riding in trucks and jeeps. Throngs of Chinese and Shanghailanders once again lined the parade route and greeted these men as enthusiastically as they had the Kuomintang soldiers. My sisters and I, like other foreigners, were hugely excited to see these soldiers, especially the Americans in their smart khaki uniforms and peaked caps, chomping on their eternal chewing gum, waving and whistling at the women and acting the same as their counterparts had in pre-World War II

Shanghai.

September 2, 1945, was a memorable day in Shanghai, as Japan signed a peace treaty with the United States, England, the Soviet Union and the Republic of China. Flags of these countries, which entrepreneurial shopkeepers had secretly sewn, fluttered from windows, lamp posts and rooftops. The most popular flag was the American flag – not always with the correct number of stars – which I, too, proudly attached to the handlebars of my bicycle.

Social activities resumed and Shanghailanders recaptured their *joie de vivre*, confident that the city would revert quickly to its pre-war heyday of successful business endeavors and leisurely lifestyle. Many of the buildings, including our Collège Français, were returned to their owners. In September my parents invited 50 people for a buffet dinner for Riva's twentieth birthday. My mother, Amah and two cooks from another household prepared the feast while our houseboy cleaned the house from top to bottom. Our German neighbor Muschie, who was awaiting repatriation to Germany, came that morning to give Riva some writing paper and envelopes although she knew that neither she nor her brother were invited to the party. My parents felt it would be prudent since some guests (and I) might make derogatory remarks about the *sales Boches*. However, I felt a twinge of pity for Muschie, the native Shanghailander who, with her parents and brother, were bound for a devastated Germany, a country the siblings had never seen.

That evening bejeweled women in long brocade and silk, dresses and men in "smoking" (tuxedos) arrived by rickshaw and showered Riva with the pre-war standard gifts – necklaces, bracelets, French perfumes, American handbags and Chinese silver dollars as souvenirs. After dinner Jackie played several classical pieces on the piano and also performed a couple of Hungarian and Gypsy dances, decked out in a so-called Eastern peasant dress sewed by Lao Papa. Some of our male guests, having imbibed much vodka as the evening wore on, sang

American, English, French and Russian songs and national anthems accompanied on the piano by Jackie. They and the other guests repeatedly raised glasses to Riva's health and happiness – which now meant "catching" an American husband. By two o'clock in the morning the exhausted guests deemed it was time to return home, leaving behind big *cumshaws* (tips) for the servants who had worked tirelessly before and during the party, and who would have to spend many hours washing dishes and cleaning the house.

A few days later my mother was making preparations for a luncheon for her lady friends to celebrate her forty-second birthday. She had to cancel it at the last minute, however, when my cousin Julie called to ask her help in transporting Uncle Ralph's and her belongings from the internment camp to temporary housing in the St. Joseph Cathedral near the Bund. When my mother saw the living conditions in the camp she was so shocked that she immediately asked our relatives to spend a few days with us before settling down in their new quarters.

Soon after, Julie invited us to join her and other British internees for a party given in their honor by the British Royal Navy aboard one of their cruisers anchored on the Whangpoo River. My sisters and I were keen on going for we had not yet met British soldiers or sailors – whom we noticed were much less aggressive in trying to pick up or meet women than their American counterparts. Since Jackie and I were free that afternoon we went by rickshaw to the Customs House jetty on the Bund, where a great number of cruisers from various nations were crowding the river. A launch took us to the HMS *Belfast*, which had just arrived from Taiwan, and once aboard we were led to the canteen to pick up gifts of biscuits, chocolate bars, marmalade and cigarettes. Jackie and I, however, did not have the patience to wait in line in the stifling heat of the lower deck – unlike the former internees used to queuing up during their years of confinement. Instead we decided to tour the ship and were escorted by a young officer who later brought us tea and biscuits from his mess room. But to our disappointment he did not ask for our telephone number like the Americans would have, whether they meant to call or not.

The phone rang endlessly, however, for Riva. Her calls were mostly from American officers she met at parties, while I accepted invitations for dates from enlisted men I encountered in the street or at the YMCA. To my astonishment, I discovered that many enlisted men spoke ungrammatical English. They filled the cabarets and bars, especially in "Blood Alley" where, as before World War II, the American Military Police were often called in to stop fights or take the rowdy and often drunk men back to

Lily driving date in pedicab

their billets or ships. One evening while my friends and I were cycling along the Bund we saw American sailors, some rather inebriated, laughing and shouting like cowboys on their steeds as they cycled pedicabs with the astonished Chinese drivers in the passenger seats. The latter were even more surprised when the Americans compensated them generously as they rushed to the jetty on the Bund. Shore Patrol announcements blared over a public address system, directing the sailors to take the shuttle tenders to their respective ships. I wondered how such "boys" could have won a war!

Many of these young military men squandered their pay checks very quickly and, after exchanging their remaining dollars in the thriving black market, resorted to selling cigarettes, whiskey, canned food, sweaters, boots and the very popular Eisenhower-style field jackets to eager Chinese merchants and Westerners. Art connoisseurs among them traded their government-issued clothing or other small items for local artifacts and antiques – real or fake – to take back to the United States.

Riva and I were very selective of the Americans we dated or invited to our home for meals, always making sure, for our parents' sake, that they were well-mannered and did not pick their teeth or chew gum too loudly. The ones we brought home always thanked my mother profusely for her excellent cooking while I plied them with questions about their country, as I hardly knew anything about the history of the United States. America was barely mentioned in our history classes at our Collège Municipal Français – except the important role France played in helping the thirteen colonies gain their independence and some superficial reading about its *Guerre de Secession,* the devastating Civil War over slavery and states' rights.

There was never any fear that women would be mistreated by these young men, who usually behaved like friendly teenagers. The most they would ask for was a long goodnight kiss, which I readily offered, but we never furthered our amorous desires since I was terrified that I could become pregnant. If their desires

Lily in military Jeep

were too great they could always be satisfied by the hordes of Chinese, Korean and White Russian "taxi dancers" and "sing-song girls" waiting for them in the cabarets and nightclubs. My dates, the enlisted men, Jerry, Dick and Richard from the army, navy and Marines, took me for rides in their jeeps, always complaining about having to drive on the left side of the road. I was scared as they drove erratically, barely missing cars, rickshaws, bicycles, wheelbarrows and jaywalkers, who would swear at these "foreign devils" in uniform. Traffic was constantly brought to a standstill by US army jeeps, weapons carriers and lumbering trucks competing for space with all other forms of local transportation. I repeatedly warned my dates to slow down but to no avail, even when I reminded them that an American soldier had recently driven his truck on the wrong side of the road and slammed into a pedicab, killing its driver and two passengers, and injuring several pedestrians. Repeated accidents of this kind led to negotiations between the Chinese authorities and the Americans, who were obliged to pay monetary compensation, whether they were at fault or not, to families of victims injured or killed in the streets of Shanghai.

These incidents, the heavy American presence in China and the US military aid provided to the Kuomintang government may have been the catalyst for changing the vehicular traffic pattern in Shanghai from the left to the right side on January 1, 1946. England's political and economic power in China – and now even its rules of the road – which had spanned a century, was clearly being replaced by that of the United States of America.

Political Rumblings

NEW YEAR 1946 was electrifying – it was the first time in nearly four years that we could celebrate happily and loudly, and not worry about curfew hours. The Kuomintang and the communists had agreed on a ceasefire, with a coalition government as a possibility, thanks to the mediating efforts of General George C. Marshall, President Truman's special representative to China. In February the Shanghainese celebrated their New Year with much gusto, and continuous noise from firecrackers and the banging of drums and cymbals. Our amah and houseboy, dressed in their best clothes, left to spend a few days with their families and friends in their villages in "Ningpo mofa" ("further than Ningpo"). My mother gave them year-end bonuses in bright red envelopes to help pay off the debts they complained about and start the year with a clean slate.

Our school was closed for Chinese New Year so Jackie and I decided to ride our bicycles to Avenue Joffre, still called "Yaffee Lu", to watch the colorful celebration. Middle-class Chinese women were dressed in their *qipao* – the high-collared silk brocade and satin dress slit at the sides – while the men wore long black gowns, although more were now attired in European-style suits. Small boys in black gowns and skull caps topped with red glass balls, and little girls in bright red dresses, wearing lipstick and rouge, walked sprightly with their parents, decked out in their holiday outfits.

All day and all evening firecrackers sizzled and sputtered in the streets. Many shop owners set them off at the entrances to their flimsy wooden stores in the belief that launching them at their place of business would augur a successful financial year. The fronts of the closed stores were decorated with bright red streamers with characters expressing best wishes for the New Year, long life and much wealth. Street vendors were selling food and Jackie and I stopped at various stalls to purchase hot chestnuts, *da bing* and *you tiao*, as well as sweet rice wrapped in palm leaves and buns colored red for the occasion. We spent the evening strolling in the crowded streets, watching dragon dances and tumbling acrobats, and hearing musicians play various stringed instruments, flutes and cymbals that were all very jarring to our ears. Foreign nationals, especially the Allied internees, were also in a festive mood following the return of their homes and businesses.

France's Third Republic officially signed a treaty with the Kuomintang government in February 1946, abrogating all French extraterritorial rights in China, the earlier treaty between Vichy and Wang Ching-wei's puppet government not being considered legally valid. The former employees of the French Concession were shocked to learn they would not receive any remuneration for their long years of service in Shanghai because they were hired under contract by the municipality in the Concession – which no longer existed – and not by the French government. Many had no choice but to leave Shanghai and seek work in the French colonies in Africa, Asia or the Pacific islands. The small French garrison also left the city, presumably bound for Indochina. Retribution by the few Gaullists in Shanghai against the pro-Vichy majority was rare but early that year someone painted a large red swastika on the door of the home of my anti-Semitic classmate Michel Guillemin. With this badge of shame for a virulent pro-Nazi French family there for all the neighbors to see, his father Charles Guillemin subsequently committed suicide.

Chinese students and workers demonstrating for political and economic causes held many parades in Shanghai in 1946. They demanded the Soviets, China's wartime ally, return Dairen and the nearby Port Arthur fortification (built during the Czarist era), and criticized them harshly for dismantling the Japanese factories in Manchuria and removing the machinery to the Soviet Union. However, the Sino-Soviet Treaty, signed after the end of World War II, stipulated that the Soviets could keep their troops in Manchuria until they signed a peace treaty with Japan. I sided with the Chinese because the USSR had become a worrisome enemy in the brewing Cold War between capitalism and communism. The demonstrators also protested the conduct of drunken American soldiers in Shanghai, and vociferously criticized the assistance provided by the United States to a defeated Japan.

Chinese workers held demonstrations to complain about their wages, which could not keep pace with the rising cost of living and galloping inflation as the Chinese National Currency issued after the war rapidly lost its buying power. In September 1945 the exchange rate for one US dollar had been 500 CNC yuan but within four months the rate had ballooned to 4,000. The general public quickly became disillusioned with the Kuomintang government, which could not control inflation, was ruining small businesses and was corrupt at all levels. There were also serious concerns on the political front – the civil war had resumed in early 1946 and the communists seemed to be gaining military strength. Chiang Kai-shek's army and supplies had to be airlifted by US military planes into the north because many of the routes were now controlled by Mao Tse-tung's army. Rumors were rife that the United Nations Relief and Rehabilitation Agency's food relief for the poor had been diverted to the Nationalist army.

Despite these economic and political events, members of the various foreign communities returned to their private clubs, attended symphonies, ate in the best restaurants in town and drank in noisy cabarets packed with the militaries of various nations. Riva and I continued to go out with the Americans we met at various parties. One afternoon we saw in our living room two very handsome English navy petty officers, drinking tea and chatting with our mother. We were not too surprised to see strangers in our home since our matchmaking mother never hesitated to invite "gentlemen" over to meet her two older daughters. She had not picked up these two Englishmen, though – they had called on our family to extend regards from Aunty Riva in Sydney, where their ship had last docked. She sent with them gifts of Australian wool blankets and sweaters, remembering too well the damp and cold Shanghai nights.

Riva cancelled her date that evening for she, like all of us, was charmed by the two Englishmen, Dennis "Barry" Barrett and Ronald Martin, who were invited to stay for dinner. They described the countries they had visited and regaled us with stories about the native people of the British colonial empire, imitating their accents. They described their encounter with the Queen of Tonga, who had informed the ship's crew that "King George is very, very good man". When my mother discovered that Barry and Ronald enjoyed classical music she quickly produced Jackie to play some pieces on the piano and before they left my parents asked them to return, and also extended an invitation to some of their friends aboard their ship, the HMS *Euryalus*. On many subsequent evenings there were at least half a dozen English navy petty officers in our home, with whom we sang songs, played Chinese checkers and talked late into the night. My parents were delighted with these "true gentlemen" who did not chew gum or put their feet on our coffee table like our American dates and, to my father's delight, spoke grammatically correct English in such a pleasing accent!

Barry, a tall and very handsome dark-haired man with a warm smile and glistening white teeth, resembled the heart-throb movie actor Tyrone Power. Barry and Riva were quickly smitten with each other so I no longer insisted on joining them; instead, I went out with several of the English petty officers who had become regular habitués of our home. Jackie, then 14 years old, was elected by these men to be the unofficial mascot of their ship. She and I spent much time with them, going by rickshaw to the

British Club to see plays, variety shows or to the newly reopened movie theaters in the French Concession. On weekends we often accompanied them to the Racecourse to watch them play rugby and cricket, which we found strange and extremely boring.

Our patience at these games was rewarded, however, when Jackie and I were invited to spend an afternoon aboard their ship. As I stood on the deck of the HMS *Euryalus* I closed my eyes and imagined I was sailing to America without encumbrances such as passports and visas. We had tea in the petty officers' mess hall at a table laden with scones, biscuits, marmalade and pineapple juice, which we had not tasted for many years. The highlight of the tour was a visit to the radioman's cubicle, where a sailor placed a microphone in front of us and asked us to speak into it while a tape was whirring away. When he played it back Jackie and I were surprised to hear that we spoke English with a slight British intonation.

A few days later we were even more surprised, and then elated, when Riva, whose dates now called her Rebecca or the diminutive Becky, told us that Barry had asked her to marry him; however, she needed to discuss it with our parents since Barry was a Catholic. Surprisingly there was no objection from them since Riva indicated her children would be brought up in the Jewish faith and my father saw how happy she was. Barry readily acquiesced. Blinded by love, I believe he set aside all thoughts of excommunication if his children were not brought up in the Catholic faith. The engaged couple very soon had to part, however, when, after a one-month stay in Shanghai, the HMS *Euryalus* set sail for Hongkong. Barry wrote daily to Riva but she would never show the letters to Jackie or me, which we thought was unfair since we shared with her the amusing letters we received from our group of petty officers on the ship.

Three months after the departure of the HMS *Euryalus* from Shanghai, my mother received a letter from Barry's mother and shared it with Riva. When Riva read it she rushed to our bedroom crying uncontrollably. My mother told us that Barry's mother had written that no son of hers would marry a Jewish girl, that Barry had given in to her wishes and that the engagement was off. A few days later Riva received a letter from Barry, who also sent me a brief note asking that I relay to our family how sorry he was to have hurt us all. I never found out what he said in his last letter to his "darling Becky".

Riva slowly recovered from the sting of Barry's mother's letter and from her lost love after the US Army hired her as a secretary-stenographer. The American military was hiring English-speaking Russian, Hongkew refugee and Macanese men and women as truck drivers, clerks, stenographers, secretaries and sales clerks in the Post Exchange stores; the Chinese mainly worked in jobs that did not require any linguistic ability. The Chinese employees at the army and navy bases quickly learned the art of going on strike whenever they wanted a salary increase since the Americans always gave in to their demands, but Riva received US$95 a month, a princely salary at a time when the Chinese currency was spiraling out of control. Her income was especially welcomed because my father had just lost his job at Sun Life. This office, which had reopened a year earlier on an optimistic note, had closed down because many potential clients, especially the French, were leaving Shanghai. Riva's income, coupled with my mother's small entrepreneurial endeavors, helped defray expenses until my father could find a salaried position.

Riva was assigned to the American Graves Registration Service (AGRS) in the Wheelock building in the former Settlement where many US government agencies were located. The purpose and goal of the AGRS was to find the remains of American aviators and flight crews whose planes had been downed in China. Riva told us the commanding officer of her unit, Colonel Charles Kearney from the strange-sounding city of Dubuque in Iowa, and his team encountered difficulties in locating and recovering the bodies, that they had to build flimsy rope bridges to cross rivers, sail on sampans and makeshift rafts, or climb very steep mountain passes. Riva explained that Lolo tribesmen in the border regions between French Indochina and China often cooperated with the American recovery teams and took them to the sites where US planes could have crashed, but during the war years Chinese officials, under threat of death from the Japanese, rarely kept records of any downed American planes. In addition to these obstacles, the AGRS had to cope with Chinese bandits who "kidnapped" skeletons from unmarked graves and held them for ransom before selling them to the recovery teams. The latter soon discovered that in many instances these remains were not those of American fighter pilots or their crews anyway and stopped paying for skeletons, forcing the bandits to seek their fortune elsewhere.

The officers and men at AGRS checked and compiled clues on the crash sites and Riva typed reports once the remains had been identified. She often cried at her desk when letters were sent to families notifying them of the confirmed death of a son or husband. The grimness was dispelled in the evenings, however, by Riva's whirlwind social life with the officers she met at work. The AGRS office was open seven days a week even though it was becoming more difficult to send teams to areas where fighting between the Kuomintang and the communist forces had erupted. Riva worked on Sundays but had two days off during the week that gave her the opportunity to shop for clothes and spend her evenings dining and dancing until late at night.

Riva took a rickshaw or a pedicab to work but there were always co-workers and dates willing to drive her home in a jeep or in an army truck. She brought us copies of the *Stars and Stripes* – the US Armed forces newspaper – and American movie magazines, from which we learned about the romances of Hollywood pin-up girls and their handsome leading men. We got a rosy concept of America from their magazines and movies, where secretaries led charmed lives and, once married, prepared mouth-watering meals for their families in spotless kitchens replete with the latest gadgets. As in old Shanghai, mothers sent their husbands off to work and their children to school and then spent the day drinking coffee, playing cards and gossiping with their neighbors. In the movies the housewife was often helped by a black maid who spoke in a screechy and childish voice with an accent we could not understand.

My social life with the Americans was not as hectic as Riva's but I did date Mac, a private in the Marines, and later Preston then Don, both army corporals. They took me to the Enlisted Men's Club where we ate hamburgers, drank Coca Cola, watched American movies, and danced to orchestra music and songs by Frank Sinatra, Dick Haymes, Vaughn Monroe and the Andrew Sisters. When my date took me home we would say good-bye at the front door, kiss each other on the cheek and sometimes on the lips – and if he had drunk a little too much he might dare to give me a "French kiss", which I would readily return.

I received several marriage proposals – but after my eager acceptance these men inevitably disappeared and never called me again. In one instance, however, Private First Class Tom Noble and I did get engaged informally, and soon after his departure he sent me a Western Union telegram from San Francisco that said, "Chop, chop to America. STOP. Will write. STOP. Love. STOP. Noble." He never wrote though, and the opportunity to settle in America disappeared with him. I had no idea what married life entailed beyond what I had observed of my parents and their friends. At the age of 20 I was living in a cocoon in the comfortable last vestiges of colonialism, with parents who supported me financially, servants who catered to my whims, and with men who flattered me. I was emotionally immature.

While European women from "good" families were in great demand as dates among the American military temporarily stranded in Shanghai, satisfaction of their sexual needs generally only came from bar girls and prostitutes. A brother of one of my classmates told me that doctors at the US army hospital, worried about the increase of gonorrhea and syphilis in the armed forces, issued condoms and tubes of medicinal cream. Obviously, these precautions were not often followed carefully given the large numbers of advanced cases of venereal disease. The proliferation of unused condoms was a boon, however, to street vendors, who sold them as balloons to little children who held them aloft on a string, running around gleefully with their new toy.

Despite our exciting social life, my friends and I became concerned that this would end soon when more American soldiers, sailors and Marines were sent back to the United States to be discharged, while the civil war continued unabated. In July 1946 General Albert C. Wedemeyer, in his capacity as Special Envoy to President Truman, came to renew peace negotiations between the warring parties.

General Wedemeyer stayed in Shanghai in a big house next to our complex on Route Delastre, as had General George Marshall. I never did get a glimpse of our famous neighbor but on several occasions I did see General Wedemeyer's olive green staff car whizzing by and waved wildly to get his attention, to no avail. With the two Chinese political sides diametrically opposed, one backed by a disenchanted army led by corrupt officers, the other by intensely disciplined soldiers indoctrinated in their goal to "liberate the masses" from abject poverty in a feudal society, Wedemeyer's talks did not succeed. Chiang Kai-shek would not consider relinquishing any power to Mao Tse-tung, and by November 1946 the fighting had resumed in full force, but now the communist revolutionary army was acquiring American war materiel left on the battlefields or purchased from Kuomintang deserters.

We could no longer ignore this civil war.

23 Immigration and Exodus

WITH THE civil war escalating and the economy in a downward spiral, the time had come to leave Shanghai – but how?

My parents, my sisters and I trooped over to the crowded American consulate, confident that we would receive an immigration quota number in the near future thanks to Aunty Brania and her husband in San Francisco, who had offered to sponsor us. This in effect guaranteed that we would not be a financial burden on the United States government. We discovered, however, that the quota numbers were based on an individual's place of birth, meaning we could not leave as a family unit since my mother was born in Russia, my father supposedly in Romania and my sisters and I in China. In addition, the immigration law was based on the ethnic composition of the population of the United States in 1921. My mother could immigrate rather quickly since the Russian quota was wide open as no one could leave Stalin's Soviet Union, but my sisters and I came under the National Origins Act of 1924, which severely restricted immigration from outside the Western Hemisphere.

I checked an encyclopedia and learned about the Chinese Exclusion Act of 1882 that barred the immigration and entry of Chinese laborers to the United States. The Asiatic Barred Zone Act forbade Asians from entering the United States and later the Immigration Act of 1917 disallowed those living in the United States permanent residency status. With China an ally of the United States in World War II, the Chinese Exclusion Act was repealed in 1943, the same year America abrogated all its extraterritorial rights in China. This repeal, however, was a token gesture since the quota for Chinese immigrants was limited to 105 individuals per year. More relevant to our family was the fact that a separate quota for Caucasians born in Asia was just as restrictive.

Riva and I were affected by this ruling but not Jackie, who could immigrate as a minor under my mother's Russian quota number. My father, who upon his arrival in China had listed his birth place as Chisinau, Romania and not Radomyshel, Ukraine, could not apply as a Russian quota immigrant. The American consul explained that no quota system had yet been established for Romania since no official peace treaty had been signed with that country, a wartime ally of Nazi Germany. He reassured my father that once my mother was in the United States he could apply for the preference quota as the husband of an immigrant. The American official then suggested to Riva and I that, while waiting for our "White" China quota, we should consider applying for student visas to the United States. He added jokingly that perhaps both of us could save some time if we married American men and left for the United States as war brides. Riva's flirting with him during the interview had surely given him the opportunity to make such an undiplomatic remark.

By January 1947 the US government had realized the futility of further mediation in the civil war and decided to withdraw all its troops based in China. That spring, Riva met a young American civilian, a former lieutenant in the United States Navy who, after his military discharge, had remained in Shanghai as an advisor to the Chinese navy. John Quimby, as striking in his looks as Riva's first love Barry, told our family he had graduated from Cornell University as an engineer and that he was from Sheboygan, Wisconsin, a state unfamiliar to us. My father commented that claims by Americans of their good upbringing and good schools were often just exaggerations, for these men could in reality be dish-washers or waiters in some small town with a strange Indian name. He soon realized, however, that John was in fact educated. Riva started going out exclusively with John and he became a regular visitor in our home, sharing many meals with us. Jackie and I wondered whether they would get married and whether my parents were willing to accept, once again, that Riva marry a Christian.

While romance was in the air in our home, Shanghai was being affected economically by the raging civil war in the north and the blatant corruption of the Kuomintang government. The millions of US dollars destined for agricultural programs in China and the shiploads of rice provided by the UNRRA for the poor and starving Chinese were waylaid by top government officials who hoarded the food in warehouses and later sold it on the black market. The UNRRA could not stem the tide of corruption because all assistance programs had to pass through Chinese government agencies before anything trickled down for distribution to the poor. It was believed that much of the relief went to the Nationalist army battling the communists in the north.

The Chinese "Big Four Families" – those of Chiang Kai-shek; Minister of Finance H.H. Kung, who married the oldest of the Soong sisters; T.V. Soong, the sisters' Harvard-trained brother, a financial advisor to the President; and the brothers Chen Li-fu and Chen Guo-fu – enriched themselves even more rapaciously after the UNRRA transferred the administration of its holdings to the Chinese government. The United States government, under pressure from Congress and the powerful China Lobby enamored of Madame Chiang Kai-shek, was obsessively worried about a communist takeover of China. Fearing encroachment and the "domino effect" of other Asian countries possibly being taken by the "Reds", Congress continued military aid to the Kuomintang.

I saw wealthy Chinese and many government officials riding in American-made cars – their favorite was the Cadillac – while on the streets of Shanghai increasing numbers of Chinese adults and children begged for food. Chinese and Westerners continued to flaunt their wealth in restaurants, cabarets and bars, where food and drinks were plentiful. My father, although cautious by nature, decided to form a partnership with two friends to open a nightclub called "The Four Aces" on Bubbling Well Road. It was immediately successful, frequented by foreign and Chinese men and women who spent the evenings eating Russian food, drinking vodka and whiskey, watching the nightly floor show by Russian dancers and dancing to jazz played by our neighbors, the two Hungarian musicians. The nightclub, listed as "In Bounds" (i.e. acceptable) by the American military police, was always crowded with servicemen spending money into the early hours of the morning. It was strange for my sisters and me to think that our staid father was now the owner of a nightclub but we were pleased that with the profits he was able to purchase a rental apartment building in the former Concession with several partners.

It was a sad time, however, for our family. Uncle Ralph, Julie and Ronnie left for Australia, while my classmates whom I had known since kindergarten were sailing to France or its colonies in Africa and Asia. Although the French were relieved to leave a China in political turmoil, they were nevertheless worried about their future since they did not know what awaited them, especially in France, a country they barely knew and which was slowly recovering from the war. The European refugees from the Designated Area in Hongkew were also leaving as they were now considered "displaced persons" by the International Refugee Organization and consequently received collective immigration visas to the United States, Canada and Australia.

The White Russian stateless émigrés were not considered "displaced persons" and their only recourse was to wait for immigration visas to Australia, Canada and, preferably, the United States. When the USSR Consulate offered them Soviet citizenship and entry to Russia, over 4,000 White Russians opted to return "home" despite some trepidation that their bourgeois background would be an anomaly in Stalin's Russia. It was no longer possible for the émigrés to go overland from Manchuria to the USSR because of the Chinese civil war in that region. Instead they sailed on Russian passenger ships from Shanghai to Vladivostok – and many were never heard from again. Soon after their arrival in the USSR the Soviet government stopped all mail services and telephone connections between the returnees and their friends in various countries. A number of young Russian women married American servicemen and some, who could not find a marriageable partner, paid US$10,000 for sham marriages to leave Shanghai as post-war brides. But a number of servicemen left behind fiancées and girlfriends with promises of marriage that never materialized.

My mother decided to start a small import-export cottage industry with her sister Brania in San Francisco. Brania sent plastic handbags, belts and nylon stockings, which were much in demand, and my mother sold them rapidly to eager customers. One of Riva's supervisors, an American colonel who came regularly to our home, gave my mother permission to use his Army Post Office address to correspond with Brania since the Chinese mail system was very erratic. A few months later, however, the colonel was reprimanded by his commander when it was discovered that Aunty Brania had used his mailing address to send goods to my mother. Fortunately the colonel managed to wriggle out of this dilemma but Riva berated my mother. After that she used the regular shipping route and, despite high customs duty on American imports, she was still able to make a substantial profit. As more of her European customers left China she succeeded in selling her goods to wealthy Chinese women keen to display the latest American acquisitions.

In April 1947 the departure of the American military was accelerated when Chinese communist soldiers attacked the artillery supply depot of the 6th Marine Regiment in Tsingtao, hoping to secure the stored ammunition. That month I read in the *China Press* that six Marines were killed in a separate "Red" attack and 16 wounded in a "surprise communist raid". To me this seemed a brazen act against the United States and I wondered why the Americans did not retaliate when attacked without any provocation. One month later, in the May 3 issue of the *China Press,* I read that Admiral Louis Denfeld, in charge of naval facilities in China, had declared all naval bases would be closed by July 1,except for a small detachment of Marines in Tsingtao. By now, the communist armies were defeating the Kuomintang forces on all fronts and were moving down from the north.

Inflation was out of control; wages and salaries paid in Chinese currency had to be spent or exchanged for US Dollars immediately. Workers in many factories began receiving their wages in goods and food lots in lieu of bank notes that lost their value by the hour. Bank clerks tied bundles of one million CNC yuan notes together and then placed a wax seal on the top of these "bricks", as they were mockingly called. These seals were rarely broken because of daily, and oftentimes hourly hyperinflation. When my mother, my sisters and I went shopping we placed bundles of banknotes on the back of our bicycles and not in the front baskets since they were not large enough to contain them. Very few urchins and beggars chased after us as we maneuvered our bicycles with the dangling bulky bank notes because even they knew that this currency did not have much buying power. It was more beneficial for them to steal food from the street vendors or beg American servicemen for nickels, dimes and quarters. Chinese workers continued to demonstrate for livable wages but they could not hold political rallies to denounce the civil war destroying China, fearful of being accused of siding with the "Reds". One political rally, however, was allowed in Shanghai in April 1947, when thousands of Jewish residents gathered in a park to protest the hanging in British-mandated Palestine of four members of Irgun Zvai Leumi, a militant Zionist group that fought for the establishment of an independent Jewish state in that country. My mother, fearful of anti-Semitic counter-demonstrations, a carry-over from her days in Czarist Russia, forbade us to attend.

By the end of the summer of 1947 I had finally, at age 20,

finished high school. I immediately looked for work as I was tired of asking my mother for money, always having to explain how I would spend it and hearing her complain about the out-of-control inflation. By August 1947 the exchange rate was 60,000 CNC yuan to one American dollar. I signed up for typing and "Gregg" shorthand lessons since I wanted to be a secretary and work for the American military, but by the time I finished these courses the Americans were no longer hiring so I had to apply for office jobs in the private sector.

I was interviewed by the manager of a French trading firm but failed the typing test since my training in this skill was not in the French language. I was also interviewed at an insurance company by a Macanese manager who asked me if I would mind working directly for him. Both he and I, born and bred in Shanghai, were very conscious of the fact that Europeans did not work for Eurasians. Our racial prejudices still prevailed in 1947. It was natural for him to pose such a question and polite of me to lie that I did not have any qualms, but I turned down his offer.

Walter Kerr, the Secretary of the Trusteeship Committee of the British-owned Racecourse on Bubbling Well Road, finally hired me in the fall; here I would look up, ethnically, to my boss. Though horse races were no longer held, one of the small buildings was used as a Racecourse Club for members of various nationalities, including English-speaking Chinese, all of whom could use the basketball and tennis courts, and play mahjong, ping pong and card games. Members also could use the swimming pool in an adjoining club administered by the Welfare and Recreation Office of the United States Navy, appropriately named the "WROndez-vous Club" for its American civilian employees. Sometimes they invited me for dinner or to the movies but I quickly discovered they were not as generous as their military counterparts.

I worked as Mr. Kerr's private secretary and office manager, supervising two Macanese women who collected dues from the 3,000 foreign and Chinese club members. These clerks noted the monthly membership fees on cards, while I typed letters for my boss and persuaded delinquent members to pay their dues on time. Since membership was dropping as foreign members left Shanghai I cajoled Westerners I met at social events to join our club. I spoke to them in their native language, in French or Russian, reminding them that our Racecourse Club was one of the few foreign clubs left in Shanghai and, more importantly, it was the least expensive. Mr. Kerr, ever the English *taipan*, bemoaned the end of extraterritoriality – as did I. He constantly reminded me that China would soon be taken over and controlled by communist "bandits". I disagreed with him since I was confident that the American government, fearful of communism, would continue to help Chiang Kai-shek despite his continued losses in the civil war.

I believe the only time I saw Walter Kerr smile was on a day in November of 1947 when we heard on the radio a replay of the wedding ceremony of Princess Elizabeth to the Duke of Edinburgh. Shanghailanders were thrilled to hear pleasant news, even from afar, since most of them believed the People's Liberation Army would inevitably win the civil war and the communists would rule China.

Economic and Political Debacle

IN EARLY 1948 Shanghai residents, Chinese and foreign, worried about the communist army's advance southward, did not celebrate Chinese New Year with the same gusto as in the past two years. Runaway inflation, corruption and mismanagement by the Kuomintang clique and their acolytes continued unabated. It was common knowledge that Madame Chiang Kai-shek's brother, T.V. Soong, and her older sister, Soong Ai-ling, controlled the four largest banks in Shanghai as well as the various expropriated foreign utility companies. They enriched themselves by buying US dollars at the official low rate of exchange, and selling these dollars on the black market at exorbitantly high rates, and then purchasing more dollars at the low official rate. Subsequently they deposited millions of US dollars into secret bank accounts in Switzerland. The "Four Families" played this currency scam over and over again while the general public bought US dollars on the black market since very few could be purchased at government banks. The only family member who stayed out of this plunder was Soong Ching-ling, the widow of Dr. Sun Yat-sen.

This cycle of greed, corruption and speculation continued relentlessly as more Chinese refugees, fearful of the civil war that was approaching their villages and towns, streamed into Shanghai, where many died of hunger and the cold during the winter months. There were no foreign missionaries or English and French municipal agencies to help alleviate the situation, as had been the case a decade earlier during the Japanese bombardment of Chapei, and more and more beggars were dying of starvation on the sidewalks.

One afternoon as I was looking for a bench at the Racecourse on which to eat the sandwich Amah had prepared for me, a young boy jumped from behind me and snatched my lunch box – not my purse, for even beggars did not bother to steal the useless Chinese currency. I squelched my initial reaction to chase after the child, realizing that this starving urchin would at least eat that day, unlike his emaciated brethren with bloated stomachs who were too weak to run after pedestrians. At this time I became aware of the desperate poverty of the Chinese in the streets in comparison with the speculators and government officials flaunting their ill-gotten money in restaurants and nightclubs. I did not, however, dwell on the similarity between their indifference to the poverty of the lower classes and the indifference of the *taipans*, and most foreigners including myself, during a century of extraterritorial privileges and exploitation of China.

In August 1948 Chiang Kai-shek tried to remedy the chaotic economic situation by sending his son Chiang Ching-kuo to correct it. My mother and her friends believed that Chiang Ching-kuo, trained as an engineer in the Soviet Union where he married Fania, a Russian woman, would perhaps start thinking more as a Westerner and thus solve the country's economic problems. The press and citizenry welcomed the Generalissimo's son since he had never been part of his father's inner circle of wheelers and dealers. Chiang Ching-kuo's first order was the issuance of new bank notes, known as the Gold Yuan Dollar, to replace the former currency and hopefully control inflation. The US dollar was pegged at four Gold Yuan. I carried several bundles of the old notes to the bank and received one Gold Yuan Dollar for three million of the old currency. It was much easier now to keep my money in my wallet rather than dangling the "bricks" off the back of my bicycle or on the handlebars. Next, Chiang's son also began enforcing laws to stop currency speculation, imprisoning offenders and executing several of the most flagrant ones. However, Madame Chiang Kai-shek forbade her stepson to investigate the illegal business dealings of her sister Ai-ling, her husband the finance minister, and their son. She even made Chiang Ching-kuo apologize to one of her friends for having "mistakenly" imprisoned their offspring. The financial reformer had lost his battle against "the family" and members of his father's inner circle.

The Gold Yuan currency rapidly lost its value, but shop owners were not permitted to increase their prices; in order to circumvent this untenable situation they demanded payments in US dollars or one-ounce gold bars for their higher-priced items. Before long I once again had to carry my bi-monthly salary of Gold Yuan on my bicycle in bundles similar to the old "bricks". All workers suffered financially when the government imposed a freeze on their wages despite the daily and sometimes hourly inflation.

In 1948 there was also much unrest in the Chinese-owned textile factories, where managers could not buy the necessary raw material with their now-worthless Gold Yuan currency. Foreign and Chinese firms with headquarters in Hongkong were forced to send them US dollars and British pounds to subsidize their poorly functioning factories. They were not allowed to close or dismiss their idle workers, who threatened managers and sometimes "imprisoned" them in their offices until their demands for higher salaries were met. One exception was the British-American Tobacco factory, which was able to pay in hard currency for American tobacco leaves imported from the state of Virginia.

Chiang Kai-shek's government also had to contend with communist cadres infiltrating factories, unions and universities. When the People's Liberation Army was rushing towards Nanking, martial law was imposed in Shanghai. Communist agitators, however, managed to speak in private sessions about the bosses' and foreign imperialists' "exploitation of the masses" and arouse the curiosity and political awareness of workers and university students in and around the metropolis. These cadres organized mass demonstrations against British-owned factories and shipping companies, but their criticisms of the Kuomintang government were subtle due to the draconian measures in place against all political dissent.

On May 1, during May Day celebrations, approximately 10,000 students and workers marched on the main streets of Shanghai and shouted slogans cleared by the Kuomintang officials. As I leant on my bicycle and watched these marchers demonstrate against American assistance to Japan, an English-speaking Chinese passerby suggested I not remain in the area because my "white" face could increase their anger against foreign imperialism. I responded that I was neither British nor American, and for the first time in my life I relished being stateless, though I could not have proved it to the demonstrators. As the shouting got louder I reluctantly decided to leave, though there had been other times when I did linger; I witnessed demonstrations against Japan over the Nanking Massacre a decade earlier and in late 1945 against the Soviet Union for their plunder of Japanese factories in Manchuria and continued control of the South Manchurian Railway and the port of Dairen.

As raw material from communist-held areas ceased to reach Shanghai a number of government-owned Shanghai factories closed down and thousands of workers lost their jobs. The salary freeze and mass unemployment did not endear the workers to Chiang Kai-shek's regime, and inevitably they were ready to listen to the communist rhetoric from the Communist Party adherents in their midst. The Nationalist government, fully aware that communist cadres had infiltrated factories and workers' and students' organizations, began to restrict demonstrations, which they suspected were led by "Red" instigators. A curfew was imposed in Shanghai from midnight to five in the morning, during which time the Kuomintang secret police raided homes and dragged out men denounced as communist adherents.

The political and economic unrest were matched by the frenzied evacuation in mid-summer 1948 of most of the remaining British, American and French nationals as the People's Liberation

Army captured towns along the east coast. Despite pressure from the powerful pro-Kuomintang China Lobby in Washington – business leaders, missionaries and the powerful voice of Henry Luce, the owner of the very popular *Time* and *Life* magazines – the United States armed forces were pulling out of China. Only then did I fully appreciate that the "Reds" would inevitably take Shanghai.

American war materiel, rolling equipment and billets were being transferred to the Kuomintang while a small contingent of US Marines remained on standby in Tsingtao to evacuate American nationals, mainly missionary families still in the hinterland. Foreign wives and children paid heed but approximately 1,000 US nationals remained behind, some who were trying to close their firms and others who believed that they could continue under communism.

When the new country of Israel came into being in May 1948 many European Jewish refugees opted to settle there out of newly-found patriotism or because they were too tired of waiting for the elusive US immigration visas.

While our stateless friends rushed from one consulate to another to inquire about visas – any country would do – the Willens household temporarily set aside all thoughts of immigration to concentrate on the upcoming marriage of Riva and John in April. Since no Orthodox rabbi would marry a Jewish woman to a Christian, they were married by an American minister in a very brief ceremony witnessed by two American friends. That evening my parents held an elaborate wedding party at the Chinese Naval Officers Club, where our relatives and friends whispered that they had rarely seen such a handsome couple. All evening the guests, young and old, danced to music from a small orchestra playing tango, foxtrot, and waltz tunes and the ubiquitous "Lambeth Walk" accompanied by much singing.

The newly married couple stayed overnight at the Cathay Hotel (Peace Hotel) on the Bund and left the next morning on the two-hour train ride for their honeymoon to the lake town of Hangchow (Hangzhou) about 100 miles southwest of Shanghai. When they returned a few days later Riva described the beauty of that area, which none of us had ever thought of visiting. Next month Riva, under a special immigration quota for war brides, sailed with John to America on the USS *General Randall*, with ports-of-call in Guam and Hawaii, from where she sent us pictures of herself sunbathing on Waikiki Beach. The ship's manifest for Alien Passengers listed Riva's "calling or occupation" as "housewife" and her nationality as "stateless". Her race was typed first as "white", then crossed out and replaced with "Romanian"; perhaps the purser thought Romanians were Gypsies and therefore not ethnically white. Riva and John were on their way to Cambridge, Massachusetts where John, under the G.I. Bill, would be studying at the Harvard Business School.

Further happy news reached our household when the American Consulate informed my mother and Jackie that they would receive their immigration quota number by the end of 1948. My father and I were determined to wait for our American visas in Shanghai and not apply for immigration to any other country. Since three members of our family would be living in the United States we felt this would place us in the "preference" quota category and hasten our departure from Shanghai.

The 25 Waiting Game

BY THE end of summer 1948 the jittery and paranoid authorities, fearing attacks by communist adherents, imposed a strict curfew, starting at dusk and lasting until dawn. The only entertainment for Jackie, my friends and me, besides gatherings at our respective homes, was an occasional American movie. However, I was highly irritated at being required, before the picture started, to stand and pay homage to a large picture of Chiang Kai-shek projected on the screen while the Chinese national anthem blared away. Jackie had to tell me to lower my mutterings against the Generalissimo which perhaps could be understood by Chinese patrons sitting nearby. Because of the curfew we no longer had time afterward to go to our favorite restaurant, Sun Ya, to enjoy succulent Chinese food and talk about the film.

Life became a grim waiting game. When would the People's Liberation Army take Shanghai? The citizenry waited fatalistically for the arrival of the communist soldiers – and possibly a new government without repression and corruption. My mother and Jackie hoped my father and I would receive our US immigration visas before the communists entered the city. According to Lao Papa and Amah there was no reason to fear them. Our servants were told by their friends that they were disciplined and helpful to the people, in contrast to the retreating Nationalist soldiers who stole food from the peasants and shop owners. The Kuomintang soldiers, who had not been paid for months, were now selling their guns and ammunition, which had been provided by the US government, to whoever would purchase them. They deserted whenever they could, usually by disappearing into the crowd of refugees escaping from the war zone. Kuomintang conscripts were mostly young peasants or poor villagers who did not have the means to escape the draft by bribing officials, as did men with money. These rather dazed-looking recruits, wearing rumpled khaki uniforms and cloth shoes or straw sandals, would parade through the city, tepidly applauded by pedestrians, who had been rounded up by the police to watch these soldiers being sent off to fight the communists.

In October 1948 the communist army neared Nanking, and refugees from that area clambered aboard the few trains still running to Shanghai. American and British missionaries were moving in from the interior to embark on evacuation ships to Hong Kong and from there to their home countries or elsewhere. The US Consulate warned its citizens to leave Shanghai on these ships, which would likely be the last ones before the communist army arrived. The American military had abandoned their base in Pootung, leaving behind trucks, jeeps and war materiel worth many millions of dollars.

Despite the continuous losses, Chiang Kai-shek repeatedly assured the Chinese people, the United States and the world that he would fight the communists to the last man. The US had given millions and millions of dollars to the Chinese government since VJ day – Victory over Japan, August 15, 1945 – but the aid had been squandered by the mismanagement, corruption and theft of KMT officials and leaders. In November 1948 Madame Chiang Kai-shek flew to the United States to appeal for more aid but President Truman was no longer willing to help. And her husband, the Generalissimo, could not call on the three treaty powers and Chinese businessmen to help him defeat the communists as he had done in 1927 during the era of extraterritoriality.

In a burst of energy the mayor of Shanghai, General Chen Liang, warned citizens it was their patriotic duty to report all communist infiltrators and money speculators. When caught, the accused were subject to sham trials, sent off to prison, and many were tortured and executed – all very reminiscent of the "justice" Japan meted out during its occupation of China. Some so-called criminals were shot in the streets, with passersby forced to watch. Amah was forced to witness such an execution on one of her shopping expeditions to the market but she closed her eyes before the victim was shot. Despite these measures, black-marketeers and speculators reappeared furtively in the streets, some lives were even spared when a presiding trial judge could be bribed for a substantial sum of money.

In Hungjao, in the outskirts of the city, where the British and the Americans had abandoned their homes and summer villas, KMT soldiers were now building bunkers, digging trenches and erecting a wooden fence topped with rolls of barbed wire. This log-hewn 10-foot fence was the butt of many jokes but seriously expensive for business owners, who were heavily taxed for the construction of this flimsy barricade that I dubbed the "Maginot Line". All these fortification activities were simply means by which the military authorities extracted more money from the citizenry. In a supposedly patriotic act, the mayor offered small plots of land for vegetable-growing called "Victory Gardens" – in the winter! – to city dwellers who had never held a hoe in their lives. Many Shanghainese living in crowded domiciles quickly accepted this offer – not for its intended purpose but to erect shacks for themselves.

By the end of the year a quarter of a million Kuomintang soldiers were captured by (or surrendered to) the Red Army. Despite posters and newspapers claiming victory on all fronts, I heard on our short-wave radio about the communists' enormous territorial gains and the Nationalists' heavy losses. Chiang Kai-shek retreated from Nanking to Canton and back then to Chungking in the far-off western province of Szechuan (Sichuan). On January 21, 1949, two weeks before the Chinese New Year, he resigned as President of China. Ten days later the communists took Peking. Soon after, the acting President of China, General Li Tsung, tried to negotiate a ceasefire with the communists but it was too late. The tragicomic bravado within the Kuomintang continued unabated, for suddenly Chiang Kai-shek returned from retirement to "save the nation" from communism, declaring himself once again President of the Republic of China, with a cabinet headquartered in Taiwan.

In January 1949 the International Refugee Organization began processing documents for stateless White Russians in limbo, waiting for immigration visas from countries willing to accept them. The organization finally sent 5,500 of them by ship to holding camps in Samar on Tubabao Island in the Philippines, where they lived in tents for the next two years before gaining passage to Australia, Canada and the United States.

Chinese New Year, in early February, was a very quiet one in Shanghai since firecrackers, which could be mistaken for gunshots, were forbidden. The usual families strolling about in new clothes were nowhere to be seen as the general shortage of money and apprehension about the future did not warrant any celebration. Monthly price increases were averaging 300 percent; my friends and I declared that we could now call ourselves millionaires! Thievery by Kuomintang officials was rampant, as they openly and stealthily "looted" Shanghai wherever possible. Late one evening, from his office on the Bund, a former classmate noticed coolies silently – not in their usual singsong *he ho, he ho* fashion – hauling crates from a building guarded by armed soldiers to a ship berthed on the Whangpoo River. The next morning the night watchman told him these crates contained gold bars and hard currency bound for Taiwan.

At home my mother and Jackie, who had just received their US immigration visas, were busily packing for the sea voyage to San Francisco. My mother bought Chinese carpets and several pieces of carved mahogany furniture to sell in America while she looked for work. My father and I were hopeful of following them very soon. It was with a mixture of joy and sadness that my father, our relatives and friends and I went to the wharf on a cold and windy day in March 1949. We boarded the President Line SS *General W.H. Gordon* to help my mother and Jackie settle in their cabin. This turned out to be, to our great surprise and greater disappointment, a large room with bunk beds stacked one above another on three tiers for 30 women passengers. The *General Gordon* had been used after World War II as a transport ship to return troops to the United States. Also on this voyage, I discovered many years later on the ship's manifest, was a 29-year-old Canadian journalist from Montreal, Pierre Elliott Trudeau, the future Prime Minister of Canada.

Within a few days of my mother and sister's departure, the People's Liberation Army crossed the mighty Yangtze River in an armada of small boats; they could not use the bridges leading to Nanking, all of which the retreating Kuomintang army had dynamited. By the end of April the communists had captured with ease the cities of Soochow and Hangchow, both abandoned by the Nationalists. They were now poised to take the most symbolic prize of imperialism, "my" city of Shanghai.

Although Chiang Kai-shek was now in Taiwan, he ordered his elite US-equipped shock troops to remain in Shanghai and defend it. But neither this, nor Chiang's patriotic exhortations, could stop the enemy's advance. I saw thousands of bedraggled Nationalist soldiers marching to and from their billets – requisitioned factories, schools, hotels and office buildings large enough to shelter them. While they were waiting to go into combat their high-ranking officers and government officials sailed with their families to Taiwan on American Landing Ship Tankers, Landing Craft Infantry ships and Liberty ships loaded with crates of personal belongings, furniture, household goods, silver dollars, gold bars and American currency, much of it acquired illicitly through corruption and theft after World War II. Of course the worthless Gold Yuan notes were left behind. Wealthy Chinese industrialists and businessmen transferred their assets to Hongkong and hurriedly left for the Crown Colony or Taiwan.

In April 1949, I could hear the detonation of bombs and the noise of artillery fire. Despite the ominous sounds in the background, Kuomintang parades were still being held in the streets of Shanghai, where women, children, and old men standing in open trucks held aloft pictures of Chiang Kai-shek and dispiritedly waved their Kuomintang flags. Soldiers were ordered to lead "victory" parades while shopkeepers and people working in high-rise buildings had to hang flags from their office windows. When these parades were over, however, owners of department stores and shops quickly pulled down the metal grates and shuttered or boarded the display windows, fearing looting by disgruntled Nationalist soldiers left behind to defend the city. In the meantime these men were ordered to place pill boxes, sandbags, barricades and barbed wire in the streets, and machine guns on the roofs of hotels and high rise buildings. Fortunate were the ones we saw riding in trucks towards the wharf and the ships sailing for Taiwan.

In May the noise of artillery guns became louder and louder, and I could see smoke from the gunfire in Woosung (Wusong) on the Yangtze to the north, and across the river in Pootung. Despite the hopeless situation, the KMT officers forced their remaining soldiers to hold another victory parade on May 23 with banners proclaiming the defeat of the communists, accompanied by a marching band that tried but could not drown out the sounds of artillery fire. The bewildered populace watched this futile, final act in silence while the communist soldiers in Hungjao quickly pushed aside the wooden fence and barbed wire that were supposed to protect Shanghai.

At dawn on May 25, 1949, the People's Liberation Army quietly returned to Shanghai, twenty-two years after Chiang Kai-shek, their ally at the time, had betrayed and massacred them during the "White Terror" episode.

A week before the arrival of this victorious army, I exchanged one US dollar for half a million Gold Yuan.

26
Communist "Liberation"?

VERY EARLY that Wednesday morning Amah woke me and told me to dress quickly, "chop, chop, come see" the soldiers of the People's Liberation Army marching nearby on Route Pichon (Fenyang Lu). I rushed out of the house and saw a column of soldiers in faded, greenish-yellow uniforms, leggings, canvas shoes and, on their shaved heads, peaked caps adorned with a small red star. Each man carried a rifle and a rolled backpack from which dangled a small teapot, a tin bowl and a cup. The soldiers glanced furtively at the large brick homes along our tree-lined street and I imagined how awestruck they would be at the sight of the Bund and its imposing row of high-rise buildings. The soldiers were quiet as they marched, but from time to time they burst into song upon orders from men who did not wear any rank insignia, and also sometimes made cadence calls I understood, such as *"Da dao mei diguo zhuyi"* ("Down with American imperialism").

As I stared at the column of victorious warriors, I could only shake my head in wonderment at how these ill-equipped fellows could have defeated the US-backed Nationalists. I could only surmise that they really believed communism would alleviate the suffering of the Chinese people and unify their country. From their appearance I concluded most were from poor peasant families who toiled in the countryside. The communists had helped the peasants plow their fields, built schools for their children, and set up free infirmaries staffed by young and compassionate "barefoot doctors". Meanwhile, the Chinese intelligentsia had pleaded for reforms in Chiang Kai-shek's Kuomintang government to enable it to do the same – but to no avail. Not only were their suggestions ignored, some were even accused of collaborating with the communists.

I learned later that Kuomintang soldiers had started firing on the communist procession from the rooftop of the 19-story Broadway Mansions apartment building (now the Broadway Mansions Hotel) near the Garden Bridge, but these hapless defenders, running out of ammunition and any desire to fight, soon began to wave white flags. Amah, Lao Papa and I, talking to each other in our limited Pidgin English about this surrender, agreed that the cowardly Nationalist army commanders *en route* to Taiwan had abandoned their men.

Several friends called me to tell that they too had seen the "Red" soldiers and that a column of men near their house had stopped marching and, obviously exhausted, were sleeping on the sidewalk. Kuomintang flags, buntings, banners and posters of Chiang Kai-shek – which the day before hung from windows, lamp posts and trees – had been replaced with red flags dotted with five yellow stars, and colorful banners with yellow and black characters in praise of the People's Liberation Army and Communist leaders.

After all of the gunfire had ended PLA soldiers with fixed bayonets patrolled the streets looking for pockets of resistance from Kuomintang adherents. During the first couple of weeks of their arrival pedestrians were not allowed to walk behind the soldiers on duty at street corners, otherwise they would be shoved in the back with a rifle butt. I avoided the streets where these soldiers were posted.

Most of the five million Chinese and the remaining 1,500 Westerners in Shanghai were actually relieved at the takeover of the city. Any vestige of sorrow for Chiang Kai-shek's government in Taiwan quickly disappeared when, in June 1949, Nationalist planes appeared in the sky and attempted to bomb a power station but missed, killing instead residents living nearby. In July I saw a large "Liberation" parade enthusiastically greeted by the

Shanghainese. The latter desperately hoped for stability and an end to economic chaos that would allow Shanghai to regain its role as a thriving center of business and its *joie de vivre*. I did wonder, however, how the new rulers would behave towards that segment of the population steeped in Westernized commercialism and materialism, anathema to communist ideology. The hotels, banks and office buildings along the Bund would be glaring reminders of a century of foreign presence, domination and – in their ubiquitous parlance – "exploitation of the masses by the bourgeoisie and foreign imperialists".

The city was now adorned with colorful posters and banners praising brotherhood and nationalism, and heralding liberation from the Chiang Kai-shek regime and capitalism. Male and female soldiers performed rudimentary plays in the streets, dazzling pedestrians, especially the poor, with their music, dances and acrobatics. Various workers' groups marched every week with banners berating the "running dog" Kuomintang leaders and their collaborators. Walls were plastered with tracts urging the populace to buy "Victory Bonds" to help the People's Liberation Army liberate Taiwan from illegal occupation under the renegade Kuomintang. I could see along the Bund bright red banners with black and white characters hanging from buildings; they were translated for me as, "Long Live the People's Republic of China," and, "We Embrace World Peace." These peace-loving words were in contrast with the bellicose slogans all over the city.

During the first three months of "Liberation" the local authorities were more concerned about eradicating the health problems of the populace than brainwashing the materialistic Shanghainese. In the name of national pride they denounced the unsanitary habit of spitting, blowing noses without a handkerchief and urinating in the street. Health stations were set up on street corners to inoculate the population against smallpox and cholera, and presentations given to passersby to explain the dangers of unsanitary conditions. Small parades were held where the lead person carried aloft a very large broom to symbolize cleanliness while other street campaigners attacked the ills of gambling, opium and prostitution. Prostitutes had been quickly sent to reeducation camps to become useful citizens such as factory workers or street cleaners.

Socialistic morality, imposed by the government, was now in full force. The authorities placed portable libraries on many streets, stacked with comic books for illiterate adults and children. It may have been the first time many of them had held a book in their hands, and they smiled or laughed at the drawings of Chiang Kai-shek and overfed landlords sitting on sacks of money or being trampled by a communist soldier. These comic books were valuable propaganda tools, while authorities also reminded the literate public about past humiliation and "exploitation of the masses" by the imperialists.

Mainland China was now governed by leaders who showed they were fair in their dealings, even respecting the rights of landlords to collect rent arrears from delinquent tenants. The latter discovered they could not pay "squeeze" to the new bureaucrats in the tax division office and were forced to settle quickly all rental claims against them. Real estate owners were required to register their holdings with the municipality and foreign nationals were reassured that their properties would not be expropriated, despite rumors to the contrary. My father and his two partners who owned the apartment building on Miller Road (Emei Lu) in the International Settlement were pleased with this turn of events for they were now able to collect the overdue rents from the last two years of the Kuomintang regime.

In a few months' time, however, the reason behind this efficient registration procedure became clear when astronomically high taxes, arbitrarily calculated, were levied on all real estate holdings. In most instances rental income was not sufficient to defray this sudden increase and many owners had to abandon their properties, which were then "legally" confiscated by the municipality for non-payment of taxes. My father and his partners suffered the same fate: the tax assessment on their apartment building was much higher than the resale value of the property so they were obliged to "give" it to the local authorities.

After "Liberation", a word used over and over again to denote freedom from the Kuomintang regime, the People's Republic of China tried to reform the monetary system to stop inflation. They issued a new currency, the Jen Min Pi (JMP), at the rate of one US dollar for 100 JMP. Within a few months, however, the exchange rate for the dollar had risen dramatically to 23,000 JMP, a currency whose initials I named "Just More Paper". The cost of living also increased due to goods having to be transported to and from the north by rail rather than sea because of the Kuomintang's continued blockade of the entrance to the Whangpoo River. To leave Shanghai foreigners now had to take the train north to the port of Tientsin and wait for a ship sailing to Hongkong.

On October 1, 1949, Mao Tse-tung announced in Peking the birth of the People's Republic of China from atop the Gate of Heavenly Peace (Tian An Men) at the entrance to China's imperial palace. Though the country was not yet free of the Kuomintang forces in the south, massive parades were held in Shanghai, where thousands of enthusiastic marchers carried the communist flags and posters of Mao Tse-tung and Sun Yat-sen. Ten days later the Kuomintang in Taiwan celebrated the Republic of China's national day – the "Double Ten", the 10th of October – with Chiang Kai-shek vowing to take back Mainland China from the communists. That month the Soviet Union recognized the People's Republic of China as the legitimate government of China.

Foreigners were relieved that they could place international calls and send and receive letters from abroad, even from countries which had not as yet recognized the People's Republic of China. On my parents' 25th wedding anniversary, also in October, my mother called from San Francisco and inquired how we were being treated by the "Reds" who, she whispered, were being lambasted in the American press. We reassured her that not much had changed – my father did not inform her that their rental apartment building had effectively been confiscated. My sister Jackie told us she had just enrolled at San Francisco State College and was taking piano lessons in a private music school. My mother then asked to say a few words to Amah who was thrilled to "talkee with Big Missee in Amelika", informing her that she cleaned our house and cooked our meals "same fashion Missee" ("as usual") and that "evelyting good Delaste Lu, no ploblem".

That fall I had my first glimpse of Soviet advisors, who were helping the People's Republic establish a number of municipal agencies in the city. Sullen-looking Russian men walked about in pairs or in groups, never alone, wearing long leather coats, wide bottomed trousers, leather boots and large-brimmed felt hats. I was highly irritated whenever I saw the Soviets riding in the American military jeeps, trucks and cars left behind by the retreating Kuomintang army. They seemed to avoid all fraternization with Chinese and foreigners alike, rebuffing with cold stares and silence the Shanghai Russians who tried to speak to them in their own language. The Soviets lived in villas in the Hungjao district, once home to wealthy British and American "imperialists" and now a fenced-off compound, off-limits to the general population.

I learned about the comings and goings of these advisors from Amah's husband, a barber who went to some of their homes on a monthly basis to cut their hair. He was issued a special permit to enter the compound, guarded by sentry towers, and once he finished his tonsorial work he was escorted out to his bicycle. Although Chinese domestic help was very cheap and readily available, the suspicious Soviets brought Russian staff to serve as cooks, chauffeurs and gardeners. Their only foray out of Hungjao was to "raid" the stores in downtown Shanghai to purchase American goods still available on the market. Many shops quickly added signs in Russian offering *skitka* (discounts) to entice the Soviet advisors during their feverish buying sprees. They singled out jewelry stores, especially Michael Sukenik's, with whom they bargained relentlessly. The jeweler, who was waiting for an immigration visa to Canada, told my father and me that he tried to question the Soviets about their country but they ignored him, examining instead the silverware, Swiss wristwatches and diamond rings, and only spoke to discuss prices.

While the Chinese in Shanghai gave wide berth to this dour new category of "foreign devils" I wondered how the People's Republic could justify its friendship with this "big brother" that had not yet relinquished control of the Chinese port of Dairen. On the contrary, the Chinese government was loud in its praise of the Soviet Union, which had recognized the People's Republic of China upon its establishment. The Chinese leadership expressed its gratitude by including posters of Stalin, Lenin, Marx and Engels with those of Mao Tse-tung, Chou En-lai, and Chu Teh (Zhu De), the Commander-in-Chief of the People's Liberation Army, during the massive parades in Shanghai. I was amused that the Chinese would show their respect to these new "devils" but not too surprised, remembering how, when I was growing up, I could not understand why Chinese Catholics paid homage to pictures of a blond and blue-eyed Jesus Christ who resembled the despised *nakoonin*, the foreigner.

Six months after "Liberation" the enthusiasm of the populace of Shanghai had begun to wane, and it disappeared entirely as the authorities cracked down with more rules and regulations – especially on entertainment. Dancing and drinking in nightclubs were criticized as parasitic bourgeois activities, and American movies were slowly replaced by dull Soviet ones of brawny young men on tractors falling in love with girls, also driving tractors. However, I did also see more realistic Russian films depicting the sacrifices of the Soviet people and their army during their Great Patriotic War against the Nazis. By the end of 1949, a growing realization and increasing fear of the communist

Park Hotel with banners "Long Live the PRC – Support Peace in the World"

regime's authoritarianism reminded many Chinese of the beginning of the Japanese occupation and the last years of the Chiang Kai-shek regime.

In January and February of 1950 Kuomintang planes returned to bomb military installations and aviation fuel depots; some workers were killed and many wounded. I saw the sky lit with an orange hue and in the morning puffs of gray smoke were still floating in the sky. Another intended target of the Kuomintang pilots was the former French power company in Lukawei (Lujiawan), but once again they missed and the bombs fell on nearby squatter huts. Radio broadcasts from Taiwan announced that the planes had hit the utility company and did not mention that over 1,500 residents were wounded or killed. The former International Settlement and some parts of what had been the French Concession were without electricity and water for several days, though our area was not affected as it was close to a hospital with its own generator. I was surprised to learn from friends who had short-wave radios that the Voice of America did not mention this bombardment by Kuomintang planes that had killed so many innocent people.

After the aerial attack I sent a letter to Riva, now living in Akron, Ohio, telling her that we were well protected by communist antiaircraft batteries surrounding Shanghai, but urging her to procure "visas to anywhere" as soon as possible for my father and me. I wanted to leave Shanghai, not from fear of bombing – I had acquired some sort of psychological immunity from the time when American planes attacked during the Japanese occupation – but out of anger over the increasing repression of the Chinese populace by their "liberators" and our inability to leave China.

The Bamboo Curtain 27

THE FIRST Chinese New Year celebrated under the People's Republic of China in February 1950 was a morose and drab one; any hope for economic betterment and political freedom had evaporated in the city, now in the iron grip of the authorities. Uniformity of thought was the law of the land and, even during the Chinese New Year, the celebrants donned their obligatory blue Mao suits. The lenient policy of the first half-year of "Liberation" was replaced by political orthodoxy. The People's Republic of China, now ideologically in the Soviet camp, was shunned by the United States and the other major Western powers with the exception of England, which had recognized the new government in January.

A strict puritanical code was instilled in which bribery was a crime and all *cumshaw* (tips) were considered an insulting and demeaning gesture. Nightclubs and bars were closing down. Laws were passed giving women the same rights as men. The few remaining rickshaws were replaced by three-wheeled pedicabs since the sight of a man pulling another man was abhorrent in this new society – as it should have been in earlier times.

Mammoth parades were held on a weekly basis with men and women wearing their unisex dull blue cotton trousers, jackets, pants and caps; tight-fitting *qipaos* disappeared and the women never wore makeup anymore. This sea of blue clothing contrasted with the palette of red, blue and gold banners and colorful portraits of Mao Tse-tung, which the marchers carried during their parades as they sang and shouted for the glory of the Party, the demise of the Kuomintang and the return of Taiwan to China.

I could not help but think back to less than a year before when marchers were holding pictures of Chiang Kai-shek and waving the Nationalist flag. At first these parades and demonstrations were a pleasant diversion for the idle population but now it had become obligatory to stand, shout and clap for many hours until permitted to disperse. Factory workers, shop owners, clerks and high school and university students seemed to spend more time marching and eulogizing the new regime than working or attending classes. Former prostitutes, freed from the re-education camps, were now wearing unattractive genderless Mao suits too, a stunning contrast from their days and nights strutting about in tantalizing qipaos wearing heavy makeup and high-heeled shoes.

Calisthenics and shadow boxing were deemed important for the physical and mental well-being of the masses, so at dawn young and old participated in exercises to music blaring from loudspeakers perched in trees or on the pavement. Nearby residents' sleep was now cut short by loud, repeating songs. I was amazed at how obedient and cowed the Chinese seemed to have become, sensing perhaps that any behavior deviating from the Party's code of conduct would be met with reprimands or punishment.

Compulsory political meetings and study sessions were held to reeducate a population too long exposed to Chiang Kai-shek's corrupt regime and Western lifestyle. The strong tradition of family closeness and respect for elders was now secondary to Party loyalty. Fidelity to communism and the new family (the Party) had to replace all superstitious and decadent Confucian beliefs. The duty of every citizen was now to be vigilant and report immediately to leaders in their community any infraction by neighbors, fellow workers and even family members. Spreading rumors favoring the "enemy" was considered a criminal offense, as it had been during the Kuomintang regime and the Japanese occupation. The authorities extended their reach to everyone by establishing neighborhood watch committees that had a list of all the residents in their lane association. A fence was built around our housing complex on Route Delastre with only one opening, guarded around the clock by watchmen who kept track of everyone entering or leaving the area.

Walls and fences were plastered with drawings of overfed Kuomintang and Western men being kicked on their backsides by heroic communist soldiers or alert citizens. Crowds gathered around these pictures – efficient visual propaganda tools, readily understood and enjoyed by the illiterate masses. Although I considered these portrayals ridiculous and childish, I was more annoyed by the strident music of cymbals, drums and flutes played by musicians to announce street plays. The performers, who were usually soldiers, acted on any available patch of land where pedestrians were corralled to watch and applaud vigorously. As a foreigner I was mercifully left out since these indoctrination plays catered to a Chinese audience, although the theme could easily be understood by a non-Chinese speaker – or even a deaf person. There were always scenes of a soldier placing his foot on the protruding belly of the "enemy" lying on the ground, with legs in the air. The same themes were continuously repeated: the corruption and greed of the Kuomintang clique, and the exploitation and brutality of former Western colonialists and Japanese invaders, while praise was heaped upon the Soviet Union. Higher education courses, once taught in English and French, were now being given in Russian since the USSR was donating textbooks on law, medicine, the sciences and Marxism. University students had to study Russian in order to read these texts and in secondary schools pupils abandoned English classes for the newly imposed Slavic language.

Although I was irritated by the crudely drawn wall posters and the noisy, infantile, and propagandistic street performances and parades that obliged me to find alternative routes to work, I became concerned when I witnessed the measures taken against people denounced as Kuomintang collaborators and saboteurs,

Sino-Soviet Friendship stamps

exploitative landlords, money speculators and common thieves. I saw open-ended US army trucks transporting small groups of people with their hands tied behind their backs while around their necks hung narrow wooden boards upon which were painted, I was told, the person's name and his or her crime. These terrified individuals were taken to large parks and sometimes to the former Racecourse – renamed People's Square (Renmin Guangchang) – where the masses would decide their fate at "Speak Bitterness" meetings. The organizers of these gatherings emphasized at the outset that it was "the people", not the government, who would decide the fate of the accused. This semblance of socialist democracy was a sham since the defendants were always found guilty. I shuddered whenever I heard the roar of the crowds from these meetings at the Racecourse, where I still worked in the small building.

It would perhaps have been dangerous for an "imperialist" to be seen among the frenzy – but my curiosity got the better of me. I stood once – and only once – at the edge of the crowd and could see from afar a defendant standing on a large improvised stage. I was later told that this man, and all the others, always confessed to numerous crimes, true or not, and subsequently begged for forgiveness. In these Kafkaesque trials the crowd yelled and cursed at the hapless individuals with cries of *ta, ta* (hit, hit). When they became hoarse and the defendants too weak to stand any longer, this jury of thousands was finally allowed to announce its verdict. The signal to end the trial was arranged by communist cadres in their midst. Many people attending these public trials were made to believe they were the ones who sealed the fate of the unfortunate defendants, although in reality the government was judge and jury. Nevertheless, it must have given people an awesome feeling of power they had never before possessed – although they must have realized that it might have been themselves on the stage, accused by the authorities.

While most of the defendants were men, a small number of women were accused of black marketing, of hoarding rice for speculation or, worse, plying surreptitiously their trade as prostitutes. In many instances they were denounced by jealous neighbors, who resented their material comfort or had quarreled with them. If found guilty, they were sent to reeducation camps to mend their ways, while blackmarketeers, speculators and thieves were sent to prison. The harshest treatment was meted out to Kuomintang "running dog" collaborators, who received long sentences of hard labor in desolate and harsh regions in northern China. Those accused of spying for the "enemy" automatically received the death sentence as the authorities became increasingly paranoid about threats from Taiwan to re-take mainland China, along with the continued antagonism of the United States. The People's Republic of China, for its part, wanted to invade Taiwan but Party leaders realized this was not feasible since the island was protected by the US Seventh Fleet.

At home my father and I read the now heavily censored *North-China Daily News* to check on who was leaving Shanghai and laugh at the stories from Beijing and from the Soviet Tass News Agency deploring the "dangerous lies" from capitalist countries. In a more serious vein, we read about Chinese-owned office buildings and houses being confiscated for non-payment of taxes, the majority of whose owners had fled to Hongkong or Taiwan. It was whispered – but never reported in the newspapers – that some prominent Chinese businessmen in Shanghai who could no longer cope with the reversals in their lives had committed suicide. We also heard from the few friends still in possession of short-wave radios that the powerful adherents of the pro-Chiang Kai-shek China Lobby in the United States were relentlessly lobbying Congress against recognition of the People's Republic of China.

Our amah, who lived in the servants' quarters attached to our house, had to attend weekly neighborhood meetings headed by a Party cadre and had to report how my father and me spent our time, including whether we listened to news on a short-wave radio or received phone calls from overseas. Since Amah's English was very limited it is doubtful she could have provided much information beyond that my father read newspapers, tended to our garden or visited acquaintances and relatives, that I worked at the Racecourse and socialized with my friends, and that we received occasional phone calls from my mother and sisters in the United States. Amah said she usually dozed off in the meetings, bored by the latest sayings and statements by Mao Tse-tung and the harangues against possible collaborators and spies.

What seemed to bother Amah the most was donning the unbecoming blue Mao "uniform", especially the cap, which she felt looked silly: "Why have hat, when no lain (rain)?" she asked me. When she returned from these meetings she rapidly changed into her black trousers and white jacket since she spent most of her time in our house or in her room. On her shopping trips, however, she felt it would be safer to wear the blue outfit to blend in with the crowd and avoid becoming a target for disparaging comments about working for foreigners.

As a lark, I asked our tailor Lao Papa, who would come by whenever we needed him, to sew a blue Mao outfit for me, which I wore while I bicycled on weekends or visited friends in the neighborhood. Lao Papa could not understand why I wanted to wear the Mao Tse-tung "dless" (dress) and grumbled that I now looked like "Led soja" (Red soldier). The many pockets of my jacket, however, were useful to hold the wads and wads of Jin Min Piao notes for my shopping excursions. The Chinese passersby were quite surprised to see this *nakoonin* pedaling away in the standard people's outfit – minus the cap and its little red star for I had no desire to display this symbol of what I saw as a repressive ideology. I despised the rigidity of the new regime, the nonsensical propaganda, the endless trials and punishments; but what also fueled my anger was the realization that our lives of privilege as white people had truly ended. Thanks to the gold bars my parents had saved – which my father could now only sell to departing Europeans as gold bars could not be bartered under the communist government – he and I were able to retain a somewhat similar standard of living as before "Liberation". We still had a servant, our amah, who still preferred working for us than in a factory at lower wages.

While the Chinese were subjected to regimentation and brainwashing, the foreigners in Shanghai were generally ignored. The communist government developed an obsessive fear, however, of Protestant and Catholic missionaries, especially of the highly educated Jesuits, who posed an ideological threat to China's new atheist society. For close to a century American, English and French proselytizers had cultivated a relationship with the peasants in the hinterland, speaking their dialects and converting many to Christianity. A number of missionaries were now under house arrest or incarcerated as spies, the government disregarding the fact that, contrary to the former privileged foreigners in their extraterritorial settlements, these proselytizers in remote villages had fed the poor, cared for the sick and taught basic reading.

Our only contact with the Chinese authorities was visits to the Internal Bureau to secure application forms for exit visas, a tedious bureaucratic chore the Chinese communists must have learned from the Soviets. Foreigners had to wait approximately six weeks for the authorities to check police and tax records before their names appeared in the *North-China Daily News* to indicate that they could leave China. British and American managers of factories, banks and trading firms knew it was useless to apply until their companies had no longer any assets or their headquarters in Hongkong or overseas refused to send any more funds. This treatment of the *taipans* was a form of punishment for their past exploitation of workers. Business was at a standstill, however, with Kuomintang ships still blockading the entrance to the Whangpoo River.

When Soong Ching-ling, the Western-educated widow of Sun Yat-sen, was named Vice President of the People's Republic of China in 1950 Shanghailanders and Chinese businessmen hoped trade would once again be allowed to flourish. This did not occur; foreigners finally realized there was no future for them in communist China, and all now wanted to leave the country as quickly as possible. My father was confident the American Consulate would soon call to issue him an immigration visa since his wife and two daughters were now living in the United States. Not fully aware of immigration rules and regulations, I believed that once my father reached San Francisco and rejoined his family I too would receive a visa. In early February 1950 my father and I went to the American Consulate in the Glen Line Building on the Bund. We were elated to learn that my father was finally placed on the "preference" quota list. My "White" Chinese quota, too, would be forthcoming quicker than expected. That evening we visited my father's relatives to celebrate and drank a toast to our impending departure, hopefully within six months, on a ship to San Francisco.

Our optimism was shown to be premature when, on March 15, 1950, the American Consulate suddenly cancelled all dealings with the public and then shut down the following month. We learned that Secretary of State John Foster Dulles had ordered the closure of the United States Embassy in Beijing and all consulates in China. (Another 30 years would pass before the American Consulate General reopened its doors in Shanghai in a mansion on the former Avenue Joffre.) The closing of the

American Consulate in Shanghai may have been an irritation to the Americans, who would now have to be helped by British consular officials, but it was a shattering blow for us stateless foreigners waiting for visas to the United States. American and British nationals were informed that the last evacuation ship would be leaving Shanghai in May.

Russians, Portuguese Macanese and I, all born in Shanghai, now had two things in common: our quota ranking under the Chinese Exclusion Act, and our great desire to leave communist China. However, the Macanese, as Portuguese citizens, could have left for Portugal but they had no intention of going to a country they had never seen, where they did not speak the language and had no familial ties. In addition, Portugal was ruled by the dictatorial Salazar regime and beset with economic difficulties and colonial wars in Africa.

Immigration to the United States was no longer possible for my father and me. We decided to apply for immigration visas to Canada and to Australia, from where we would eventually rejoin the rest of our family in America. We had no choice but to wait for what seemed an interminable length of time for visas from one of these two countries.

My usually positive view on life slowly disappeared, and was replaced by feelings of despondency and isolation. I felt like one of the birds I had seen in the marketplace with Old Amah, flying round and round in its small wooden cage looking for a way out.

28
Romance

SHANGHAI IN 1950 was becoming more oppressive for the Chinese and depressing for my friends and me. However, I was cheered when Amah's brother invited me to his son's wedding. I had never attended a Chinese wedding before, and enjoyed the brief Buddhist ceremony without understanding what was said. The couple was bedecked in European-style clothes, setting aside their Mao suits for this festive occasion. Approximately fifty people sat down for a sumptuous banquet at a restaurant on Mohawk Road (Huangpi Bei Lu) near the Racecourse, gulping down the various dishes, tea and the amber-colored *shaoxing* wine, and repeatedly toasting the newlyweds with *bai jiu*, a powerful white liquor. The working-class couple and guests in their best clothes obviously enjoyed themselves in this "decadent" atmosphere, and perhaps forgot for a short time the restrictive world outside the restaurant.

I was leading a very quiet life, not having dated since the departure of the American military from Shanghai. After work I bowled and played ping pong at the former YMCA or went out with my few remaining friends to see American and British movies – all reruns since new ones could no longer be imported. I was surprised and pleased they could still be shown at all. The prancing, skimpily-attired Hollywood pin-up sirens were a stark contrast to the puritanical edicts now enforced in Shanghai. To the great disappointment of the authorities, Chinese moviegoers largely stayed away from the stilted acting and long patriotic tirades of the Soviet films shown in most of the movie houses. I went to several of them with my Russian-speaking friends for the sole purpose of laughing at the ridiculous storyline and heavy propaganda. It was not surprising the Chinese avoided such films since their own daily lives were a constant barrage of propaganda; they went instead, in droves, to see Hollywood musicals in Technicolor and especially "Westerns", depicting battles between colonialists and Indians that did not require any understanding of the English language. At the colorful movie "Bathing Beauty" they "oohed" and "aahed" at the sight of the aquatic prowess of Esther Williams and her bevy of bathing beauties plunging in synchronization into the bright blue waters of an Olympic-size swimming pool.

My lethargic social life was unexpectedly brightened by my friendship with Sergei, a White Russian with whom I regularly played ping pong and who often joined us at the movies and at gatherings in our respective homes. I soon realized that I was attracted to the sharp intellect as well as the looks of this blond, blue-eyed, Slavic young man, feelings that surprised me for I had never dated a "Shanghai boy" of his ethnicity. We discussed domestic and international politics, differing in opinion about the Soviet Union, which Sergei felt would flourish once Stalin left the scene. Sergei and his parents had become Soviet citizens and he often pondered leaving for the USSR as the prospect of emigrating to America and other democratic countries was very bleak. We enjoyed riding our bicycles, stopping to eat at open-air stalls, where Sergei would insist on paying for my bowl of noodles despite the fact he worked only sporadic odd jobs whereas I worked full-time. Besides these nocturnal meals with Chinese workers and coolies, we went several times to the reopened Cercle Sportif Français with a Macanese woman and her French boyfriend, who invited us to his club for dinner and dancing. For the club's Bastille Day celebration Lao Papa sewed me an evening dress in which I swirled and fox-trotted on the ballroom dance floor, feeling lighthearted dancing cheek-to-cheek with Sergei.

On a warm day in May Sergei suggested we ride our bicycles

out of the city and relax in the countryside, which we had never seen, and discover whether normality had returned there in the aftermath of the civil war. Amah prepared us a lunch basket with sandwiches, fruit, bottles of juice and water. She also made me take a blanket for our picnic and a can of "Flit", the anti-mosquito spray foreign households kept in every room. She cautioned us to avoid the soldiers patrolling in and around the outskirts of Shanghai. Sergei and I rode for several hours, breathing the fresh air and enjoying the silence around us, interrupted from time to time by the chirping of birds in the trees and the croaking of frogs in nearby creeks. We occasionally stopped to watch farmers plowing their fields with the help of water buffaloes while women worked knee-deep in rice paddies.

We picnicked in a field close to several miniature brick structures in the shape of a house but without doors or windows, the above-ground graves where peasants buried their dead. We munched on our sandwiches, drank the juice (which had become rather tepid under the noon sun) and took pictures of each other and the countryside. Sergei recited a Pushkin poem in Russian while I recited a stanza by Racine from my French classical repertoire. Both of us, romantics at heart, were inebriated by the fresh air, the calm and the greenery surrounding us, and we decided to ride to a village where we could taste the local food and wash it down with beer for Sergei and tea for me. We rode another couple of hours, the wind in our hair, singing a medley of songs in several languages, free from the endless cacophony of noises in Shanghai, especially the strident martial music from loudspeakers in the streets.

At a bend in the road, the peaceful atmosphere was suddenly interrupted by two soldiers pointing their guns in our direction and barking at us to stop. We quickly dismounted and I instinctively took my camera from the front basket of my bicycle and put it in a pocket of my skirt. The soldiers came towards us speaking a dialect we did not understand; they did not understand our replies in our limited Shanghainese. They sounded very angry, but also curious, about these two Caucasians riding in the countryside. We understood by their gestures that they wanted to see some documentation that allowed us to travel in this area. Sergei and I knew that no one could travel out of Shanghai – or anywhere in China – without permits from the local authorities, and now realized we were in a predicament which could have serious repercussions. We had broken the law and it would be too risky to try to bribe these two communist soldiers – unlike Kuomintang soldiers, who would have eagerly accepted money. We tried to make ourselves understood, with gestures, that we had been riding in the countryside to be away from the noise and dust of Shanghai. Although I tried to keep a calm composure I was extremely nervous and worried that perhaps I should not have hidden my camera, which if discovered would suggest we were spies; we were living in an era when all Westerners were considered potential spies.

Sergei, who remained calm during these tense moments, suddenly whipped out his Soviet passport, its cover adorned with the hammer and sickle, and showed it to the soldiers. He took off his wide Russian army hat which he had recently bought in the market and pointed to the metal star above the visor. The two soldiers suddenly smiled and said *hao, hao* (good) since the passport and the army hat with a star were obviously from a communist country. Sergei emphasized the friendship between the People's Republic of China and the Soviet Union by joining two fingers and repeatedly saying Mao Tse-tung and Stalin's names. The soldiers understood "Stalin" but not, at first, the name of the Chinese leader since neither Sergei nor I could pronounce Mao's name correctly in Chinese.

Sensing that Sergei's limited conversation with the soldiers might not persuade them of our innocence, I opened my purse and showed them its contents, explaining with gestures that the lipstick was used to redden my lips, the face powder to whiten my cheeks. Then I asked them to try my thick-lensed eyeglasses, which they did laughingly but quickly returned to me, perhaps wondering why I wore glasses through which they could not see anything. The soldiers were ready to let us go, and when Sergei offered them some fruit they refused and waved us off with wide smiles. This was probably the first time they had interacted with foreigners, surely an amazing event for them but a nerve-racking one for us.

After we said our many goodbyes my imagination ran wild. I told Sergei that I could have been raped and he shot or, in a less dramatic vein, taken to their commanding officer who, probably more sophisticated than his men, would question us as to why we were in the countryside without a permit. I repeatedly thanked him for his quick thinking in showing his passport. If we had been investigated, I said, as a Soviet he would eventually have been let go while I, as a stateless individual, could have been incarcerated..

Since I was trembling and too upset to continue riding, Sergei suggested we rest against a nearby burial structure to talk about the incident and try to relax. When we were ready to return to Shanghai we realized that we would be riding in the dark on country roads without our bicycle lamps, and decided to spend the night at the foot of a tree where we placed the blanket to lie on. We lay close, side-by-side, but Sergei never touched me except to kiss me "goodnight" on the cheek. We went no further as I was terrified of becoming pregnant and he of the consequences. We were both exhausted psychologically and soon fell asleep under a moonlit and silent night.

This incident with the communist soldiers must have affected me strongly, as I began dreaming in a jumbled way about the movie "Outlaw", in which the actress Jane Russell was defending herself against a very aggressive man. It was now I, and not the Hollywood siren, who lay disheveled on the haystack pushing off Sergei, pleading "no, no" and hoping the two Red soldiers would rescue me and save my virtue. When I woke up I was too embarrassed to tell Sergei how he had misbehaved in my dream. Reality took over, however, and at dawn we rode back

Lily with Sergei

to Shanghai to our respective beds to recover from our first real encounter with soldiers, fortunately naïve ones, from the People's Liberation Army. My father did not ask me where I had spent the night, probably believing that I was at a friend's home.

That month I had seen thousands of soldiers marching in the streets for the 1950 May Day celebration of a unified People's Republic of China. A friend and I saw from the balcony of her apartment on Nanking Road a riot of colors stretching for miles, with soldiers in their khaki uniforms, civilians in their blue suits holding bright red banners imprinted with yellow characters, and hand-drawn posters of beloved communist figures, Chinese and foreign. A Chinese neighbor joined us on the balcony and translated the slogans on the banners, which praised the Chinese and foreign communists, and denigrated Chiang Kai-shek and Western imperialism. He angrily complained that China was once again under dictatorship, but one more frightening than the Kuomintang regime. The persona of Mao had become a cult, he said, his speeches read and learned in schools and workplaces and his portrait plastered all over town, in homes, shops, factories and offices. After this May Day parade the nonsensical stories and lies about America in the *North-China Daily News* angered me. I began to feel trapped.

By summer 1950 there were no more than 400 foreigners left in Shanghai and often I was the only Caucasian shopping or riding my bicycle. The Chinese simply ignored me, for I was not yet an oddity in Shanghai, where the "foreign devils" had lived and reigned for so long. The Chinese did not display any hatred or resentment towards me as a symbol of past colonialism and exploitation, though I would have understood such feelings in a country under an anti-foreign communist dictatorship.

The following month I heard that North Korean soldiers had invaded South Korea on June 25, 1950, crossing the 38th parallel, the demarcation line established after World War II. In Shanghai this conflict would lead to the Chinese bamboo curtain's replacement with an iron one.

The "Police Action" in Korea

ANTI-AMERICAN PROPAGANDA in Shanghai intensified when General Douglas MacArthur was named commander of the United Nations Forces in South Korea to repel the North Korean invaders. China decried this action against its friend and ally, whose intent was to "liberate" the South Koreans from the corrupt and dictatorial regime of President Syngman Rhee. Mammoth demonstrations ensued, and I also saw an unusual parade of men in well-pressed Mao suits with paper flowers in the buttonhole of their jackets, marching and singing martial songs. These men had volunteered to fight for their North Korean "brothers" under attack by the United States and twenty other nations. The sight of the men prepared for war disturbed me; I wondered if China was planning to send regular troops to fight in this so-called "police action".

My mother called from San Francisco, extremely worried as to whether the fighting in Korea was affecting us, but we assured her we were far away and that China would surely remain neutral since it did not have the means to attack the United Nations. I saw more and more parades by these "volunteers" in the streets of Shanghai, who seemed eager to fight with their Korean brethren against enemy forces led by "imperialist America".

On a happier note, in July we received a telegram from Cambridge, Massachusetts, announcing the birth of Riva and John's daughter Roxanne. My father and I wondered why her parents had chosen such an uncommon first name and I opined that Riva must have had in mind the heroine, Roxanne, from Edmond Rostand's play "Cyrano de Bergerac", which she had read in school. (My theory, however, was not even close; Riva later explained it was because her husband's ancestors, the Brewsters, who left England in the 17th century for the American colonies, had named one of their children Roxanne.) Riva telephoned and told us she was filling out affidavits of support for us to immigrate to the United States and that we needed to get to another country to wait for our visas. To my surprise, after only three years in the United States Riva had completely lost her Shanghai English accent and now spoke with an American accent – which, I thought, fortunately did not resemble the one used by men I had dated from the southern states.

Although Sergei and I often talked and argued about politics, especially about the Soviet Union, I also had the opportunity to discuss the world situation with my father's friend Frank, a 40-year-old Australian who still believed private enterprise could function in a Communist system. A risk-taker by nature, he had not turned in his short-wave radio to the authorities, and shared with me the latest news, that General MacArthur's forces had landed in the port of Inchon, taken the capital city, Seoul, and were advancing north towards the 38th parallel. Frank and I were sure that the North Korean forces would capitulate and the war would end quickly. The military reversal by the West against the North Koreans was not mentioned in radio broadcasts or newspapers, though more articles appeared in the *North-China Daily News* about the need to help China's "brothers" in the north.

This materialized when we learned that Chinese communist forces had rushed down to the 38th parallel in November 1950 and invaded South Korea. The People's Republic of China explained that its intervention was necessary to protect the Chinese border from possible invasion by enemy forces. In the fall Frank had told me US intelligence was warning MacArthur that Chinese soldiers were massed along the Chinese-Korean border, poised to attack, but the general assured President Truman that neither China nor the Soviet Union would enter the war. After the

Americans crossed the 38th parallel, China, now considering the United States an aggressor, sent waves of Chinese soldiers in armed with rifles and grenades. The Americans were forced to retreat below the 38th parallel as their defensive positions began to crumble. Frank's Chinese business partner told us this onslaught by Chinese "volunteers", and the American retreat, was hailed in every newspaper and on the radio, although no mention was made of the one million Chinese soldiers who had been wounded or killed. In Shanghai more large and very noisy parades and anti-American demonstrations were held to celebrate this victory, and paper maché effigies of Truman, MacArthur and Uncle Sam, and American flags were burned to the amusement and delight of gawking passersby. I wondered again how the crowds of people busily marching, parading and haranguing, ever found time to work. I read some signs in English, presumably for the edification of the few remaining foreigners in Shanghai, saying "Death to America". Past incidents involving American military personnel in Shanghai were revived – drunken soldiers causing road accidents, destroying property and supposedly raping young girls. Interestingly, as hard as the authorities tried to stir anti-American feelings, the marchers did not appear to be angry towards the United States, and still no antagonism or hatred, verbal or otherwise, was ever directed towards me.

This non-belligerent attitude of the Chinese public towards the West was reflected when, to their great disappointment, American movies were banned: they were immoral, sinful and pornographic, said the authorities, especially the public's favorite, "Bathing Beauty", with its women swimmers in bathing suits. The depleted stock of American-made goods was also replaced with shoddily-made Russian goods and foodstuffs, though inexpensive red caviar became a staple in our home as a delicious appetizer on dark brown bread.

Despite Frank's optimism about business under communism, the authorities clearly wanted foreigners to leave. My father's sister, Sonia, and her daughter's family had just left for Australia, assuring us they would sponsor us once they had settled there. Although we were not too eager to go to Australia, where we heard life was difficult for new immigrants, we had to leave China. My father wrote to the Sun Life Assurance Company in Montreal, asking them to rehire him and provide him with a work permit to facilitate his entry to Canada. His aim was to eventually cross the border into the United States and be reunited with my mother and Jackie. We discovered, however, that Australia and Canada would not issue visas to stateless people unless they had a "final destination" visa that guaranteed they would leave upon the expiration of their transit visa or temporary work permit.

To resolve this problem my father decided on a course of action that was very difficult – and most distasteful – for him to do. He decided to apply for Soviet citizenship. At the height of the Cold War, my father and I trudged over to the Soviet Consulate to become citizens of the USSR, a repressive communist country we both abhorred. This was the first time my father had indicated on an application form that he was born on Russian soil in Radomyshel, Ukraine, since he left the country. The Soviet consular official posed questions about my father's birthplace, the present whereabouts of his wife, why we wanted to become Soviet nationals and whether we were thinking of leaving immediately for the USSR. My father simply replied that he was born in Russia and believed that he had a right to acquire Soviet citizenship. The consul ended the interview, looked at my father with his cold blue eyes and stated bluntly, "You really do not want to return to the Motherland, you simply need a passport." He was right, of course, and we left with mixed feelings, somewhat disappointed but strangely relieved that we would not become Soviet citizens.

My father and I still needed a "final destination" permit and discovered the Israeli consul, Moshe Yuval, who came to Shanghai at the end of 1948, would issue visas to Jews who wanted to settle in Israel. Several White Russian families had applied unsuccessfully for these visas, as proof of a Jewish background had to be verified and certified by the remaining members of the Ashkenazi congregation. In November 1950 my father and I received visas to Israel, valid for six months and renewable. We had no intention of going to Israel of course, but thanks to our "final destination" permits we were now able to reapply for entrance visas to Australia and Canada.

While awaiting the outcome of these applications I noted with disgust the ever-increasing paranoia of the authorities towards Chinese who had once worked for foreign organizations. They were looked upon as traitors for having associated with imperialist "running dogs". Xenophobic propaganda and vitriolic comments about American imperialism appeared daily in long articles in the *North-China Daily News*. The press now seemed to blame the United States for not only the Korean War, but all the past ills of the Chinese people; I still have the clippings as a reminder of a time when the world had gone mad.

Many of these articles, written in very poor English, attacked Christian religious orders – especially the Catholic priests and nuns "for deceiving, doping and imbuing in the minds of the Chinese people with subservient ideas aimed at the moral enslaving of the Chinese people [sic]". The meaning of these bombastic words was often difficult to comprehend, although the anti-religious intent was very clear. Another article in the *North-China Daily News* declared, "American subsidized Chinese religious bodies should be brought under the complete management of Chinese believers. The Government should encourage their movement to become independent, self-supporting and self-preaching . . ." – which meant teaching communist ideology. Chinese Christian nuns and priests were relentlessly harassed and sent to re-education camps, while a number of foreign missionaries and priests were incarcerated on trumped-up charges of being spies, and their church properties confiscated. American teaching nuns from the Legion of Mary order in Shanghai, who had always led secluded lives, were repeatedly interrogated by the authorities on politics with which they were not familiar.

Educational and medical relief organizations originally established by American non-government entities were heavily criticized for their past collaboration with the "bourgeois imperialists". According to the *North-China Daily News*:

> Teachers, students, medical workers, and employees and workers in missionary schools, churches and hospitals in various places have everywhere held patriotic anti-American elements of reactionary and disruptive activities. These organizations needed to be taken over by the government or transformed into bodies completely operated by Chinese people. These undertakings became especially active after American imperialism invaded Korea and Taiwan and when the 'Resist America, Korea campaign' of the Chinese people was widely developing [sic].

Ironically, in these articles the Chinese Communist Party was now holding the United States, rather than Britain (which had by now recognized the People's Republic), solely responsible for the past colonialism and exploitation of the Chinese people, through the very newspaper that had been the voice of British imperial interests in China since the 1860s.

As the war in Korea progressed during the second half of 1950, the editorial attacks became more virulent:

> U.S. imperialists sucked the blood and sweat of the Chinese people and vainly hoped to buy the hearts of the Chinese people with a view to spiritually numbing the Chinese people. For over a hundred years, the U.S. imperialists have invaded and robbed China; they have directly helped Chiang Kai-shek to massacre several millions of Chinese people. The U.S. imperialists are completely mistaken in thinking that they can really buy the hearts of the Chinese people with a few of their dirty dollars stained with blood.

The newspaper editor explained that American assets were being expropriated because "under the leadership of the Central People's Government, the Chinese people can manage these institutions and can certainly manage them still better by relying on their own strength".

These chauvinistic propaganda statements complemented the lies and distortions of life in the United States in the *North-China Daily News*:

> America is going underground with different departments of the government in Washington tunneling below earth to set up offices that will function during any atomic war. There has been a big national boom in caves. Slick real estate merchants are helping to spread panic among the bourgeoisie and cashing in by offering for sale dry, deep, livable caves in Arizona and other remote spots . . . papers and periodicals published articles and advertisements to the effect that white dresses and sheets and white paper will act as protection against atomic bomb effect [sic].

In addition, American politicians and businessmen "threaten any who sign the Stockholm peace appeal with loss of jobs . . . Young men and women asking passersby on the streets to sign petitions are often arrested for disturbing the peace".

While Western imperialism was castigated in the streets, in newspapers and on the airwaves, the Chinese bourgeois class suffered the loss of their properties, their freedom and in some instances their lives. Life had become untenable for merchants, whose properties were being confiscated on the pretext that the owners had gained their wealth by exploiting "the masses", a tiresome, ubiquitous term. More businessmen and others jumped from office buildings, from the roof of the Park Hotel or drowned themselves in the Whangpoo River.

My Australian friend Frank told me he and a colleague had recently seen, with binoculars from the top floor window of the

Shanghai Brewery building, ghoulish scenes taking place in a nearby walled compound. A man's hands had been tied behind his back and a rope placed around his neck; his head was then pulled back and he was shot by a firing squad, an execution which Frank said was repeated on another prisoner. Most likely these men had been rounded up for pro-Kuomintang activism and, as "enemies of the people", had paid the ultimate price, probably without any semblance of a trial.

During the second half of 1950, I saw an inordinate number of ambulances rushing down the streets with shrill sirens blaring. Amah told me these vehicles were actually run by death squads. Masked stretcher-carriers, she said, entered homes in broad daylight, shot the person they were seeking and then carried the body to the ambulance – which did not go to a hospital but disposed of the body elsewhere.

A friend who lived in the Park Apartments on Rue Lafayette called me to relate, with much trepidation, how she had witnessed a "trial" from her apartment window facing the front yard of her building. The yard was being guarded by soldiers, who then ordered the tenants to turn off their lights. Suddenly the gates to the complex were opened to let in a group of people who were ordered to sit on benches facing a mournful-looking man sitting on a low stool, dressed only in his underpants and undershirt. Bright lights shone on him while the newly arrived "witnesses" testified that he was a collaborator of the Kuomintang. After several hours of haranguing by the attendees and many apologies by the defendant, he was declared guilty, to everyone's relief since all were hoarse and exhausted at this late hour. The man was led away to prison and possibly to his death.

The year 1950 ended sadly for me when Sergei announced that he was leaving for the Soviet Union. I argued with him that he would never be able to leave that tyrannical country, but he had become convinced and somewhat enamored of the post-war Russia he was reading about in pamphlets and books he picked up at the Soviet Consulate. He looked forward to enrolling in an engineering school and helping to rebuild the "Motherland" he had never seen. He promised to write to me once he arrived in the Soviet Union but I never heard from him again.

The Paper Chase

DESPITE THE deteriorating economic situation and the constant criticism of bourgeois materialism in Shanghai, I was surprised to see advertisements in the *North-China Daily News* inviting readers to celebrate the Western New Year 1951 in grand style at the "popular, foreign-owned nightclub, restaurant and bar *Reno* at 689 Avenue Joffre, which in the past had successfully accommodated their patrons on Christmas and New Year Eves". Readers were assured that "in 1951 they will find at the place the same quality of food, drinks and music they have enjoyed in previous years". In another advertisement, the *First Avenue* shop in Sassoon House (offices and stores in the Cathay Hotel) offered:

> ...a selection of imported articles de luxe including rare French perfumes of such renowned manufacturers as Guerlain, Langevin, Rocha, Houbigant, English lavender by Yardley, costume jewelry, the sight of which keeps every woman glued to the counter, toilet sets, woolens in latest designs and other novelties too numerous to be mentioned.

I wondered who the customers could be since most of the foreign women had left Shanghai, and the Chinese avoided stores selling "decadent bourgeois" items out of fear. Another store, the Standard Rug Company on Nanking Road advertised "cheap prices for Tibetan, Peking, Tientsin and blue/white Mongolian carpets and rugs", while the Avenue Joffre Flower Shop offered corsages "for the festive season going on and many parties still to come". What optimism! Another flower shop, the Forget Me

Not, reminded the public, "Your sentiment, your condolence, your happiness can be expressed best with a floral tribute."

Surprisingly, the streets listed for these stores and restaurants were the former English and French names from the Settlement and Concession, and not the new Chinese ones. After reading these advertisements I felt for a brief moment that I was back in the old Shanghai before "Liberation".

In January 1951, while still waiting for immigration visas to Canada and Australia, I received an uplifting letter from Japan from my parents' close friend Jacques Picciotto, offering me a secretarial job at his trading firm in Tokyo. He explained that he could get a work permit for me without any difficulty from the American authorities in occupied Japan since English-speaking secretaries were in demand. He added that once I moved to Tokyo I could apply for an entry permit for my father. We were elated; I called the few friends still in the city about this unexpected turn of events and immediately started to apply for the necessary documents to leave Shanghai.

My chase for the numerous application forms and visits to various offices began in earnest, but I never imagined how time-consuming, cumbersome and frustrating it would be. The process started out smoothly enough; I was able to procure a travel document from the office of the Far East Mission of the United Nations International Refugee Organization. My timing was most fortuitous, for this office was closing and its employees were issuing as quickly as possible the required documentation and giving financial assistance to stateless foreigners leaving Shanghai. This organization gave me a "Certificate of Travel" that stated I was a *bona fide* refugee headed for Israel.

I was surprised to discover that I now belonged to the category of "refugees". The comfortable life I was leading – my salary at the Racecourse and having a servant taking care of all household chores – seemed contrary to the life generally led by refugees. I did not relish my new status, but as a practical person I was very pleased that all my travel and hotel arrangements, and expenses to Japan would be taken care of by the International Refugee Organization.

In early February, during Chinese New Year, I received another letter from Jacques Picciotto informing me that the US Occupation authorities in Japan had issued me a work permit. I read and reread his letter several times for I could not believe that I could finally leave China. I called my friends and they called theirs about this momentous news, and I invited several of them to a Chinese restaurant to celebrate this very special event and my eventual departure. But ships still could not sail from Shanghai because the Kuomintang had placed mines around the estuary of the Yangtze River; I would have to take a train to Tientsin and from there sail to Japan. The thought of additional documents for the ship stopped me cold, however, and I decided the least complicated and most direct way to leave Shanghai was to take the train to Canton and Hongkong, then embark at a later date on a ship sailing to Japan. I had to apply for an exit permit from the local authorities, then get a transit visa for Hongkong from the British Consulate, now reopened to the public. Once I obtained these two visas and purchased my train ticket to Canton, the International Refugee Organization would book my hotel room in Hongkong and my passage aboard a ship to Japan.

I first went to the Chinese Bureau of Foreign Affairs office on the Bund to get the application for an exit permit, which had to be filled in triplicate, then to the police station on Bubbling Well Road for my security clearance permit. In addition, I had to prepare a list of items I intended to take to Japan and, strangely, bring all my photo and stamp albums. The examiner at the Foreign Affairs office, dressed in a black military uniform, spoke to me first in Chinese, but switched to impeccable English when he discovered I did not speak the language. He admired my stamps, especially the ones I had bought recently that showed Mao Tse-tung side by side with Stalin. I was intrigued that I needed to show our family pictures but quickly understood the reason when the examiner removed one of the pictures from my album. It was of Riva and me, the two little Caucasian girls on each side of Old Amah wearing her white jacket and black pants. Her "uniform" as a servant of white colonialists was unacceptable in an era of extreme sensitivity about past colonialism and daily ranting against "the exploitation of the Chinese by foreign imperialists".

Despite my explanation that Old Amah had been with us for over a decade and was my "second mother", the examiner would not return the picture to me. I was angrier with this "theft" than the fact he would not tell me when I could expect to receive my exit permit. His sullen reply was that I needed to look in the *North-China Daily News* for my name and the date I could pick up the permit from his bureau. I knew of instances where it took about six weeks for foreigners to learn whether or not they were granted this valuable document – and, if refused, no reason would be given. While I was now sure that I would eventually leave Shanghai, I felt sorry that the Chinese could not leave their country. Many of them desperately tried to reach British Hongkong or Portuguese Macao.

My next appointment was with a British consular official to apply for a transit visa to Hongkong. It was generally known that the British were very reluctant to issue visas to stateless persons, even under the auspices of the United Nations, fearing they would want to remain in the Crown Colony to apply for immigration visas at the various consulates in Hongkong. I presented to the British official my travel document issued by the International Refugee Organization and the Israeli immigration visa proving I would not stay in Hongkong since I had an "end country" destination. The consul looked askance at my birth certificate, for it was simply a piece of paper typed by my father seven years after my birth that stated, "Mrs. Anna Schwartz, Midwife, Licensed by the French Municipal Council, attended to my birth at 3.40 p.m., August 5, 1927, at my parents' home at 640 Avenue Joffre, Shanghai [sic]." This delayed birth certificate had been necessary when I started kindergarten at the Collège

Municipal Français.

While waiting for all these visas and permits I decided to brush up on my secretarial skills for the job in Tokyo with a crash course on Gregg shorthand from a Chinese teacher who had taught it before "Liberation". I asked Lao Papa to return to our house to sew dresses for my trip and went on a spending spree, purchasing brocade jackets and silk material for more outfits. I feared I would not be able to get clothing in Japan, still reeling from its devastation by relentless wartime air raids and the atomic bombs dropped on Hiroshima and Nagasaki.

Although a very limited amount of foreign currency could be taken out of China, my father beat the system by taping US$20 bills under the front and back covers of my hardback school textbooks. These bills were so well hidden that I had no fear they would be discovered by customs officials. Once I reached Japan I would send them to my mother and Jackie; they had told us my father's account at the Anglo California National Bank in San Francisco was "frozen" because he was living in communist China. Only after he left communist China would the bank be able to request a license from the US Treasury Department to unblock the account. We were somewhat relieved, however, to learn that my mother and Jackie had acquired enough money for their living expenses by selling the Chinese carpets and other artifacts they had taken with them from Shanghai. My mother also informed us they were moving from San Francisco to Boston to be closer to Riva and John, and their one-year-old child, Roxanne.

Every morning before leaving for work I purchased a copy of the *North-China Daily News*, not to read the endless nonsense about the glory of communism and the decadence of the West, but to see if my name was on the list of exit permits. I did not expect to be denied, as had several British and American *taipans*, who had then been held hostage in their offices for several days by their employees until hard-currency funds were received from Hongkong to pay the workers. I had the necessary documents to enter Japan, including a residence permit from the office of the Supreme Command for Allied Powers (SCAP), General MacArthur's headquarters in Tokyo.

Amah helped me pack while my father typed a list of every item in my suitcases, to be translated in Chinese. I mailed a copy to my mother, asking her to let me know whether I needed additional clothing for my eventual arrival in America. Since I did not know how I would fare financially in Japan or the United States, I packed two big leather suitcases to the brim with a dozen dresses, several skirts and blouses, many of which Lao Papa had made, pedaling all day long on the sewing machine. I also purchased a dozen pairs of shoes and handbags, two woolen overcoats and a Chinese mink coat (which I was later told was simply rabbit fur).

The policeman who checked this list seemed to shudder with disgust at the numerous items of clothing I was taking with me at a time when the entire Chinese population was dressed in their blue cotton outfits. I also bought a carved camphor wood chest, and had a case built for it since it had to be sent by train to Hongkong and then by ship to Tokyo. This piece of furniture needed to be delivered, inspected and stored at the Customs House on the Bund, and I had to sign several documents to ensure that the chest would be transported to the Shanghai North Railway Station (Bei Zhan) on the day of my departure.

I shouted with joy one cold morning in February 1951 when my name – spelled incorrectly – jumped out at me in thick black letters from the *North-China Daily News'* list of exit permits granted by the Bureau of Foreign Affairs. There was, however, a three-day waiting period to allow any complaint to be filed against me. It took me some time to realize that finally, after two long years of waiting, I would be able to leave my communist "paradise". My friends and I celebrated at the "Silk Hat", a nightclub now frequented exclusively by foreigners. Not surprisingly, upper-class Chinese did not want to be seen at these places of entertainment.

I sent a telegram to my mother and Jackie in San Francisco and to Riva in Cambridge, Massachusetts. Riva called within a few days, excited about my impending departure to Japan, where I could apply for an immigration visa to America. She also told me that as a new aunt I could be proud of Roxanne, a very cute and alert baby.

I purchased a train ticket to Hongkong from the government-owned China Travel Service and resigned from my job at the Racecourse, where I had worked for three-and-a-half years. I received very little separation pay but a rather flattering letter of recommendation from my boss, the staid Englishman. "Miss Willens' efficiency on matters concerning office routine," he wrote, "and her test in handling the delicate question of outstanding membership dues has been favourably commented upon by Members of the General Committee of the Recreation Fund Trustees." He added that I was a "competent, steady and industrious person of marked ability who speaks English, French and Russian". With such a glowing letter in hand I felt confident I would easily find a secretarial position in the United States.

My father would not be alone in our house for he had invited a family to stay with him until their impending departure to Australia. Coincidentally, the couple's adopted daughter was the child of the French girl whose pregnancy had been the *cause célèbre* at our Collège Municipal Français. I was quite taken aback to see that the little girl resembled her birth mother not only in her good looks but in the way she walked and carried herself. The couple brought along their amah to cook for them and to look after their daughter, and took over my large bedroom, while I moved downstairs to the living room couch.

Then, on a windy March day, my father and a contingent of friends loaded with flowers and chocolates came to see me off from the North Railway Station. It had been difficult for me to say good-bye that morning to Amah and especially to Lao Papa, who had been with us for over ten years. Fortunately, they would still be working, Amah for my father, Lao Papa for our friends, but I wondered how they would fare once my father and all the other foreigners left Shanghai. I was concerned that their livelihood could be affected by having worked so many years for the "foreign devils".

At the railway station customs officials and other uniformed individuals opened my suitcases but fortunately did not take out my clothing, which Amah had carefully wrapped in tissue paper. The list of the contents was carefully checked and compared but nothing was confiscated or removed, as I saw happen to several other passengers. One official slowly turned the pages of my books and also shook them, obviously looking for hidden currency, but my US dollar bills stayed firmly glued under the front and back covers. Other officials opened the wooden crate that protected the carved chest and tapped the wood for any sound that might suggest a hollow spot. I wore a diamond ring that my father had bought for me to sell in Japan in order to send money to my mother and Jackie, now in Boston. Foreigners were not allowed to take more than US$100 out of China, a ridiculously small amount for those bound for Hongkong, where they would have to wait for visas to other countries. The fate of these foreigners was no concern to the government of the People's Republic of China, which needed to control the flight of hard currency that could pay for goods and materiel from the Soviet Union.

Friends told us there would not be any body searches at the train station, so I concealed fifteen US$100 bills in my brassiere, which proved to be rather scratchy but made me look buxom! Various officials counted the ten US$10 bills I was allowed to take with me, and I was surprised that I had to surrender my Chinese JMP money. A representative from the China Travel Agency gave me a receipt for the Chinese currency and informed me it would be sent to my father. There was no doubt in my mind that this amount would disappear the moment I stepped on the train, and I simply shrugged off the small loss of "Just More Paper". Several months later, though, my father told me in a letter that the money had been returned to him.

I was somewhat tense waiting on the platform because I had heard of several incidents where passengers were informed at the last moment that they could not leave because their documents supposedly were not in order. I became even more tense and agitated when customs officials re-inspected my suitcases, and those of other foreigners on the platform. I felt sorry for an elderly American Episcopalian priest, who was being interrogated by two military men. They had discovered among his meager possessions a cloth scarf on which was painted a map of China and were questioning him about it; they finally let him get onto the train as the whistle shrieked and the locomotive's engine rumbled. This priest later told me that the scarf was a parting gift from his students as a remembrance of his life in China.

I said tearful goodbyes to my father and friends, and as I boarded the train and waved to them I was relieved, but also angry that I had spent the last two years under a totalitarian regime, trying to obtain a visa to anywhere. My paper chase, which had started under the postwar Chiang Kai-shek regime, had lasted five long years. As the train pulled away from my "hometown" I began to calm down, comforted by the fact that at the end of the 1,500-kilometer ride was the British Crown Colony of Hongkong. I had to admit, too, with much reluctance, that the communist regime was changing China. Despite the lack of political freedom – which the majority of Chinese had never known under their emperors, foreign invaders and their own 20th century rulers anyway – there were no longer beggars in rags dying of hunger and cold in the streets of Shanghai. Illiterate adults and children were being taught to read and write, albeit with propaganda cartoons, pamphlets and books, and they could survive if they obeyed the laws, and praised Mao Tse-tung and his oppressive regime. None of this, however, concerned me anymore. My train was carrying me to freedom.

The Ride to Freedom

31

IN THE New China, where class distinction was supposedly eliminated, foreigners on the train to Canton were obliged to purchase first-class sleeper-cabin tickets. High-level Chinese officials also travelled in comfort for I saw several of them in our section of the train. It would have been extremely uncomfortable and tiresome to sit on wooden seats for two nights and three days in a train crowded with workers and peasants, holding onto their bundles of clothing and food packages, smoking, spitting and noisily gulping down their food. While the Chinese passengers ate where they sat, foreigners could choose European or Chinese meals in a very clean dining car exclusively for their use. The communists now segregated us from the masses, a situation which in my mind perpetuated the superior economic status of the "white man" versus the Chinese.

Chinese train attendants walked up and down the aisles all day, carrying enormous thermos bottles or kettles of boiling water that they poured into glasses with small amounts of tea leaves. We, the "capitalists", had our own attendant to fill our glasses, who refused our tips with many gestures of protestation, since this form of "bourgeois subservience" was strictly forbidden.

The first passenger I encountered in our four-berth cabin was a young French woman who had worked at the French Embassy in Peking, but I was quite surprised when two young Englishmen, also from the diplomatic corps, introduced themselves as our cabin mates. As proper gentlemen they suggested that we take the lower bunks to avoid climbing the rickety ladders, and darted out of the cabin whenever we needed to dress, undress or wash and brush our teeth in the small sink by the window under a collapsible table. The toilets in a nearby passageway were always kept clean, in contrast to the ones in the other cars, where a hole in the train floor irrigated the ground between the tracks. From early morning until dinner time the passageways and the dining room resonated with the sounds of music and speech I could not understand. The refrain I was hearing over and over in my mind in cadence with the wheels of the train was, "I can't believe, I can't believe, I am leaving communist China."

I quickly discovered that my three cabin mates had radically differing political views from mine; while I pointed out how dictatorial and repressive the new regime had become, they praised the communists. It was ironic that these three diplomats, representatives of governments that had enjoyed for nearly a century all the privileges of extraterritoriality, were siding now with the communists. As our arguments became more and more heated, I felt I was witnessing the end of rivalry between the two historical enemies – England and France. Eventually I decided to withdraw from the verbal battles and instead spent time looking out of the window.

Outside, peasants were tending rice paddies, sometimes knee-deep in muddy waters, hoeing the dark brown earth or trudging behind their reluctant buffaloes, nudging them along. At times deep valleys and high mountains rushed by but generally the land was rather desolate and strewn with rocks and scrawny shrubs. In villages and hamlets poorly-clothed children played near small huts with thatched roofs. Whenever the train stopped, local vendors rushed to our cabin windows to sell food and small homemade artifacts – still allowed in those early years of the People's Republic. I purchased several small cloth dolls for my niece Roxanne and some food reminiscent of that which I had always eaten in the streets of Shanghai – buns, dried mangoes, and succulent green and black olives. But no one sold my favorite foods, the delectable *da bing* and *you tiao*, which I learned was a specialty of Shanghai.

Grim-faced military guards entered our cabin several times to examine our travel documents and check off our names on their roster of foreign passengers. When I handed them my exit visa permit and a sheet of paper – my certificate of identification – adorned with the seal of the International Refugee Organization and the consular stamp of the British Consulate, they seemed somewhat puzzled that I did not have a passport like my cabin-mates, but the photo on the document did resemble me and my name was printed on their list.

We reached Canton after three days and two rather sleepless nights; I had often woken to the sound of whistles and the grinding noise of wheels at station stops along our route. When we got off the train in Canton we had to open all our suitcases on the station platform for inspection by officials as serious-looking as their counterparts in Shanghai. Many of the young examiners, in their blue Mao suits, were obviously from the countryside and could not hide their surprise, especially the women, when they saw the contents of our suitcases. They scrutinized my textbooks with their hidden American dollars, and seemed interested in the pages with pictures and drawings. They again counted my ten US$10 bills, holding them to the light as if questioning their authenticity. They seemed to understand their value as I heard a sigh from one of the young guards as he handed the dollar notes back to me. I was in a very light-hearted and expansive mood and thought of giving several US coins to the guard closest to me, but then realized that such a generous act could be misinterpreted as a form of bribery and consequently judged a crime.

Once the inspection was over a local representative of the China Travel Service took all the foreigners by bus to the New Asia Hotel, located in a very noisy section of Canton, as there were no trains to the Hongkong border until the next morning. After a quick bath and a hearty Chinese lunch we were taken to the Bureau of Foreign Affairs to register our arrival in Canton, and the police station to register in advance our departure the next morning for Shamchun (Shenzhen), the last outpost on

Chinese territory.

I spent the afternoon walking near my hotel with a small group of foreigners, one of whom spoke the Shanghai dialect and another who spoke Mandarin, but their linguistic skills proved useless since Cantonese was the *lingua franca*. The People's Republic of China had already established many schools where Mandarin was the primary language but these reforms would need time to take effect in the southern provinces. Passersby never approached us. After dinner I went out alone for a walk near the hotel to take in the sights, sounds and odors of this crowded city with its narrow streets and lanes teeming with residents. Pedestrians stared at me, this lone foreigner in their midst, but I felt very safe since their expressions revealed no animosity; and with many soldiers and militia men with red armbands patrolling the area, no one approached me.

Realizing that this would be my last night in China, I celebrated by purchasing dumplings filled with black beans, which Old Amah used to buy for me so many years ago during our walks in the markets of "Chinese" Shanghai. Before returning to the hotel I sat down at a food stall to eat a bowl of noodles next to surprised workers and pedicab drivers.

The following morning we were awakened at 4 a.m. for a breakfast of tea and dumplings followed by a 15-minute bus ride to the train station. I wondered why we had to get up so early, since the train to the Hongkong border was leaving at 7:30 a.m. The reason became clear when we reached the station; men and women in shabby greenish-yellow uniforms patted us down, presumably searching for hidden gold bars, silver objects or currency above the permissible US$100. I watched them closely as they carefully counted my $10 bills since I felt these very poorly paid government officials could be tempted to remove one of the notes with a slight of hand. Although I was distrustful of the communists, I had not realized that while their faults were numerous, dishonesty was not among them. We were joined at the platform by a party of 15 harried American men and women, missionaries being expelled.

There was much confusion, with militia and passengers milling about while the customs officials examined our suitcases even more closely than their counterparts had twenty hours earlier when we arrived in Canton. I believe they wanted to make sure that there were no antique artifacts or other illegal goods we might have surreptitiously purchased during our brief stay in the city. We boarded the train on schedule, and two hours later reached the end of the Chinese railway line and were hustled onto a bus to the border town of Shamchun, where we lined up while guards examined our exit visas, and counted and recounted our US dollar bills.

After two more hours' close scrutiny of our luggage and documents we were ready to enter British territory, and the Chinese border police took away our travel permits – proof for the bureaucracy in Shanghai and elsewhere that the "foreign devils" had left China. We walked for about ten minutes to a bridge, accompanied by coolies who carried our suitcases to the entrance of the British customs office.

As I was crossing the rickety bridge over the Shamchun River and into Hongkong I felt an overpowering sense of relief – and at the same time disbelief that I was finally leaving my "prison without walls". Behind me were olive-green-clad soldiers and the red flag of the People's Republic of China flapping in the wind; facing me were Englishmen in their neat khaki uniforms and the blue, red and white Union Jack. This symbol of freedom seemed to greet me personally on that cool, sunny day in March 1951, and the contrast between the sullen-looking Chinese border guards and the friendly British customs officials was striking. The musical refrain, "I can't believe it, I can't believe it," which had played in my mind during the train ride from Shanghai to Canton returned spontaneously. For many years whenever I took a train or a subway I could still hear this refrain in cadence with the clacking of wheels.

As we entered the customs shed on Hongkong territory, an

English border guard told us, "You are free and can go anywhere you want." I had a lump in my throat when several of the American missionaries sobbed uncontrollably, before the British customs officials helped us board a train for the 30-minute ride to Kowloon. At the final stop I was pleasantly surprised and moved to see Riva's classmate René Ballerand waiting for me. I had written to him about my arrival in Kowloon, although I had no way of knowing if my letter had reached him. René, who was working in Hongkong, drove me to a hotel in Kowloon where the International Refugee Organization had reserved a room for me. He invited me for dinner so that we could catch up on the latest news about China and talk about the former students of the Collège Municipal Français, most of whom were now living in France and whose parents had had a difficult time finding work and adjusting to a new life style.

The next morning I walked around Kowloon and took a ferry to Hongkong, where I soon felt I was back in the International Settlement of Shanghai. British policemen in their khaki shirts and shorts and soldiers and sailors from various nations were walking about in the crowded and noisy streets. Many of the office buildings resembled the Art Deco buildings of Shanghai while Kowloon's main thoroughfare, Nathan Road, with stores stocked with food, clothing and gadgets from around the world, reminded me of the once-bustling Avenue Joffre. I felt I was in a time warp as I looked at the people hurrying about, cars clogging the streets and the many ships anchored in the harbor. The Shanghai I had just left was a city without cars, shops without buyers and wharfs without ships. I took the cable tram to the Peak, where stately homes clung above hillside hovels and sampans bobbing in the water, similar to the ones I used to see in Shanghai's Soochow Creek. In the unseen distance, I realized with a shudder, was communist China.

As I walked about, no longer able to find my bearings, I approached a young English policeman to ask for directions to my hotel. He asked if we could get together in the evening and

I readily accepted. We went out for dinner and endlessly talked about the Cold War and the future of the colonies in Asia and Africa. My date felt strongly that Hongkong should and surely would remain British since it was not only a bastion of democracy facing Red China but also a strategic port for the British navy in the Far East. He hoped to remain in Hongkong for he felt it would be very difficult to find employment in England so soon after the war. I was flattered to be courted by this Englishman, a gentleman similar in behavior to the polite American soldiers I had dated in Shanghai. He did not ask me to spend the night with him, but gently kissed me goodnight at the door of my hotel. I went out with him every evening during my five-day exhilarating stay in Hongkong and also saw René Ballerand in his office to reminisce again about "our" Shanghai that no longer existed. We both wondered whether we would ever again see our classmates, now scattered around the world.

A representative from the International Refugee Organization called me several times while I was out, leaving messages to return his calls but I ignored them. I wanted to remain as long as possible in Hongkong where I had regained my freedom and was squired around town by an attractive Englishman, and where I returned to the privileged era of the "white man" in extraterritorial Shanghai. The representative felt quite differently when he finally reached me, informing me that I would leave on March 21 on a cargo-passenger ship for Yokohama, Japan. My suitor tried to console me by saying that schedules for cargo ship changed very often and that my departure could be delayed. Unfortunately he was wrong. I kissed him goodbye, packed my suitcases, made arrangements to send the carved wood chest aboard my ship the SS Straat Sonda, a cargo-passenger ship bound for Yokohama, Japan. I consoled myself, however, that my stay in Japan would be the springboard for my entrance into the United States.

Out of "Red" China

32

AS THE *Straat Sonda* started pulling away from the pier, I waved goodbye to my life in China. I spent a relaxing week on a calm sea with ten passengers and Dutch ship officers, who plied me with questions about "Red China" during our meals, which were served by an Indonesian crew. Our first port-of-call was Kobe, where the ship had to dock for three days to unload and pick up cargo. The ship's officers recommended that I take the electric train to the quaint and ancient town of Kyoto, which had not been bombed by American planes during the war. As I was strolling along Kyoto's narrow, cobblestone streets, admiring the intricately carved wooden Buddhist temples and Shinto shrines, I suddenly saw, to my great amazement, a Shanghailander, my friend and Jackie's classmate, Laura Topas. We shrieked with joy, repeatedly hugged each other and talked endlessly about our families and friends who had immigrated to various countries.

Laura and her family were living in Tokyo waiting for their immigration papers to the United States, and they had come to Kyoto for the day. I spent the early afternoon with them, reminiscing about Shanghai and our classmates and our teachers, and later took the train back to my ship. When I went aboard an American who identified himself as an official from the Supreme Command for Allied Powers in Tokyo asked me about my two-year stay under the communist government in Shanghai. He wanted to know whether I had noticed any military maneuvers in or around Shanghai (I answered that soldiers were always patrolling in the streets) or whether there were gunboats anchored near the Bund (I explained that because of the mines at the mouth of the Yangtze there were only a few fishing boats and sampans on the Whangpoo River.)

When our ship anchored in Yokohama harbor on April 1, 1951, I once again had to pinch myself. My new employer, Jacques Picciotto, was waiting for me at the pier and, on the ride to Tokyo in a chauffeured car, he mentioned that I would be paid $150 a month – a princely sum for me – working as a secretary/typist in his import-export firm, the John Manners Company. Jacques had reserved a room for me at the Tokyo YWCA, but added that he and his wife Aline would like to invite me to stay for few days in their home before starting my new life in Japan. I readily accepted, and found the Picciottos' elegantly decorated house on a hill overlooking Tokyo an ideal place to relax. I was pampered by my hosts and their many servants – a cook, three maids and a gardener. As had happened in Hongkong, memories of old Shanghai life flooded my mind.

Although my arrival in Tokyo was near the end of the US occupation of Japan, the Western colonialism with which I was so familiar still reigned in full force in Tokyo. Once again I felt that I was in a time warp; the Japanese were not allowed to go into stores and restaurants that catered to foreigners, nor were they permitted to ride in the first-class section of subways and trains reserved for Americans and other Caucasians. Instead, they were pushed and shoved into overcrowded carriages, from where they stared at me as I sat, often alone, in my "off limits" section. I was amazed by the lack of angry expressions – there were only passive ones. They seemed cowed but surely relieved – and perhaps surprised – that they were, by and large, not mistreated by the American occupiers.

Japanese women were eager to work as maids for $8 a month, while others earned substantially more working as bar girls or prostitutes catering to American servicemen. Although I did not have an official pass to go aboard US army busses for military and civilian personnel, I boarded them without any difficulty simply because I was a Caucasian. Once again, I was the privileged white person in Asia.

After my stay at the Picciotto's I moved into the YWCA, where I realized with some trepidation that I was now on my own in a strange land without my parents or my sisters, and with no amah to wash my clothes. This was the first time in my life – at the age of 25 – that I would have to look after myself, pay bills and make decisions without any of my family's advice or arguments. The "Y" was a residence in the Shihoda-ku residential section and catered to foreign women who worked in or passed through Tokyo. I paid $50 a month for my room, which included breakfast, a weekly change of sheets and towels and maid service. Since we were forbidden to use the communal bathroom to do our laundry and I did not care to hang and dry clothes in my room, I hired a young woman to wash and iron my clothes for 50 cents a week. Whenever I overslept or was too lazy to eat breakfast at the YWCA I boiled water on a hotplate and enjoyed my morning tea and a piece of fruit while listening to the radio. Food that needed to be refrigerated was kept in a refrigerator in the big communal kitchen, where I met other residents of the "Y".

I learned to be very frugal with my $150 monthly salary and sent some money every month to my mother and Jackie. I even managed to set aside $5 every month in an envelope marked "transportation" for my eventual departure by ship to the United States. As a very proud aunt, I splurged $2 on a Japanese doll for my niece Roxanne's second birthday, and later that year I purchased a baby kimono for $1.20 for her newly born sister Renée. I ate dinner across the street from the "Y" at a US housing billet for American civilians working for the Department of the Army; once again because of my Caucasian features no one asked me for any US government identification. I often purchased the latest delicacies from the United States and other countries from specialty stores reserved for foreigners only.

Several of the women at the "Y" were young American missionaries eager to convert the Japanese to Christianity or awaiting assignment to South Korea, the Philippines or Taiwan.

They were a happy-looking group, in contrast with the older missionaries at the "Y", who had recently been expelled from China but still believed they would return to their former missions. They were encouraged by Chiang Kai-shek's statements from Taiwan that his army was ready to invade and take back mainland China from the "Reds". My perception of staid and prudish missionaries, which I had acquired in China, disappeared rapidly when I became friendly with my young neighbor Billie, a lively young Seventh Day Adventist missionary with an infectious laugh. She went out dancing nearly every night with American soldiers, although this activity was frowned upon by the tenets of her faith. She told me the Lord would forgive her for she was intent on marrying a missionary so that both could work in tandem to save souls. Her wish was soon granted – she found a husband and both were sent to South Korea.

At the other end of my hallway was a foul-mouthed 60-year-old American journalist who swore like a drunken sailor after her daily shots of whiskey. Although alcohol was not allowed on the premises, it was easy to bring in a bottle or two and leave them in one's room since the gentle Japanese cleaning girls, who relied heavily on our tips, would not report this to Miss Mori, the "Y" manager. Several young women on my floor complained that it was ridiculous to have to meet their male friends in the reception hall and not in their own rooms. Maria, a divorcée and a White Russian Shanghailander friend of Riva, complained to me that the residents and the ambiance of our building were not to her liking. She could not afford to rent an apartment, and was looking for a man who would take her out of the YWCA's puritanical atmosphere and away from its preachy missionary residents. Maria was always heavily rouged and smoked constantly, blowing cigarette smoke purposely and disdainfully in the faces of people who irritated her. The American journalist saw in Maria a soul sister, and there must have been many complaints about them. Gentle and patient Miss Mori regularly placed signs on all the floors: "Respect your neighbors – Be quiet please – Do not slam doors." Miss Mori and the older missionaries heaved a sigh of relief when Maria left the "Y" to live with an American officer, and the journalist left for an assignment in Thailand.

A week after I moved to the "Y" two events occurred that surprised me very much. The first was when, on April 11, 1951, President Harry Truman relieved General Douglas MacArthur of his command of the United Nations forces in Korea and replaced him with General Matthew Ridgeway. It was difficult for me to understand why an experienced and brilliant military strategist, who had served so many years in the Far East and understood the Asian mentality was fired, as it seemed to me at the time, simply because he openly expressed to some members of Congress his views on the Korean conflict. MacArthur felt the United Nations forces needed to cross the 38th parallel and attack the North Koreans, while President Truman believed in containment and possibly a ceasefire as too many American soldiers had already been killed. As a fervent anti-communist I could not understand why President Truman would let go of someone who, in my opinion, could have defeated the North Koreans and the Chinese communists by bombing them to oblivion. MacArthur was regularly praised in the Japanese press, and the citizenry apparently held in awe this conquering general who could have brutalized them after the war, as Japanese generals had done to the peoples of Asia, but did not.

It must have been even more startling for the Japanese nation to hear that Emperor Hirohito had paid a visit to General MacArthur at the American Embassy to bid him farewell. On April 16, 1951, I got up at the crack of dawn, along with thousands of people waving Japanese and American flags, to see the general leave for Tokyo's Haneda airport and his flight out of Japan. Many women in the crowd were crying softly; I just shook my head. I had been so impressed with MacArthur's persona that several times during my lunch break I waited outside his headquarters in the Dai-Ichi building to see him come out and walk briskly to the drab olive-colored staff car that would whisk him away. I got very excited whenever I caught a glimpse of this general, who in my eyes was a hero battling communism in Asia.

The second event shook me emotionally and physically one evening while I was relaxing in my room before going out for dinner. Suddenly our building started swaying back and forth, and the floor began moving under my feet. Even though the tremors lasted only a few seconds they seemed to go on for an eternity and I was paralyzed with fear. When I finally recovered I rushed into the hallway and down to the lobby, where I heard the usually demure Japanese staff repeating "*jishin da, jishin da*" ("earthquake, earthquake") loudly. The foreign residents were gathered around Miss Mori, who tried to console the young women crying uncontrollably while the missionaries prayed and thanked God for sparing their lives. Miss Mori must have been subjected before to mini-earthquakes for she remained amazingly calm.

Soon after, a loftier event came to the "Y". Residents were informed that Emperor Hirohito and the Empress would be attending a swim meet at our indoor pool. Signs were posted on every floor informing us that on a certain day in May residents would not be allowed in or out as the imperial couple would be inside the building. The YWCA administrators were fearful the solemnity of the occasion would be marred by the noisy comings and goings of the foreign women, some of whom were often rather sloppily attired, wearing curlers when they went down to the lobby to pick up their mail. I decided to wait outside, armed with my camera to snap a picture of the Emperor and Empress stepping out of their car emblazoned with the imperial chrysanthemum emblem. I caught a glimpse of the emperor, surrounded by court officials, as he mounted the steps of the YWCA and gave a wave as the Japanese in the crowd bowed repeatedly. At the time I could only think of this man's troops massacring and committing heinous crimes against the defenseless Chinese and other peoples in Asia, and whose pilots flew *kamikaze* missions, all in his name.

The city of Tokyo, where American soldiers, sailors and Marines abounded, was an ideal city for a single woman looking for dates and perhaps a husband. In contrast to the dullness of my social life in communist Shanghai, I started going out nearly every night after my non-demanding work as a secretary. As usual I selected my dates for their good looks rather than for their intellect since I could not always discern their educational background. I was still amazed, however, that many of my American dates did not speak their native language correctly – the importance of which been drilled into me at the Collège Municipal Français. My dates, who had not traveled much in their own country, thought that I had a Boston accent due to my British-sounding speech inflection. To avoid endlessly repeating that I was born and brought up in Shanghai, or hearing that I did not look Chinese, I told people, whenever possible, that my parents were from Boston and had moved to the Far East soon after my birth.

On weekends whenever my date could borrow a jeep we drove to the countryside. Several of these young men tried to teach me to drive but quickly tired of my slow progress since I had much difficulty in maneuvering the stick shift. During these driving lessons I learned the latest American swear words from my very impatient teachers, who nevertheless always apologized for their vile language brought on by my mishandling of the jeep, especially the grinding of gears. They, on the other hand, scared me when they drove in the crowded narrow streets, showing off their driving skills by speeding, honking and slamming on the brakes, inevitably reminding me of their earlier counterparts in Shanghai.

American soldiers on five-day Rest & Recreation breaks from the conflict in Korea were eager to enjoy themselves as much as possible during their stay in Tokyo. Some went on wild sprees, getting drunk and going to brothels despite warnings about syphilis and gonorrhea, before going back to war in Korea. I spent time with several American soldiers who wanted simply to talk with a young Caucasian woman about their miserable life in desolate Korea, and whose only desire was to be discharged and return home as quickly as possible. On a couple of occasions we took the train to the countryside to relax in a Japanese inn, where we soaked ourselves in tub baths, swam and talked in our kimonos until the wee hours of the morning – and then retired to our separate bedrooms. One evening I had dinner with two soldiers on leave from Korea. When the restaurant closed we decided to continue our conversation at an "Off Limits" hotel. When we asked for a room the receptionist offered to find a girl for one of the men. When he refused she looked askance at me,

Lily with date in Tokyo

believing perhaps that I would be cavorting with the two men that night. We left early in the morning to the stares of the same receptionist.

Although I was giddy with my renewed social life and flattered by the men's attention, my feet were still solidly on the ground for I had to deal with a very serious mission: procuring a visa to Japan for my father. The letters he managed to send to me revealed an even more repressive China than the one I had left. I had to get my father out of "Red" China.

Behind the Iron Curtain 33

IN HIS letters my father described the deteriorating economic situation in Shanghai, the imposition of more laws curtailing people's freedom and the continued repression against individuals accused of spying for the Kuomintang or the United States. The "running dog collaborators" – landlords, black marketeers and petty criminals – were still being taken by army trucks to the Racecourse for open air trials. My father reported it was difficult for the few who still had short-wave radios to listen to overseas news because they were being jammed by sophisticated Soviet technology. I learned with sadness that the *North-China Daily News*, despite its recent communist propaganda, had closed down at the end of March 1951, just after my departure from Shanghai. First published in 1864, it was read by Westerners and English-speaking Chinese in the treaty ports and elsewhere in the Far East, where before the outbreak of World War II its circulation had risen to 10,000 copies daily. I grew up with this newspaper, first looking at the pictures, then reading it for many years, and in the process learning about a world outside the confines of Shanghai. I always found it more enjoyable than the *Journal de Shanghai* because of its satirical cartoons by the White Russian artist known as Sapajou.

Another symbol of England's colonial era, the firm Jardine Matheson, which for a century had dominated the coastal ports of China, especially in the opium trade, was no longer functioning in Shanghai. Shanghai's reputation as an important commercial center in the Far East had disappeared for good, it seemed. Extortion of what foreign firms and factories were left had continued unabated. It hurt to hear that the school I had spent so many years at, albeit difficult ones, had closed its doors and been taken over by the local authorities.

Shanghai's nightlife had disappeared; cabarets and nightclubs had closed down one after the other, and even the garish neon lights downtown were all turned off. Petty thievery, robberies, and burglaries of homes and shops had increased. When Michael Sukenik's jewelry store on Avenue Joffre was burglarized he sold the remaining stock of silverware, crystal and watches at bargain prices to his only clients, the Soviet advisors, and then closed his store. Busses, tramways and pedicabs were the only modes of transportation on streets now bereft of cars, except for the big American ones carrying Chinese and Russian officials hidden behind curtained windows.

My father noted in his letters that while Westerners were ignored by the authorities except when there was money to be extracted from them, there was no overt criticism of the approximately 200 remaining American and British businessmen and missionaries in Shanghai still waiting for their exit permits. The rights of Chinese were being curtailed drastically for now they needed permission to leave Shanghai to visit friends or relatives in "Ningpo mo fa" or elsewhere in China. My father noted that on National Day, October 1, 1951, the marchers on the parade route were given permission to wear clothing other than blue suits, and that in the evening the populace was offered a display of fireworks at the former Racecourse. He added that Amah was resenting more and more the obligatory weekly sessions of self-criticism and communist indoctrination, which she considered "vely stupid".

My father described the new campaign to fight waste, corruption and bureaucracy dubbed the "Three Antis", which the Party's central leadership launched against lower-level government workers, while the local authorities relentlessly continued their campaign against the mercantile class for its "exploitation" of the masses. Later "Five Antis" were added to this list, denouncing bribery, tax evasion, cheating in contract work, stealing state property and theft of state economic secrets. Posters attacking Chinese former property owners and industrialists began to appear on walls next to the ones decrying the use of bacteriological warfare by American soldiers in Korea. Later, having extracted all they could from these merchants, the authorities announced the purge against the despicable mercantile class was over and that the people could now begin to prosper. They did not explain how.

My father was pleased to report that some daring individuals regularly tore down the anti-American posters plastered around town. The authorities, however, quickly replaced them with more posters with the ubiquitous cartoons of rotund Western and Chinese businessmen stomping on the belly or the back of the downtrodden Chinese working class. People labeled "capitalists" were heavily taxed and fined for not paying their taxes on time, and even after paying their fines they still had to relinquish all their properties to the municipality. As usual, no explanation was given. Suicides had become a common occurrence, sometimes reaching ten a day. My father said several unfortunate pedestrians and pedicab drivers had been killed from the impact of bodies falling on them.

With regard to his own situation, my father mentioned that the International Refugee Organization office was closing and that he still had not heard from the Canadian Consulate about his visa application. When my mother telephoned him he suggested she go to Montreal to speak to someone at Sun Life Assurance Company about rehiring him and sponsoring his immigration to Canada. I later learned that my mother, now the holder of a US "green card", did not need a visa to enter Canada and took the train from Boston to Montreal. When it reached the border and the Canadian customs official asked her routine questions about the purpose of her trip she became flustered and blurted out her husband could not get out of "Red China" and that she had an appointment at Sun Life to help him acquire a visa to Canada. In

1951, at the height of the "Red Scare", anyone with a thick Russian accent who gave confusing answers could understandably be considered suspicious. It did not help that my mother's arrival in Canada coincided with the visit to that city by Princess Elizabeth of Great Britain as part of her tour of the British Commonwealth. My mother was deported unceremoniously from Canada and sent on the next train back to Boston.

With the war in Korea increasing the Chinese communists' paranoia and repression, I needed to find a way to help my father get to Japan as quickly as possible. I also decided it would be necessary to get a better-paying job to pay for my father's eventual living expenses in Tokyo and save money for travel to the United States. I checked the US armed forces' *Stars and Stripes* newspaper and saw many openings for English-speaking secretaries of any nationality, including those who were stateless. I made an appointment with Northwest Airlines, which had a contract to train Japanese personnel for the newly established Japan Airlines at Haneda airport. Though I did not do too well at the stenography test, I still passed, and the interviewer, apparently fascinated by my eclectic background, especially the fact that I spoke three languages, hired me on the spot.

That evening I wrote to Riva that "I must have talked my way into the job" since the American interviewer surely equated my knowledge of foreign languages – so common in Shanghai – to some higher form of intelligence. My salary was set at $216.25 a month plus all the privileges accorded civilians working under contract with the American occupation forces.

Meanwhile, I spoke with the owner of a life insurance company in Tokyo who was willing to hire my father, sight unseen, since Sun Life Assurance Company had an excellent reputation in the Far East and his company needed an English-speaking salesman to sell insurance to American civilians in Tokyo. Although he assured me he would fill out the necessary work permit documents I decided to go to the office of the Supreme Command for Allied Powers (SCAP) and inquire about visas to

Japan. When I told the Marine guard on duty that I needed to speak to an aide of General Matthew Ridgeway, he suggested I try to see an officer in a nearby office. While I waited, I noticed in the office on a messy desk several documents marked "Secret" that I could easily have read before a colonel finally walked in. He seemed familiar with visa problems for stateless persons and readily understood the impasse my father was in, suggesting that I prepare an affidavit of support guaranteeing he would not be a financial burden in Japan. The colonel chatted with me for some time, posing questions about life under the communists in Shanghai, and wished me luck, adding that I should call him if I needed further help. After I left his office I got lost in the corridors of the vast Dai Ichi building and, despite signs indicating that some areas were restricted and off-limits to non-military personnel, no one stopped me as I roamed around trying to find my way out. Inadvertently, I entered one of General Ridgeway's suites of offices before I asked a Marine where the exit was and quickly dashed out of the building.

I immediately contacted a lawyer, who drafted an "Affidavit of Support", which I showed to the same colonel before submitting it, in September 1951, to the SCAP. I was worried that after the peace treaty between the United States and Japan was signed, Japan as a sovereign country might not grant entry visas to stateless refugees whose sole purpose in Tokyo would be to visit various consulates for immigration visas. Recently the Japanese police in Tokyo had arrested several stateless businessmen, formerly from Shanghai, whom they caught smuggling Swiss watches and jewelry into Japan without paying customs duty. Soon after, I received a letter from my father in which he wrote that his application to immigrate to Canada was denied. This did not surprise me; the Canadian authorities must have realized he would leave Canada as quickly as possible to rejoin his wife and daughter in the United States. But "my" colonel must have pushed through my father's application because within two months he received clearance to enter Japan.

My father went into action quickly, applying for his Chinese exit permit and making arrangements for his departure with the International Refugee Organization just before it closed its doors in January 1952. He transferred the lease to our house on Route Delastre to a Chinese couple for US$2,000 "key money", the accepted financial agreement to transfer the house keys to a new renter, who could then move in without dealing with a management company and thus avoid a substantial increase in rent. This transaction could be dangerous, however, if the Communist authorities found out.

My father moved in with friends, gave Amah money to help her until she found other work, and waited for his exit permit. Within two weeks his name appeared in the newspaper, much more quickly than mine had since the authorities in early 1952 were even more anxious to get rid of "parasitic" foreigners who did not possess any property that could be expropriated. He received a transit visa to Hongkong from the British Consulate General, and made the same arrangements I had, going first by train to Canton and then by ship to Japan.

History was repeating for Benjamin Willens. Some thirty years earlier he had been obliged to leave Vladivostok because of the approaching Russian Bolshevik army. Now he was leaving Shanghai because of a Chinese communist government with a similarly repressive ideology.

End of 34 the Chase

AT THE beginning of 1952 I received a letter from the United States Consulate in Tokyo informing me that I had received a quota number for immigration to the United States. More than five years of chasing after permits and visas and filling out endless documents was coming to an end. I had already submitted a medical report to the American Consulate attesting that I was free of all imaginable diseases and a letter from the Tokyo police stating that I had not committed any crime in Japan. While waiting at the American Consulate I noticed a number of soldiers, sailors and marines filling out immigration papers for their Japanese brides or fiancées, and I was curious as to how these women, most of whom barely spoke English, communicated with their husbands or boyfriends. I also wondered how these young women would be received by their Caucasian in-laws; I had been told by my dates that the white population in America tended to discriminate against Asians, as had been the case in Shanghai.

I had also noticed in Tokyo that white American servicemen did not socialize with their fellow black soldiers and often made disparaging remarks about the "coloreds" or "niggers". What surprised me most was that black Americans were fighting and dying in Korea while in their own country they were discriminated against by the laws of their own government. I wrote to Jackie about this bizarre and unfair situation and added that it must be difficult to be a black person in the United States. She responded that in Boston blacks and whites rarely socialized, and warned me that Jews also met with discrimination – in housing, jobs, higher education – in Boston, a city where the majority of residents were Irish Catholics. She said when she enrolled as a freshman at the New England Conservatory of Music another student – a young black woman – in line behind her had helped her resolve a problem with registration. Jackie learned that this student, Coretta Scott, who was a few years older than herself, had already graduated as a music major from Antioch College and now wanted to specialize in the areas of music education and concert singing at the Conservatory. They became friends and Coretta, a mezzo-soprano, on one occasion asked Jackie to be her piano accompanist at a concert at her church. Jackie was warmly received by the congregation; however, she felt strange being the only white person in attendance, and wondered how blacks must feel in a society generally hostile towards them. Pleased with their performance, Jackie and Coretta made a recording – which Jackie still has – of spirituals and classical French songs. Jackie told me she often met Coretta and her boyfriend Martin, who had begun his doctoral studies in theology at Boston University, and several other young black men and women at parties where Jews were usually the only whites. Coretta's boyfriend was Martin Luther King, Jr.

Jackie's comments triggered reflections on our behavior towards the Chinese in Shanghai, especially our superior attitude towards them. I began to question how and why I had the right – and obviously the arrogance – to believe that I was superior to someone based on my Caucasian ethnicity. This was the first time in my life that I had ever thought that a Chinese might be equal to a Caucasian.

I was musing over these thoughts at the American Consulate when I was called for an interview with the vice consul, Dorothy Duggan, who congratulated me on receiving a quota number based on the very restrictive Chinese Exclusion Act. Attached to this long-awaited and precious visa was a list of 32 classes of individuals excluded from admission to the United States:

. . . idiots, feebleminded, insane persons, persons with

constitutional psychopathic inferiority; professional beggars; persons afflicted with loathsome or dangerous contagious disease; a crime involving moral turpitude; prostitutes, procurers; persons who believe in advocating the overthrow by force of violence of the Government of the United States or the assassination of public officials.

Although I did not belong to any of the above categories, this list of inadmissible individuals also included "natives of Asiatic barred zone" – a group to which I belonged because I had been born in Shanghai, and which had caused me inordinate grief, frustration and delays in my quest to immigrate to the United States of America.

While awaiting my father's arrival in Japan I enjoyed my new job at the Haneda Airbase, where I was allowed to use US Occupation military scrip money to purchase tax-free items at the military Post Exchange and to eat lunch for 50 cents. To keep the US dollar out of the black market, the scrip currency, equal to the value of the dollar, was issued to the US armed forces in countries they occupied after World War II. I often spent time at the airbase reading American newspapers and magazines in the library or seeing the latest movies with dates who would tell me about life in America. I was becoming Americanized without ever having set foot in the United States and many of my dates seemed generally surprised that I had never been to their country. I often asked how I would fare socially and financially in America, and was always reassured that many opportunities were available for secretaries and that Americans would appreciate my sense of humor.

I enjoyed the activities at the airbase, where I saw on the stage the Hollywood stars Danny Kaye, Jack Benny and Ginger Rogers, who were part of the USO contingent of celebrities entertaining the airmen before flying to Korea to perform for the American troops at war in that country. I liked watching the planes landing and taking off at Haneda Airbase, and dreamed of my own flight to America. On one occasion, at a farewell ceremony for a British general, I was horrified to see a plane spiral out of control and crash in a nearby field but fortunately neither the pilot nor anyone on the ground was killed. One afternoon at the airbase our Hungarian neighbors from Route Delastre appeared. They had finally received their visas for Canada and were on their way to Montreal. They gave me a letter from my father, and told me very few foreigners remained in Shanghai and that the Chinese residents, fearful as ever of the communist regime, were suffering economically because of the ongoing Korean War.

Although my four bosses at Northwest Airlines did not give me much work they never failed to thank me whenever I typed a letter for them. The manager of the station, Irl Groe, was a laid-back supervisor, who did not seem to mind when I read the *Stars and Stripes* in our office, typed letters to my mother and sisters, or chatted with the airmen who dropped by. I was often late for work after a night of dancing and drinking rum and Coca-Cola but Mr. Groe never reprimanded me. When he was transferred back to the United States he was replaced by a station manager who was very demanding of his staff, and a stickler for rules and regulations. One morning when I came late to work he fired me on the spot, obviously disgusted with my sloppy shorthand transcription, my typing mistakes, my long lunch hours and general tardiness. My pride was hurt but I was not concerned since there were many secretarial jobs available in the English-language newspaper.

I applied for a job with a shipping company because I decided it would be a good source to inquire about ships to the United States. I was hired by C.F. Sharpe & Company, which represented several cargo shipping lines to North and South America and the Far East, and went to work for their office manager, Mr. Isherwood. I was told he was related to a well-known British-born American writer whom I, not surprisingly, given my education at the Collège Municipal Français barely touched upon American literature, had never heard of. I enjoyed working for my new boss, who had a sense of humor and, just as importantly, did not have much work for me. I had become rather lazy at my Haneda Airport job. Mr. Isherwood, who knew I would be immigrating to the United States, told me that as an employee of the shipping firm I could book a ticket at half price on one of the cargo ships sailing from Yokohama to New York.

In early 1952, despite my pleasant social life and relaxed working conditions, I was anxious to leave Japan before it became a sovereign country later in the year. My privileges as a Caucasian would then end, just as they had when Chiang Kai-shek took control of China after World War II. I was also getting annoyed with anti-American demonstrations in Tokyo and in other cities by communist and left-leaning Japanese students who ranted against American imperialism. I was horrified that they could believe in the restrictive communist ideology under which I had lived in Shanghai. It was time for me to leave Japan but I had to wait for my father's arrival, hopefully before the expiration date of my immigration visa to the United States.

In early February my father left Shanghai for Canton and Hongkong, where Jacques Picciotto, then on a business assignment in the city, greeted him. He sent me a carbon copy of a long letter to my mother, typed on his faithful Remington

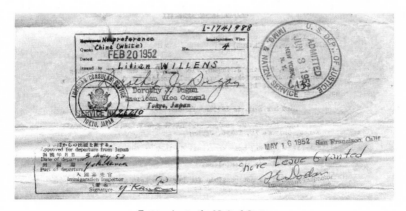

Entry visa to the United States

typewriter, describing the train ride from Canton to "freedom". Foreigners could no longer take out silver, diamonds or jewelry and were only allowed to have US$30 if in transit to Japan and US$50 if traveling to the United States, Canada or Australia. Looking for his hidden money, suspicious communist officials removed the frame from the mirror that had hung in our bedroom, and even looked inside my father's hatband, but they did not find any bills. The US$2,000 "key money", in hundred dollar bills, was spread around the lining of his coat and jacket, and he had also hidden banknotes in dictionaries and grammar books. "These communists," my father wrote in his letter, "are after the American dollars, which they pay the Soviets for military materiel." He ended his letter, "I am a free man again . . . and now I think with disgust about Shanghai and am so glad to be out of that awful hole, where the coolie is your boss."

On a happier note he wrote that on the eve of his departure from Shanghai Riva had called to tell him that she and John had moved with their growing family to Akron, Ohio, where she wished she had Old Amah to look after her two little girls, Roxanne and Renée. When I finished reading the letter I felt drained, reliving life in Shanghai but relieved to be far away in Tokyo.

My father sailed from Hongkong to Japan on the Dutch cargo ship *Tasman*, of the Royal InterOcean Line, the same route I had taken. I greeted him with joy at the Yokohama pier and we took the train to Tokyo, where I had rented a room for him at the YMCA. My father was not ready to talk about China but was eager to go to the US Consulate to inquire about his immigration visa to the United States. He was relieved to discover that he could now register under the wide-open Russian quota because his fictitious place of birth, Chisinau, had become part of the USSR. It was quite ironic that the vice consul had to ask my father, who had struggled so hard to leave a communist country, whether he had ever been a member of the Communist Party or had any connection with Party officials in Shanghai. She then warned me that I had to reach American shores before the expiration of my quota number or I would have to start the immigration process anew. I assured her that I had booked a passage on a cargo ship and would be leaving for the United States within two weeks.

When we left the consulate my father remarked how amazed he was that a representative of the United States government would write with her left hand! This comment was not surprising – when I was a child my father had noticed that I held a pencil in my left hand, a physical aberration, in his opinion, that needed to be corrected at home and by my kindergarten teacher. But neither father nor teacher was entirely successful for I continued to use my left hand in non-writing related activities – and still do.

35

To America, To America

I WAS leaving behind my life in the Far East, where I had lived for nearly a quarter of a century as a privileged Caucasian. It was only during my one-year stay in occupied Japan that I had started to develop a sense of uneasiness about some of the privileges I had regained in Hongkong and Japan simply because I was white. The US occupation of Japan reminded me of the century of subjugation the Chinese had endured under Western and Japanese military might and gunboat diplomacy. I now felt twinges of embarrassment at riding in empty subway cars while Japanese passengers were packed into overcrowded ones. I remembered similar inequalities that had existed in extraterritorial Shanghai and began to question the racial and cultural prejudices of Westerners towards Asians in general. Discrimination against the Chinese was a natural part of my upbringing and environment, and it seemed strange to me that only after I had left Shanghai had I become aware of the injustice and humiliation that the colonialists, Western and Japanese, had inflicted on China. Slowly I began to overcome these shameful feelings of superiority based on ethnicity and culture.

On March 12, 1952, my father, accompanied by Jacques and Aline Picciotto and Laura Topas, took me to the pier in Yokohama, where I embarked on a Norwegian cargo ship, the *Lisholt* of the Ivaran Line. I was confident of starting a career in the United States as a secretary/stenographer. I also had the financial means to start my life without the initial difficulties generally encountered by immigrants, taking with me US$1,500 in cash, many clothes and several Chinese carpets to sell. I had discovered in Tokyo, however, that the diamond ring that I smuggled out of China was not worth anything since it turned out to be ordinary glass. As I boarded the ship I was very excited to think of the various ports-of-call – San Francisco, where I would first set foot on American soil, then Long Beach and far south to the Panama Canal, up to my final destination, New York City. My six-year struggle to reach America was ending.

As the *Lisholt* started pulling away from the Yokohama wharf I threw several rolls of colorful streamers to my father and friends as I waved goodbye. When everyone disappeared from view, I went to my cabin to compose a telegram to my mother informing her of my arrival date in New York City. I then located the cable room and handed my sheet of paper to the officer on duty, a blond, blue-eyed young man, who greeted me with a dazzling smile and a thick Norwegian accent.

I cannot remember whether it was the rocking of the ship or the sight of this very handsome young man that made me feel faint – but that's another story.

Afterword

THE PEOPLE'S Republic of China remained closed to the West for approximately a quarter of a century after its establishment in 1949, but a crack in the iron curtain occurred when President Richard Nixon met with Mao Tse-tung in 1972. A few years later China slowly opened up to tourism from the West after the end of the Cultural Revolution of 1966-1976. At that time I had no desire to rekindle memories of my last two years in Shanghai, where I had witnessed the repressive measures taken against the Chinese population. I was not ready psychologically to visit the China I had left behind with such great relief. Many, many times over the years, however, I had thought of Old Amah, Shao Wang, Lao Papa and our last amah, and hoped they had not been hounded for having worked for us, the "foreign devils".

The various nefarious programs of Mao Tse-tung and the decade of madness that was the Cultural Revolution did not surprise me since the seeds of frenzied mass hysteria were sown at the "Speak Bitterness" rallies and trials I had witnessed at the Shanghai Racecourse.

It was only in 1996, 45 years after leaving Shanghai, that I was able to convince myself it was time to revisit my past in China. My Chinese friends in Washington suggested I spend a few days with their relatives in Shanghai to get over any initial shock, before settling down in a hotel in my "hometown". It seemed strange that I did not know anyone in a city I had grown up in, gone to school in and lived in for the first 25 years of my life.

When my plane landed at Hongqiao Airport I was amazed to see a modern terminal staffed by efficient customs officials – although their yellow army uniforms reminded me of that fateful morning in May 1949 when the victorious People's Liberation Army walked into Shanghai. My Chinese hostess met me at the airport and as we rode by taxi through the two former foreign settlements, I was taken aback to see modern skyscrapers on nearly every corner of the main streets of Shanghai competing architecturally with the magnificent 1930s Western-style office buildings and hotels on Nanking Road, Bubbling Well Road and the Bund, reminders of the heyday of Western colonialism. As we drove towards my hostess' home in the former French Concession, near the Koukaza Park, where I played as a child under the watchful eye of Old Amah, the Art Deco apartment buildings were in place as I remembered them, though they now looked very shabby. I could not get over the fact that the communist China I lived in, which had ranted and raved against the decadence of imperialist capitalism, was now home to a flourishing capitalist economy. That night I could not sleep. I felt a strange tinge of apprehension at feeling alone in the city where I was born. I did not know a soul. To add to my uneasiness, I was the overnight guest of a Chinese family – a social situation that would not have occurred during the era of extraterritoriality, when Chinese and foreigners lived in Shanghai in two very separate worlds. The Communist Party government, whose establishment I witnessed in 1949, was still in place, but with the advantages of a free-market society. I was in awe of the leaps and bounds that the destitute country I had lived in for 25 years had made. My last thought as I finally fell asleep was to ask myself when and if political freedom would triumph in the People's Republic of China.

After a few days with my hostess and her family I asked them to reserve a room for me, not in a hotel exclusively for foreigners, as was the law, but in one for Chinese patrons only. I wanted to feel that I was back in China as a former resident and not as a tourist. I knew I was breaking the law thanks to my friends' *guanxi* (connections), a very useful but often corrupt custom of bypassing the myriad regulations of China's very centralized form of government. The hotel staff was intrigued that I wanted